The Rule of Law and Automated Decision-Making

Markku Suksi
Editor

The Rule of Law and Automated Decision-Making

Exploring Fundamentals of Algorithmic Governance

Springer

Editor
Markku Suksi
Department of Law
Åbo Akademi University
Turku/Åbo, Finland

ISBN 978-3-031-30141-4 ISBN 978-3-031-30142-1 (eBook)
https://doi.org/10.1007/978-3-031-30142-1

This Springer imprint is published by the registered company Springer Nature Switzerland AG
The registered company address is: Gewerbestrasse 11, 6330 Cham, Switzerland

Preface

This volume grew out of the Åbo Akademi University Law School's second conference on automated decision-making, entitled *The Rule of Law and Automated Decision-Making at Public Authorities*. The conference was held on 24 August 2021 and took place online due to the COVID-19 pandemic, underscoring the increasing impact of digitalization in our lives. This second conference on automation followed an inaugural meeting of scholars in 2019, which addressed the topic of *Opening the Black Box – Regulatory Perspectives on Automated Decision-Making*.

All contributions in this volume have emerged from the second conference in 2021, except for Mr. Sarlin's entry, which has its origins in the first conference of 2019. I would like to offer my sincere thanks to the contributors for their excellent work and patience through several rounds of review.

I also wish to thank Mr. Reagan M. Sova for his thorough linguistic proofing of the contributions, and the Finnish Section of the Nordic Federation of Public Administration (Nordiska administrativa förbundets finska avdelning r.f.; NAF) for a grant that made the linguistic proofing possible. Furthermore, I would like to express my gratitude to Ms. Raija Hanski for her skillful technical editing of the text. From all of us who contributed to this book, we are grateful to Springer for arranging a useful review process prior to their publication decision, and for publishing this volume.

Åbo, Finland
November 2022

Markku Suksi

Contents

Contributors

Lena Enqvist Department of Law, Umeå University, Umeå, Sweden

Anna-Sara Lind Faculty of Law, Uppsala University, Uppsala, Sweden

Cecilia Magnusson Sjöberg Faculty of Law, Stockholm University, Stockholm, Sweden

Yannick Meneceur Council of Europe, Strasbourg, France
Faculty of Law, University of Strasbourg, Strasbourg, France

Markus Naarttijärvi Department of Law, Umeå University, Umeå, Sweden

Tuomas Pöysti Chancellor of Justice, Helsinki, Finland

Riku Sarlin Former Chief Architect of Social Benefit Systems, Social Insurance Institution of Finland, Helsinki, Finland

Markku Suksi Department of Law, Åbo Akademi University, Turku, Finland

Introduction

Markku Suksi

Abstract The theories underlying automated decision-making date back several decades, but rules of public law, particularly administrative law, have only started to develop in this area over the past ten years. Different states regulate automated decision-making to varying degrees, and in some countries, prohibitions against automated decision-making may exist, or stipulations that only allow such decision-making under certain circumstances. The creation of automated decision-making systems may take place in-house, or such systems can also be purchased by public authorities, as applications made by software companies or as licenses from software companies. In such cases, the computer programs should typically be purchased by means of public procurement. Software of this kind may be a proprietary program owned by the software company, not by the public authority. Case law covering different facets of automated decision-making is still in its inception, but several interesting cases have already been resolved by courts in various jurisdictions.

Keywords Automated decision-making · AI law · Procurement of software · AI case law · Rule of law

The truism that government must be under the rule of law has been increasingly challenged by the development of algorithmic decision-making techniques. Such techniques are already widely used in the private sector, and in European countries, the use of automated processes in administrative decision-making has existed for several decades.[1] Additionally, other countries, such as the United States and Australia, have taken steps toward incorporating automation in governmental decision-making. However, in the context of this trend toward automated

[1]For the evolution of theories and various applications of automation and artificial intelligence in various contexts of law, see the thematic issue of *Artificial Intelligence and Law*, more specifically Bench-Capon (2022), Sartor et al. (2022), Araszkiewicz et al. (2022). For analyses of service automation in the public sector from a non-legal perspective, see Juell-Skielse et al. (2022).

M. Suksi (✉)
School of Law, Åbo Akademi University, Turku/Åbo, Finland
e-mail: markku.suksi@abo.fi

M. Suksi (ed.), *The Rule of Law and Automated Decision-Making*,
https://doi.org/10.1007/978-3-031-30142-1_1

decision-making, it is important to take note of what Dag Wiese Schartum has said about automation that has been in use in administration since the 1960s: "[M]any of the basic legal questions related to automated decision-making have principally remained unchanged."[2] Therefore, it is now high time for lawmakers, citizens, and scholars to reflect upon how automated decision-making in public law contexts relates to the rule of law, and thinkers and scholars of today must also reflect upon how to ensure the rule of law in an environment where automated decision-making processes are increasingly utilized by public authorities.

In a 2020 review of the use of algorithmic techniques in administrative decision-making, Rónán Kennedy observes that until recently, the adoption of information and communications technology (ICT) by bureaucratic institutions has received relatively little study, although this development poses important questions concerning, inter alia, the rule of law. Kennedy thus identifies a lack of academic attention and makes the point that scholars have failed to pay sufficient attention to the role and impact of ICT in the governance process.[3] From the vantage point of this volume, it is possible to agree with Kennedy and conclude that luckily, during the past five years, the academic study of automated decision-making in public administration, and legal issues surrounding such decision-making, have started to flourish in many countries.[4]

However, it is not only academics who have taken notice of automated decision-making processes implemented by public authorities. At the international level, in institutions such as the Council of Europe, the matter is prompting action.[5] Lawmakers have also become more active in shaping automated decision-making processes, and by doing so, they have occasioned responses from the legal community concerning various issues surrounding automated decision-making in the service of governmental entities. Now, it appears that countries may be divided into two categories depending on the stringency of the legislative response to automated decision-making of a general nature: there are countries with a more relaxed attitude towards automated decision-making in public authorities, and there are countries with a more demanding legal order on the use of algorithmic systems. Countries such as Sweden, and perhaps also Germany, appear to belong to the first group, while countries such as Finland and France appear to have positioned themselves in the second group. However, within each group, significant differences between the

[2] Wiese Schartum (2020), p. 303.

[3] Kennedy (2020), pp. 221–222. However, see Suksi (2021), pp. 100–105, for an account of complications between automated decision-making and the rule of law.

[4] By way of example, academic analysis is provided by such works as de Vries and Dahlberg (2022), but it is also extremely important that works intended for students of law and AI are published, such as Noll (2021), to satisfy the need for readings at university courses.

[5] See, for instance, "Governing the Game Changer – Impacts of artificial intelligence development on human rights, democracy and the rule of law," Council of Europe Conference in Helsinki on 26–27 February 2019 and Conclusions from the Conference, at https://rm.coe.int/conclusions-from-the-conference/168093368c (accessed on 8 September 2022). See also the contribution of Yannick Meneceur in this volume.

relevant countries may exist, and the existence or non-existence of general rules about the use of automated decision-making does not mean that material law on, for instance, congestion tax or social benefits would be entirely devoid of provisions concerning algorithmic decision-making.

In Sweden, the relatively recent Administrative Procedure Act (förvaltningslag, 2017:900) contains, in Section 28, a sentence which creates a very generic starting point for the use of automated decision-making by public authorities: "A decision can be made by a public servant alone or jointly by several public servants or automated."[6]

The provision thus contains a very open-ended authorization for the establishment of algorithmic systems. The inclusion of such a provision in the legislation, a provision that may cede traditional governmental decision-making by public servants to algorithms, is a potentially profound, transformative step to take from the point of view of principle. It is therefore surprising that the issue of automated decision-making appears only with a short mention in the Government Bill,[7] without an exacting analysis of the various facets of the use of automated decision-making in the preparatory documents that precede the Government Bill. At the level of local government in Sweden, transfer of decision-making powers to non-human, algorithmic systems had actually been forbidden, but an amendment to the Municipalities Act (kommunallag, 2017:725) in 2022 has made it possible to use automated decision-making in local government, albeit within relatively strictly drawn boundaries.[8] Undoubtedly, other pieces of law may impact the use of automated decision-making in Sweden, such as mandating the use of automated decision-making in a specific context, but the point of departure in Swedish law appears to be very permissive.

In Germany, the Administrative Procedure Act (*Verwaltungsverfahrensgesetz*)[9] has contained a provision since 2016 that is not quite as open-ended as its Swedish counterpart. Section 35a on fully-automated adoption of an administrative act sets up the requirement of a separate legal basis and surrounds automated decision-making with some qualitative boundaries: "An administrative act may be adopted entirely by

---

[6] Translation by MS.

[7] Regeringens proposition 2016/17:180, En modern och rättssäker förvaltning—ny förvaltningslag, pp. 179–180. The Government of Sweden concluded that the prior drafting work did not inquire into the issue, but automated decision-making has become an ever more common phenomenon within some parts of the administration. The Government points out that when the Administrative Procedure Act establishes that decisions can be made in an automated manner, it is at the same time made clear that there is no need of regulation in any particular legal act to make it possible for a public authority to use this form of decision-making. What this means is that in principle, Section 28 is regarded as a sufficient legal basis for the internal decisions of public authorities to be made using automated decision-making.

[8] See the contributions of Anna-Sara Lind and Cecilia Malmgren Sjöberg in this volume.

[9] Verwaltungsverfahrensgesetz in der Fassung der Bekanntmachung vom 23. Januar 2003 (BGBl. I S. 102), das zuletzt durch Artikel 24 Absatz 3 des Gesetzes vom 25. Juni 2021 (BGBl. I S. 2154) geändert worden ist. Translation by MS.

automated means, provided that this is permitted by law and that the matter involves neither discretion nor a margin of appreciation."

The reference to law, that is, a requirement of legal basis, is not necessarily a requirement of law in the formal meaning of the word (an Act of Parliament), but law in the material meaning of the word, which appears to mean that a legal basis for automated decision-making can also be created in a legal act of a lower order, such as a decree. The suitable qualifications for automated decision-making, which should involve neither discretion, nor a margin of appreciation, appear then to make automated decision-making relevant only for mass-decisions of a relatively technical kind.

In Finland, by October 2022 when this book was finalized, there existed no explicit rules about automated decision-making and how such decision-making could be used in administrative matters. There existed however at least one piece of material legislation that creates a legal basis for automated decision-making in the specific context of subsidies to forest owners, but attempts by the government to propose legislation in a number of other material areas caused the relevant parliamentary committee to stop legislation containing references to automated decision-making until a general regulatory framework is in place. A Government Bill to that effect was submitted in September 2022,[10] and while permitting the use of automated decision-making by public authorities, the several amendments to the Administrative Procedure Act (hallintolaki – förvaltningslag, 434/2003) and the Act on Information Management in Public Administration (laki julkisen hallinnon tiedonhallinnasta – lag om informationshantering inom den offentliga förvaltningen, 906/2019) create various legal requirements for establishing algorithmic systems by governmental entities. Approved by the Parliament in February 2023, these amendments ushered in a set of relatively detailed and demanding legal provisions from 1 May 2023 onward that seek to frame the use of automated decision-making in a manner that would satisfy, inter alia, the requirements of the Constitution. The level of detail of the provisions in Finnish law is higher than in Germany and may approach that of France (see below), although the point of departure of the Finnish provisions is somewhat different from the French counterpart.

Sections 53e through 53g in the Finnish Administrative Procedure Act establish the conditions for the use of fully automated decision-making by public authorities. According to Section 53e, a public authority can decide a matter in an automated manner if the decision to be made does not require the use of discretion on a case-by-case basis (or if such aspects of the matter have already been decided by a civil servant or some other person with similar authority). A condition of principal importance is that automated decision-making shall be based on handling rules that have been established on the basis of applicable material law, including applicable

[10] Regeringens proposition RP 145/2022 rd till riksdagen med förslag till lagstiftning om automatiserat beslutsfattande inom den offentliga förvaltningen. See Act (487/2023) amending the Administrative Procedure Act by adding a new Chapter 8 b, including, inter alia, Section 53 e on requirements for automated decision-making of a matter, in force from 1 May 2023. See also the contribution by Markku Suksi in this volume.

EU-law, and with prior consideration. According to the *travaux preparatoires* of Section 53e, this condition is to be interpreted so that the handling rules are established by a physical person prior to making use of the automated system, and these handling rules are to be documented in a public description of the automated system displayed on the website of the relevant public authority. Moreover, and most importantly, the requirement of prior handling rules excludes such technical choices for the automated system that, instead of rules based on the law, are based on probabilities, that is, on machine-learning techniques. This facet of the prior handing rules means that the provision is actually about regulation of AI by excluding machine-learning techniques of all kinds from the applications used for automated decision-making by public authorities. The software developed for use in public administration must thus always be rule-based.

Additionally, a person who is subject to an automated decision shall have the right to request a review of the decision in all its parts, while a review decision shall not be made in an automated manner. A person who is subject to an automated decision shall also be informed in the decision of the fact that this decision has been taken in an automated manner. Lastly, the individual subject to an automated decision shall receive the name of the physical person who is designated to give further information about the matter.

The Finnish Act on Information Management within Public Administration contains another set of rules concerning automated decision-making. According to Section 28d, a formal decision on the introduction of an automated decision-making system shall be made by the public authority prior to launching the application. Such a decision shall include justifications for the introduction of such a system and how it fulfils the conditions, a listing of the documentation that constitutes the foundation of the introduction of the system, the projected date for the introduction of the system, the name of the person who made the decision, and contact information of the public authority. Furthermore, a formal decision shall be made when changes take place that require a new determination of the conditions of introduction for a system that already is in use.

Section 28 of the Act on Information Management lays down requirements concerning the documentation of the distribution of tasks between civil servants in charge of the automated system. The documentation and the handling rules shall be so clear and all-encompassing that their legality can be assessed. In particular, the handling rules shall explain how the non-discriminatory nature of the decision-making process is guaranteed, how a particular matter at hand would be sufficiently and correctly investigated, including the hearing of the party, and how the decision would be motivated (or why it does not have to be motivated, as might be the case in some specifically established situations). In addition to quality assurance rules in Section 28b, including the designation of a public servant in charge of the quality assurance of the automated system, the Act contains rules for quality control and handling of system errors in Section 28c. In case an error is discovered in the automated decision-making process that may impact the content of a decision, the public authority shall implement corrective measures without delay. An error that is discovered, the consequences of the error, and the corrective measures shall be documented. A public servant with responsibility over on-going quality control of the automated decision-making system and for the handling of error incidents shall be designated by the public authority. According to Section 28f, a public authority shall, on the basis of risk assessment, implement by means of suitable technical measures that the data that is used in automated decisions is up to date and free of errors. The new Finnish provisions concerning automated decision-making are thus relatively detailed and maintain a strong connection to the rule of law. In addition to these more procedural provisions, additional provisions concerning introducing automated decision-making have been enacted in material law.

In France, legislation concerning automated procedures in administration dates back to 1978. Provisions concerning automated decision-making are included in Act No. 78-17 of 6 January 1978 relating to data processing, files, and freedoms (Loi n° 78-17 du 6 janvier 1978 relative à l'informatique, aux fichiers et aux libertés). However, on automated decision-making, the French perspective is different from that of Sweden, Germany, or Finland, where the point of departure is a positive one on the use of algorithmic systems, but with more or less stringent requirements on such systems. In France, it appears that the point of departure is negative, because under Article 47 of the Act, any decision that produces legal effects upon a person, or otherwise significantly affects them, may not be taken solely through means of automated processing of personal data, including profiling. However, in France, exceptions to this negation apply in two cases.

First, exceptions apply in the cases mentioned in paragraphs (a) and (c) of Article 22(2) of the EU's General Data Protection Regulation (GDPR), provided that the rules defining the processing as well as the main characteristics of the implementation are communicated—except for secrets protected by law—by the controller to the interested party if the interested party so requests. The second exception may be granted in cases where individual administrative decisions have been taken in compliance with Article L.311-3-1, and with Chapter I of Title I of Book IV of the Code of Relations between the Public and the Administration, provided that the processing does not relate to data mentioned in Section I of Article 6 of this Law. (For these decisions, the controller shall ensure that the algorithmic processing and its evolutions are in control, in order, and explainable, both in detail and in an intelligible form, to the data subject in a way that explains the processing that has been implemented in the subject). Although automated decisions are thus actually permitted in a number of cases in France, concerning decisions wherein the administration decides on an administrative appeal mentioned in Title I of Book IV of the Code of Relations between the Public and the Administration, these decisions may not be taken solely on the basis of automated processing of personal data. Internal complaint procedures are therefore always outside the remit of automated decisions.

The above-mentioned Code of Relations between the Public and the Administration contains specifying rules for instances in which automated decision-making is permissible. Under Article L.311-3-1 of the Code, an individual decision taken based on the algorithmic processing shall include an explicit mention that informs the interested party of the automated procedure.[11] The rules defining this processing, as well as the main characteristics of its implementation, shall be communicated by the administration upon request to the person concerned. The specific rules of application of this Article are established in a decree by the French Council of State. Under the implementation rules, the administration must communicate to the person who is the subject of an individual decision taken on the basis of algorithmic processing, at the latter's request, in an intelligible form and in a manner that does not infringe upon secrets protected by law, with a response that includes the following information: (1) the degree and mode of contribution that algorithmic processing had upon the administration's decision-making process; (2) the data processed and their sources; (3) the parameters of processing and, where appropriate, their weight as applied to the situation of the person concerned; and (4) the operations carried out during the algorithmic processing. As one might notice based on this summary, the French legislation is relatively detailed in its approach to automated decision-making by public authorities.

Of course, the use of automated procedures in making individual administrative decisions hinges, in addition to legislation, on the manner in which computer programs and software for automated decision-making are produced for public authorities. The modalities of production of automated systems software is, in many ways, the critical point of the matter, because it is at the design and programming phase that the algorithm and the source code should incorporate the requirements of a formal, procedural, and material kind that the legislation lays down.

Generally, three main ways to produce automated decision-making programs can be identified. First, a public authority or the government may choose to develop the software through in-house production. This would imply that the governmental entity has at its disposal its own capacity for the design and construction of software. This is the way in which the Social Insurance Institution of Finland has acted in relation to its software needs.[12] Such in-house development is not always possible and therefore, software used in governmental and administrative contexts is often produced by external sources. A second way that governmental agencies use to procure software for automated decision-making functions is to obtain the software from firms that act under the instructions of the procuring authority when setting up the program. This is was occurred in the municipality of Trelleborg in Sweden, where a legal case resulted in the conclusion by an administrative appeals court that because the procurement of the software had resulted in the transfer of ownership of the product from the company to the municipality, the source code of the program had therefore become a public document, and as such, should be handed over to the

[11] See Restrepo Amariles (2020), p. 285, for information of how the source code of an automated system used to allocate applicants to French universities was made available by the Ministry of Education to an association of high school students in an administrative procedure before the National Commission for Access to Administrative Documents.

[12] See the contribution of Riku Sarlin in this volume.

complainant.[13] Third, an external delivery of software can also be based on a license that the public authority purchases. This is currently the case with the Finnish Tax Administration, which formerly had its own in-house produced programs, but changed its system in a negotiated procurement procedure. Since late 2019, the Finnish Tax Administration has used a licensed product, GenTax. This product is delivered by a European subsidiary of Fast Enterprises, a US corporation,[14] which means that the algorithm and the source code is owned by a private company outside the jurisdiction where the product is used. However, it appears that the Finnish Tax Administration is involved in the continuous refinement of the software for Finnish conditions. The institutional manner of production and purchase of the software for automated decision-making may thus also have proprietary implications for the software.

Once taken into use, with or without a legal basis, algorithmic systems of administrative decision-making start to produce individual administrative decisions and, in addition, legal complications. These legal complications result in appeals proceedings before courts of law, but such complications also often result in other types of complaints to supervisors of legality, such as Parliamentary Ombudsmen or other designated administrative bodies that handle such complaints. For instance, in Finland, the main institution for receiving such complaints is the Chancellor of Justice, who used to share the supervisory competence over algorithmic systems with the Ombudsman, but as of 2022, the supervisory competence in this regard has been solely allocated to the Chancellor of Justice.[15] Because legislation concerning automated decision-making systems is relatively new or non-existent, or perhaps because individuals and business enterprises that are affected by algorithmic decision-making have yet to grasp that automated decisions may not always be as licit as they appear, there have not been very many legal cases concerning algorithmic decision-making thus far. While several of such cases are mentioned in the various contributions in this volume, some of them may nevertheless be mentioned here to highlight certain salient features therein and provide an easy entry-point for the reader to some of the legal issues that are involved in automated decision-making.

One example of a ruling that involves algorithmic decision-making is the aforementioned judgment by the Administrative Appeals Court of Gothenburg, Sweden, in a case from 2020, where the court established the public nature of the source code.[16] Another case, one that has attracted significant attention in the legal community in recent years, is the SyRI case from the Netherlands, where the European Convention on Human Rights was used by a national court to address serious issues

[13] Kammarrätten i Göteborg, dom i mål nr 6973-19, datum: 2020-02-21.

[14] For more information, see the website of the Finnish Tax Administration, at https://www.vero.fi/tietoa-verohallinnosta/verohallinnon_esittely/toiminta/valmishanke_uudistaa_verotusohjelmisto2/valmis_verotusohjelmisto_muokataan_suom/ (accessed on 9 September 2022).

[15] See the contribution in this volume of Tuomas Pöysti, who is the Chancellor of Justice of Finland.

[16] Kammarrätten I Göteborg, dom i mål nr 6973-19, datum: 2020-02-21.

that had arisen due to the use of automated decision-making in the area of fraud detection concerning social benefits, child allowances, and taxation.[17] Additionally, the French Constitutional Council considered a case on the construction of an algorithm operating in the background of a self-learning and machine-learning-based system capable of self-modification. Although the provision did not reach actual implementation by administrative agencies, this case is important in ironing out some modalities of the use of algorithms for decision-making purposes.[18]

The Court of Justice of the European Union (CJEU) has expressed itself in a preliminary ruling on automated processing of personal data in national administrative entities, where passenger name records containing data of air passengers of flights operated between the European Union (EU) and third countries are handled on the basis of an EU directive. The CJEU found that the directive is in harmony with the Charter of Fundamental Rights of the European Union but was skeptical concerning the use of machine-learning in contexts of this kind because their intransparency may deprive the data subjects of their right to an effective judicial remedy.[19] The use of facial recognition was the issue in a case from the United Kingdom, where a machine learning system was used as a support system for police, but the use of this system was blocked by a court for questions about bias in the training data.[20]

The use of an algorithmic support system for decision-making was also the topic in a UK case concerning the public services to which a disabled person was entitled, but in this case, the court upheld the system, because the decision-making body was not bound by the system's result (the result of the semi-automated system was regarded as the beginning of the decision-making process, rather than the end).[21] The non-transparency of a scoring system used by a school district in Texas, USA, to determine the salaries of teachers, and the teachers' inability to learn whether the system operated correctly, was proceeding to trial after a grant of motion for summary judgment on substantive due process and on equal rights, but the case

[17] *NJCM et al. v. The Dutch State*, The Hague District Court, judgment of 05-02-2020, ECLI:NL:RBDHA:2020:1878. See also the contribution of Yannick Meneceur in this volume.

[18] Conseil Constitutionnel, Decision no. 2018–765 DC, June 12, 2018, at https://www.conseil-constitutionnel.fr/decision/2018/2018765DC.htm (accessed on 5 September 2022).

[19] Case C-817/19 *Ligue des droits humains v Conseil des ministres*, CJEU, Judgment of 21 June 2022, ECLI:EU:C:2022:491.

[20] *R (Bridges) v Chief Constable of South Wales Police* [2020] EWCA Civ 1058, at https://www.judiciary.uk/wp-content/uploads/2020/08/R-Bridges v CC-South-Wales-ors-Judgment.pdf (accessed on 9 September 2022). See Williams (2022), pp. 476–477.

[21] *R (Savva) v Royal Borough of Kensington and Chelsea* [2010] EWCA Civ 1209, at https://www.casemine.com/judgement/uk/5a8ff7a860d03e7f57eb0e33 (accessed on 9 September 2022). See Williams (2022), p. 490.

was denied with respect to the procedural due process claim, at which point the school district settled the case and refrained from using the scoring system.[22]

And while it may seem that election administration and the administration of justice would not be appropriate environments for regular automated decision-making, one case can be mentioned in each of these respective contexts. The Constitutional Court of Germany concluded in a case concerning electronic voting machines, that the measure by the federal ministry which authorized the machines lacked legal basis, insofar as the intention of their use was to create entirely electronic voting procedures that did not guarantee transparency.[23] The use of an algorithmic system to predict the risk of recidivism among persons was, according to the Supreme Court of Wisconsin, USA, permissible and in compliance with due process rights of the US Constitution when used as a support system for the judge, and as one source of information among others.[24] Because several other relevant cases are from lower courts, it is not yet possible to say that the case law points in any definitive direction concerning the use of automated decision-making in public authorities. However, one thing is certain: there will be more cases from courts that illuminate the manner in which automation can be used by government.

In this volume, these cases, and a number of other cases and interpretations, and also laws concerning automated decision-making in public authorities, will be presented in the context of the rule of law. As a consequence of the expected proliferation of such cases and laws, the connection between the use of automated decision-making by public authorities and the principle(s) of the rule of law will become clearer but also more nuanced.

The topic will first be approached from a general perspective by *Markus Naarttijärvi*, whose contribution balances the multifaceted nature of the concept of the rule of law and its massive body of literature with the relatively recent topic of automated decision-making. Until now, our understanding of decision-making has been based on language, but automation adds at least one, potentially two, refractive layers to the procedure of making an administrative decision in a manner that impacts our traditional language-based understanding of the rule of law.

[22] *Houston Federation of Teachers v. Houston Independent School District* 251 F.Supp.3d 1168 (2017), at https://www.leagle.com/decision/infdco20170530802 (accessed on 9 September 2022). See Williams (2022), pp. 482–493, for the settlement issue.

[23] BVerfGE 123, 39, nr 2, Urteil des Zweiten Senats vom 3. März 2009.

[24] *State of Wisconsin v. Eric L. Loomis*, 881 N.W.2d 749 (2016). According to paragraph 1 of the judgment, the Conference of Chief Justices and State Court Administrators adopted in 2007 a resolution entitled "In Support of Sentencing Practices that Promote Public Safety and Reduce Recidivism." Although the resolution makes reference to the use of programs, it is not clear on the basis of it that the term is used in the meaning of computer programs, at https://www.ncsc.org/__data/assets/pdf_file/0016/25117/resolution-12.pdf (accessed on 12 September 2022). However, the resolution appears to form a basis of the use of the COMPAS system for the prediction of recidivism, developed by Northpointe corporation (making it a proprietary trade secret to disclose the inner workings of the system). Because the system is used for prediction based on multiple indicators, it is likely that the technique used is machine learning based.

With legal certainty as a key feature of the rule of law, *Tuomas Pöysti*, who has been the Chancellor of Justice of Finland since 2018, and in this capacity has been a supervisor of legality for the administration, including with automated decision-making mechanisms, develops a comparative and a theoretical approach that is connected both to actual practice and to pending legislative reform in Finland concerning automated decision-making. Chancellor Pöysti calls for a human-centric approach where the legislator, system-developers, and those who apply the law have a common task to maintain human dignity and human agency when automation is used in public administration.

Various facets of the rule of law, including the decision-making method involving subsumption or legal reasoning, are examined in *Markku Suksi*'s chapter. Suksi distinguishes between formal, procedural, and material rule of law, and his chapter subsequently details how each of these categories includes different aspects of the rule of law that should be considered when legislation involving automated decision-making used by public authorities is prepared. Suksi's contribution also covers the two main techniques of algorithmic decision-making, maintaining that only rule-based systems are compatible with the rule of law, and thus only such systems should be used for fully-automated procedures, while the use of machine learning should be limited to supporting procedures only.

A practical example from an administrative agency is provided by *Riku Sarlin*, who has served as Chief Architect of Algorithmic Systems at the Social Insurance Institution (SII) of Finland. The use of automated decision-making is put in relation to the massive volume of what can be called "mass decisions about social benefits." The point of departure at the SII is that algorithmic systems used in decision-making are rule-based, and one interesting feature of the SII is that its algorithmic software is developed in-house.

Yannick Meneceur develops a problematizing argument based on real-world situations where automated decision-making has been used. Meneceur argues that the development of algorithmic systems in public administration appears to be particularly problematic and may threaten to evolve into a rule of algorithm that is in actuality an antithesis to the rule of law. To counter such a development, it may be helpful to use a set of criteria Meneceur has collected to evaluate algorithmic systems—criteria that include such elements as application of existing positive law, keeping a human agent liable for automated decisions, managing potential bias, preventing solutionism by applying proportionality in the use of algorithmic systems, and guaranteeing the right of appeal over algorithmic decisions.

While automated decision-making is often constructed to work in environments where no discretion or weighing of proportionality takes place, proportionality in particular is posited as a core feature of the rule of law in the contribution by *Lena Enqvist* and *Markus Naarttijärvi*. The authors develop different facets of proportionality that need to be considered at the different stages of automation implementation, e.g., the legislative stage, the system implementation stage, the decision-making stage, and at the appeals or review stage. It is thus necessary to assess proportionality at different stages of implementation, and for that, human oversight and agency must be at the forefront of the process.

In a forward-looking contribution, *Anna-Sara Lind* discusses the EU proposal concerning an AI Act, a regulation that will, if adopted, impact algorithmic systems and their use in different parts of society, potentially including the public administrations of Member States. Lind raises important points throughout, but the three that conclude her chapter include challenges for how to legislate technological phenomena, the manner in which to handle the rule of law in a pluralistic legal context, and the ways in which a holistic approach, embracing several facets of the rule of law, can be created.

In another contribution that turns an eye to the future, *Cecilia Magnusson Sjöberg* draws upon historical developments to construct an observant argument involving, inter alia, digital personhood and digital citizenship. Most notably, Magnusson Sjöberg reflects on the new social roles and professions that are likely to emerge in a future society, one in which various functions are increasingly digitalized, where nascent or yet-to-exist roles contribute to shaping the law and its implementation. Magnusson Sjöberg's chapter thus anticipates the creation of roles such as legal developers, privacy protectors, data openers, technology interpreters, and security agents, all of which would likely play a part in "reading the algorithm."

The volume concludes with Markku Suksi's reflections of a more theoretical nature on a possible future, where automated decision-making in public authorities is situated within a societal context in which the rule of law has been supplanted by what might be termed as a "rule of algorithm."

The academic study of automated decision-making from a legal perspective, by necessity, involves different and varying aspects of law, including theoretical aspects. At the same time, the contributors hope that this current volume elucidates not only current issues, theories, and practical perspectives on the use of automated decision-making by public authorities, but that our volume also deepens the reader's knowledge of the theory of the law, as our authors draw from many timeless thinkers such as Alexy, Bentham, Dworkin, Foucault, Fuller, Habermas, Hart, Hayek, Peczenik, Plato, Raz, Tuori, and others. And while our volume will surely not exhaust conversations around this burgeoning area of law, we hope our entry will contribute to the timely analyses of automated decision-making from the perspective of the rule of law.

References

Araszkiewicz M, Bench-Capon T, Francesconi E, Lauritsen M, Rotolo A (2022) Thirty years of artificial intelligence and law: overviews. Artif Intell Law. https://doi.org/10.1007/s10506-022-09324-9

Bench-Capon T (2022) Thirty years of artificial intelligence and law: editor's introduction. Artif Intell Law. https://doi.org/10.1007/s10506-022-09325-8

de Vries K, Dahlberg M (eds) (2022) Law, AI and digitalisation. De Lege: Årsbok 2021 för juridiska fakulteten vid Uppsala Universitet. Iustus förlag, Uppsala

Juell-Skielse G, Lindgren I, Åkesson M (2022) Service automation in the public sector: concepts, empirical examples, and challenges. Springer, Cham

Kennedy R (2020) Rule of law and algorithmic governance. In: Barfield W (ed) The Cambridge handbook of the law of algorithms. Cambridge University Press, Cambridge, pp 209–232. https://doi.org/10.1017/9781108680844
Noll G (red.) (2021) AI, digitalisering och rätten: en lärobok. Studentlitteratur, Lund
Restrepo Amariles D (2020) Algorithmic decision systems: automation and machine learning in the public administration. In: Barfield W (ed) The Cambridge handbook of the law of algorithms. Cambridge University Press, Cambridge, pp 273–300. https://doi.org/10.1017/9781108680844
Sartor G, Araszkiewicz M, Atkinson K, Bex F, van Engers T, Francesconi E, Prakken H, Sileno G, Schilder F, Wyner A, Bench-Capon T (2022) Thirty years of artificial intelligence and law: the second decade. Artif Intell Law. https://doi.org/10.1007/s10506-022-09326-7
Suksi M (2021) Administrative due process when using automated decision-making in public administration: some notes from a Finnish perspective. Artif Intell Law 29:87–110. https://doi.org/10.1007/s10506-020-09269-x
Wiese Schartum D (2020) From legal sources to programming code: automatic individual decisions in public administration and computers under the rule of law. In: Woodrow Barfield W (ed) The Cambridge handbook of the law of algorithms. Cambridge University Press, Cambridge, pp 301–335. https://doi.org/10.1017/9781108680844
Williams R (2022) Rethinking administrative law for algorithmic decision making. Oxford Journal of Legal Studies 42(2):468–494. https://doi.org/10.1093/ojls/gqab32

Situating the Rule of Law in the Context of Automated Decision-Making

Markus Naarttijärvi

Abstract This contribution situates the rule of law in the context of automated decision-making by using leading rule of law theories to distill some key underlying values of the rule of law which carry particular significance for automated decision-making; dignity, autonomy, and democracy. While disagreement may exist surrounding specific components of the rule of law, general agreement seems to exist surrounding these core values underpinning the concept. By adopting these underlying values of the rule of law, issues with automation, such as the foreseeability of law, access to justice, or non-discrimination, can also be conceptualized as tensions between achieving automation and maintaining respect for human dignity, autonomy of the individual, and a connection to democratic processes. These tensions are finally explained and illustrated through the analogy of normative refraction occurring as automated decision-making requires legal intent to be mediated not only by the language of the law, but through additional refractive layers of code and data. While existing rule of law principles are adapted for managing the refraction added by the language of law, new approaches may be needed to manage the challenges emerging from the additional layers of code and data.

Keywords Rule of law · Automated decision-making · Dignity · Autonomy · Democracy · Normative refraction

1 Introduction

It is safe to say that philosophical and semantic challenges are bound to accompany any attempt to analyze the implications that automated decision-making might have for the rule of law. Not only will difficulties arise in attempting to clarify and analyze the technological frameworks surrounding automation efforts and their legal implications, but this task is made all the more difficult by the contested and vague nature

M. Naarttijärvi (✉)
Department of Law, Umeå University, Umeå, Sweden
e-mail: markus.naarttijarvi@umu.se

M. Suksi (ed.), *The Rule of Law and Automated Decision-Making*,
https://doi.org/10.1007/978-3-031-30142-1_2

of the rule of law as a concept (or is it a principle, an ideal, or a set of expectations?).[1] Nevertheless, certain core components about the rule of law are typically agreed upon in general terms by scholars, legal practitioners, and international actors alike.

First, there is the requirement that both government officials and citizens be bound by the law. Additionally, there are several other minimal, although important characteristics of the concept of the rule of law, including that "[the] law must be set forth in advance (be prospective), be made public, be general, be clear, be stable and certain, and be applied to everyone according to its terms."[2] Other aspects of the concept have been more contentious, such as the inclusion of human rights under the rule of law umbrella. Rather than adding to the many attempts to define what the rule of law is, or should be, I will instead attempt to distill certain elements from some of the more influential conceptualizations of the rule of law, which have become particularly interesting in the context of automated decision-making. In doing so, I will turn from the specific lists and components to certain higher order values that the rule of law can be said to implicitly (and sometimes explicitly) protect, such as individual autonomy, dignity, and democracy.

2 The Rule of Law

The rule of law as we know it today in Europe and much of the western world is the result of a long and winding historical development, emerging from the different legal traditions in which it has grown. A complete history would not be possible here, but suffice to say, the early seeds can be found in Greek philosophy, notably in the writings of Aristotle and Plato.[3] Expressions of rule of law (or at least rule by law) thinking in the enlightenment era are visible in the writings of Hobbes' *Leviathan*,[4] but there are also earlier medieval Nordic expressions of rule of law insights visible in the proclamation "*with law should the land be built*" dating back to the Norwegian *Frostatingsloven* in the year 950, and later in the Danish *Jyske Lov* from 1241.[5] While far from fully developed, these early insights give some

[1] Tamanaha (2009), p. 3; Waldron (2021), pp. 121–136.

[2] Tamanaha (2009), pp. 3–4; see also Raz (2009), pp. 212–219; Fuller (1969).

[3] See Waldron (2020). However, note that Plato seems divided on the value of the law binding the ruler; in *Laws* he states: "Where the law is subject to some other authority and has none of its own, the collapse of state, in my view, is not far off, but if the law is the master of government and the government its slave, then the situation is full of promise and men enjoy all the blessings all the gods shower on a state." Plato (1997), p. 1402 (Laws, Book V, 715 d.). In *Statesman*, he dismisses the idea of the use of law in government instead of intelligence and expertise as essentially stupid (Plato (1995), sec. 294 b-c.).

[4] See Vinx (2012), pp. 145–164.

[5] Sunde (2019). It has been speculated that the expression can be traced back to the Roman Sextus Pomponius "*Civitas findaretur legibus*"; see Sandnes (2006).

indication of the historically varied and culturally embedded values that form part of the foundation of the modern concept.

In more contemporary times, a continuous development and theorization of the concept has brought many competing and overlapping notions of what the rule of law is, or contains, or how it should be understood. These competing notions are certainly present in the debate surrounding whether the rule of law should include more substantive dimensions, such as respect for human rights. In this debate, influential theorists such as Lon L. Fuller and Joseph Raz have stayed clear from more substantive approaches,[6] maintaining the value of formal criteria, even in the face of the wrongs that can be done within a system still based upon a formal understanding of the rule of law. The approach taken up by Fuller and Raz essentially holds that the rule of law can prevent a specific set of legal problems associated with arbitrary or opaque exercises of power, which can in turn serve other values such as maintaining individual freedom and autonomy, or reducing the risk that power will be used for nefarious purposes. Others, such as British judge and scholar Tom Bingham, have argued for more substantive approaches which do include human rights protections. For a justification of this view, Bingham has pointed to the rather disquieting notion that some states are in fact complying with the rule of law when they persecute or even kill members of their population in accordance with "detailed laws duly enacted and scrupulously observed."[7]

While scholars and legal practitioners often talk of the rule of law, it is actually difficult to talk of *the* concept of the rule of law, as there have been different expressions and forms of rule of law logics at play within different legal families. One example of a distinct approach to the rule of law would be the German concept of *Rechtsstaat*, which has a statutory and bureaucratic focus on the relationship between state authorities and citizens on the one hand, and the "rule of law" concept of common law systems on the other, with the emphasis of such systems placed on access to justice "in the ordinary courts of the land" where citizens may claim their rights.[8] While nuances, discussions, and distinct approaches such as the aforementioned are sure to persist, there have been significant steps towards a more coherent, uniform understanding of the rule of law, at least in Europe.

In 2012, the European Commission for Democracy through Law, the Council of Europe advisory body on constitutional matters, more commonly known as "the Venice Commission," attempted to bridge some of the previously mentioned differences and provide a more widely agreed upon definition, what they described as a "consensus," on the core aspects of the concept.[9] One of the more significant tasks of the Venice Commission was therefore to find common ground between the *Rechtsstaat* and the rule of law. This common ground also had to accommodate and balance the many different functions of the rule of law, while remaining careful

[6] Fuller (1969) and Raz (2009).

[7] Bingham (2011), p. 67.

[8] See Meierhenrich (2021a), pp. 39–67.

[9] Venice Commission, Report on the Rule of Law, 003rev-e, 2011.

not to include too much—which would turn the rule of law into a vague collection of "everything good"—or too little, making the rule of law a narrow and formal concept unlikely to function as a bulwark against tyranny. The Venice Commission's efforts culminated in a report which included a rather succinct list of necessary components of the rule of law, "as well as those of the *Rechtsstaat*," where formal, procedural, and substantive rule of law components are represented. The Venice Commission report includes:

(1) Legality, including a transparent, accountable, and democratic process for enacting law
(2) Legal certainty
(3) Prohibition of arbitrariness
(4) Access to justice before independent and impartial courts, including judicial review of administrative acts
(5) Respect for human rights
(6) Non-discrimination and equality before the law[10]

To public law scholars, these are familiar notions. They are generally expressions of principles which can be found at the heart of constitutional and administrative law in most modern democracies. Still, the gathering of these components under an overarching umbrella concept highlights their importance in ensuring a functional rule of law, as well as the necessary interconnection between what can otherwise be seen as a discrete set of principles. This is however far from the only attempt to list rule of law components,[11] and the discussions surrounding the content of the concept are likely to continue.

Additionally, it is worth noting how the Venice Commission embraced a more substantive conceptualization of the rule of law, or as they stated, a "not only formal but also substantial or material (*materieller Rechtsstaatsbegriff*)" concept,[12] which serves as an important endorsement for including respect for human rights under the rule of law. In their report, the Venice Commission noted that "[r]espect for the rule of law and respect for human rights are not necessarily synonymous. However, there is a great deal of overlap between the two concepts and many rights enshrined in documents such as the ECHR also expressly or impliedly refer to the rule of law."[13] Accordingly, the Commission also highlighted a number of rights that most obviously connect to the rule of law, such as access to justice, presumption of innocence, *ne bis in idem*, and other procedural rights.[14] Respect for human rights was thus framed in a context of human rights having importance for the realization of formal rule of law values, although the text of the report leaves open the possibility of a wider interpretation, particularly considering the embraced substantive or material understanding of the rule of law.

[10] Venice Commission, Report on the Rule of Law, 003rev-e, 2011, para 41. See also the contribution of Tuomas Pöysti in this volume.

[11] Notable attempts can be seen in Raz (2009), Fuller (1969) and Hayek (2011).

[12] Venice Commission, Report on the Rule of Law, 003rev-e, 2011, para 41.

[13] Venice Commission, Report on the Rule of Law, 003rev-e, 2011, para 59.

[14] Venice Commission, Report on the Rule of Law, 003rev-e, 2011, para 60.

The Venice Commission report has been influential in the case law of the Court of Justice of the European Union (CJEU), as well as in the rule of law efforts of other EU bodies,[15] not least in the efforts by the European Commission to curb the dismantling of judicial independence and other rule of law safeguards in Hungary and Poland. As the CJEU stated in *Hungary v European Parliament and Council of the European Union*, the rule of law as expressed in Article 2 of the Treaty of the European Union "is not merely a statement of policy guidelines or intentions, but contains values which [. . .] are an integral part of the very identity of the European Union as a common legal order, values which are given concrete expression in principles containing legally binding obligations for the Member States."[16]

The expression "the rule of law" may connote a hypothetical end-state which exists where legal certainty prevails, and there is access to justice before independent and impartial courts, etc. However, while this end-state—a state governed by and under the rule of law—is a clear goal, we should also acknowledge that this goal can never be reached in any final or settled manner. Instead, the rule of law must be continuously maintained and protected. In this sense, the rule of law should perhaps better be described as a continuous process, a social phenomenon that is what actors make of it, through the level of respect they show to it.[17]

This process and respect involve a constant and ongoing vigilance in ensuring that the individual components are safeguarded in the face of challenging phenomena that emerges, political and legal turbulence, or attempts at weakening the rule of law as a whole or in part for temporary political or economic gains. In this process, the interconnectedness of the components of the rule of law needs to be acknowledged. As with recent developments in Poland and Hungary, the erosion of the independence of courts threatens other rule of law components as well, such as legality and access to justice. However, challenges to the rule of law do not always come in the form of blatant, publicized assaults on established institutions. Such challenges sometimes come in the form of gradual and subtle changes to how power is exercised, which in the long term may have significant implications for the rule of law. This brings us to the phenomenon currently issuing such a challenge: the growing reliance on automated decision-making within public administrations, especially in light of technological developments in artificial intelligence (AI).

[15] Clayton (2019).

[16] Judgment of 16 February 2022, *Hungary v European Parliament and Council of the European Union*, C-156/21, ECLI:EU:C:2022:97, para 232.

[17] Meierhenrich (2021b), p. 621.

3 Beyond the Anatomy of the Rule of Law: Individual Autonomy and Restraint of Power

It has been said by Martin Krygier that lawyers tend to focus on the anatomy of the rule of law: endless lists or attempts to pin down necessary components, with less focus placed on the broader aim of the legal enterprise.[18] To some extent this picture is accurate, although pursuits to identify and catalogue the anatomy of law are virtually always shaped by specific implicit or explicit moral and philosophical assumptions about the aim of the rule of law. In his influential writings on the rule of law (although he avoided that label), Lon L. Fuller delineated such overarching values that he held would, if the legal system failed to respect them, threaten the very function of law as an enterprise aimed at governing behavior. Even if a ruler seeks total blind obedience to every whim, Fuller argued that failure to respect these values would in turn undermine that ruler's ability to maintain effective obedience.

Through this approach, the clarity and promulgation of laws demonstrate legal internal "moral" values that have gained prominence through their function in the legal system. If the point of law, as Fuller argues, is to govern and guide behavior, this aim will not be met when individuals cannot adapt their behavior as a result of not knowing what the law entails. Consequently, the law needs to be transparent and clear about rules and requirements contained therein. If the law is not applied in line with the language in which it is expressed, those bound by the law will not be served by having access to it, nor will they even have the ability to understand it. If the law creates the conditions for arbitrary enforcement, those bound by it will not be able to understand or anticipate how the state will respond to particular actions, nor will subjects under the law understand how best to manage their affairs.[19] Raz and Fuller may have disagreed on the moral character of these components, but they both agreed that the aim of law was to guide behavior, and Raz's own list includes many of the same components that Fuller outlines.[20]

This ability to follow the law is however connected to further implicit aims, not only to the effective exercise of power but perhaps, more importantly, to the ability of individuals to know where the outer bounds of their own freedom lie. This in turn helps individuals maximize their freedom and act as autonomously as possible within the confines of the law, thereby creating conditions where the law respects the self-determination of those bound by it.[21] In other words, an awareness of the rules of the law leads legal subjects to focus more clearly upon what they are free to do. For some influential legal thinkers, this individual autonomy lies at the heart of the rule of law. Nowhere is this view more emphatically articulated than in Friedrich Hayek's view on the rule of law. Hayek discussed the topic under the headline, "the

[18] Krygier (2009), pp. 46–47.

[19] Fuller (1969).

[20] Raz (2009).

[21] Fuller (1969) and Raz (2009).

safeguards of individual liberty"; the function of rule of law as a protection for freedom (and property), and by extension, autonomy, is a clear focus of his writings on the topic.[22]

For freedom and autonomy of individuals to exist, however, the power of the state (and arguably, other powerful entities) needs to be placed within certain limits to avoid a slide into despotism. The role of the rule of law in placing limits on the exercise of public power has consequently also been a frequent topic of discussion among legal scholars and practitioners. Even the most formal conception of the rule of law virtually always includes limits on the *form* that the governing authority's exercise of power takes. As discussed above, more substantive conceptions place limits also on what that exercise of power *does*, such as through the protection of human rights. However, a recurring theme in such discussions is also how the rule of law aims to promote or *restrain* the arbitrary exercise of power. This restraint is in turn accomplished by limiting discretion.[23]

4 Autonomy, Automation, and Discretion

The relationship between automation and discretion is complex. On the one hand, attempts at automating decision-making in public administrations have been described in public administration research as a movement towards not only more efficient decision-making, but also as a way of limiting discretion among public servants. Discretion, in this context, can be seen as an obstacle to effectively achieving policy goals—a source of errors, bias, costs, or even resistance against policy goals.[24] These issues may suggest that the automation of decision-making could benefit the rule of law by limiting or even removing discretion, thereby producing less arbitrary, and more uniform, decisions.

The complexities of automation efforts and the roles of discretion in decision-making are however not so unidirectional. As we have seen, the limits to discretion are tied to the existence of clear and foreseeable legal rules applied in line with their legal meaning, ensuring both legality and legal certainty. While automation can reduce the human discretion of public servants, either by replacing those public servants or reducing their role to supervisors of automated systems, automation does not remove discretion as such in the exercise of public power. Instead, automation can move the exercise of discretion from the frontlines of administrative agencies to the backrooms, to system engineers and IT consultants, or automation can sometimes lead to the outsourcing of discretion to private software developers.[25] This

[22] Hayek (2011), pp. 308–329.

[23] Krygier (2009), p. 57; Meierhenrich (2021b), p. 53; Hayek (2011), pp. 321–322; Tamanaha (2021), pp. 225–226.

[24] See Ranerup and Henriksen (2020), p. 4; Bullock (2019), p. 751.

[25] See Waldman (2019), p. 627; Brayne (2021).

move is also connected to the potential for legal rules to be displaced by other normative sources, such as datasets and the algorithms used to analyze that data. Even rule-based systems with decision-trees tend to display a disconnect from the law, as the translation of legal norms into computer codes in such systems can introduce errors or be slow to adapt to changes in the legal environment that they have been designed to emulate.[26]

Hayek enthusiastically promoted the need for limits to discretion under the rule of law, but in the same context, he marked the importance of the possibility of reviewing the substance of decisions before independent courts, stating:

> This means that the decision must be deducible from the rules of law and from those circumstances to which the law refers and which can be known to the parties concerned. The decision must not be affected by any special knowledge possessed by the government or by its momentary purposes and the particular values it attaches to different concrete aims, including the preferences it may have concerning the effects on different people.[27]

Concerning discernability and special knowledge, rule-emulating systems of automation may be able to parrot the language of the law, but in the end, they apply code, rather than law. Checking for errors in such rule-emulating systems may require knowledge possessed only by their designers, or those with access to and understanding of their code base. However, systems based on advanced machine learning may be inscrutable even to experts or those who have created such systems, and even more so to the parties subject to their decisions.[28] Thus, one could be forgiven for mistakenly thinking that, in the passage above, Hayek was writing about profiling by automated decision-making, as such decision-making uses special knowledge that the government extracts from data, assigning scores and values through opaque algorithms to enable the government to decide a particular outcome, depending on the attributes of the data, as processed by the algorithm.

In this sense, the influence of automation on discretion is not one of reduction, but one of displacement. Automated decision-making shifts power and discretion from more visible areas of public administration to less visible areas.[29] In this context, it is also important to remember that legal discretion fulfills an important role in relation to the exercise of power. Legal discretion is often the site of humanity, empathy, and individual justice in the exercise of law.[30] Removing human discretion in the discretion-making stage or exchanging human discretion for *algorithmic discretion*[31] thus runs the risk of reducing humanity and empathy in the exercise of public power. The humanity and empathy with which traditional legal discretion is ideally associated must also be separated from pure expressions of arbitrariness. These human values often play a legitimate role in legal considerations through established

[26] Mohun and Roberts (2020), p. 32.

[27] Hayek (2011), p. 322.

[28] Burrell (2016); Kennedy (2020), pp. 228–229.

[29] Cf. Brayne (2021), p. 119; Lessig (2006), p. 138.

[30] See Lipsky (2010), pp. 14–15; Goldstein (1959); Binns (2020).

[31] See Musco Eklund (2022).

legal principles, e.g., reasonableness or proportionality.[32] In this sense, the legal understanding of discretion—and the attempts to manage it through automation—is an area which must account for the vital influence and role of principles. Without such considerations, there is a risk that we reduce or remove not just discretion, but our humanity.

5 Dignity and the Rule of Law in Automated Decision-Making

This brings us to another of the teleological values that the rule of law serves. Dignity has increasingly been identified as a meta-value which can be seen as both the source of all human rights, and a human right in its own respect, as acknowledged in the EU Charter of Fundamental Rights.[33] The connection between dignity and the rule of law is well-explained by Jeremy Waldron, as he highlights how:

> Applying a norm to a human individual is not like deciding what to do about a rabid animal or a dilapidated house. It involves paying attention to a point of view. As such it embodies a crucial dignitarian idea — respecting the dignity of those to whom the norms are applied as beings capable of explaining themselves.[34]

One of the strongest expressions of human dignity as a meta-value of the rule of law can be found in the German Basic Law, where dignity is placed as a higher-order value that the constitution is intended to secure, placed not only beyond the reach of the legislature, but even as inviolable by constitutional amendments.[35] While this seemingly places dignity among the added values of a substantive understanding of the rule of law, known in German as a *materieller Rechtsstaatsbegriff*, dignity shines through in the protection of more formal components, such as the protection of equality and the generality of norms.

T.R.S. Allan builds upon this notion of dignity anchored in equality before the law when he observes: "Formal equality before the law — the equal subjection of all, regardless of rank or status, to general rules — is underpinned by a deeper conception of equal citizenship: there must be equal protection of the law in the sense that rights or benefits enjoyed by some cannot be unfairly denied to others."[36] Such arbitrary discrimination between persons can be avoided only through laws general in form, applied fairly. Consequently, under the rule of law the state is limited in power through principles of constitutional justice "according each citizen the same

[32] See further Enqvist and Naarttijärvi in this volume.

[33] Dupré (2014).

[34] Waldron (2020).

[35] Tamanaha (2004), pp. 109–110.

[36] Allan (2016), p. 203.

standing and dignity as an equal member of the political community."[37] The same logic may reasonably be extended to procedural rule of law components expressing similar dignity-serving dimensions. The provision of processes in which to challenge government decisions before impartial and independent courts—checking whether legality and other rule of law values have been upheld—must be seen as similar to the recognition of the individual as an equal party under the law, one that can hold power to account.

Raz, who held a strictly formal view of the rule of law, still maintained that "observance of the rule of law is necessary if the law is to respect human dignity," which, for Raz, entails "treating humans as persons capable of planning and plotting their future."[38] This highlights the connection between autonomy and dignity, as respecting dignity, according to Raz, includes respecting individual autonomy and the right to control one's future.[39] The failures of the rule of law thus appear when the law can no longer guide people's deliberations, thus failing to respect their dignity as autonomous beings.[40] This view has certain similarities with the Kantian notion of human dignity, whereby the treatment of human beings as objects, or as a means to an end, rather than as ends in themselves, is seen as a violation of human dignity—an approach endorsed by the German Federal Constitutional Court, the *Bundesverfassungsgericht.*[41]

Automated decision-making carries many different, sometimes subtle, implications for dignity. The connection between dignity and autonomy thus implies that similar concerns can be raised involving dignity. However, the protection of dignity puts at the forefront not just one's freedom to act, but one's treatment and consideration by the state as a person with the *capacity* to act autonomously.[42] When the state employs profiling or automated risk assessments to make decisions or judgements about individuals, this essentially compares how similar the pattern of data surrounding one individual is to the pattern of data surrounding other individuals or groups. These pattern assessments are then used by the state to predict behavior, assigning attributes and drawing inferences.[43]

An example of how the state may use aggregate patterns to judge individuals would be if a traveler experiences increased suspicion of drug trafficking, based on travel routes, or booking details, that align with those of previously known drug traffickers.[44] Another example would be if an individual is denied a visa based on

---

[37] Allan (2016), p. 203.

[38] Raz (2009), p. 221.

[39] Raz (2009), p. 221.

[40] Raz (2009), p. 222.

[41] German Federal Constitutional Court, bverfg, *1 BvR 357/05*, 1 BvR 357/05, Judgment of 15 February 2006, para 121.

[42] See Raz (2009), p. 221.

[43] Hildebrandt (2010), pp. 117–118; Custers (2018), p. 112. See also GDPR Art. 4(4).

[44] European Commission, Report from the Commission to the European Parliament and the Council on the review of Directive 2016/681 on the use of passenger name record (PNR) data for the

data patterns that suggest this individual would apply for asylum if admitted into the territory.[45] These profiling efforts, along with similar ones, and risk assessments, impact dignity as they essentially hold that individuals either cannot or should not be trusted to act autonomously from a category or group in which the state has put them.[46]

With possible infringement upon one's dignity and autonomy, profiling and risk assessments might also lead to unequal treatment. In fact, one could argue that such conditions are the point of the exercise. Profiling and risk assessments are practices in choosing who, in a lineup of different people, the state should spend their resources investigating, questioning, probing, or prioritizing. The use of big data and statistical methods simply brings an objective sheen to this exercise. Whether this may be accepted under the rule of law, or find itself compatible with human dignity, will likely depend on how well we as scholars and lawyers can articulate and make visible the specific preconceptions underpinning such practices, and how vigilant we are as a society in our protection of the underlying values at stake for the rule of law.

6 Democracy

This teleological exploration of the rule of law would be incomplete without acknowledging the role that the rule of law plays in the constitutional framework of democracy. Democracy underpins the principle of legality and the associated democratic processes for enacting law.[47] This component of the law is connected both to formal validity and democratic legitimacy through the way legal rules are formally enacted through democratic assemblies. Not all rule of law definitions place such emphasis on the democratic nature of law-making, but the Venice Commission does make explicit reference to this democratic nature of law-making in their definition. Sometimes the potential conflict between democracy (understood in majoritarian terms) and the rule of law (as a limit to some excesses or expressions of majoritarian choices) is highlighted, but the rule of law is at the very least a constitutional cornerstone of liberal democracies where "democracy" is understood as exercised under a framework of the rule of law.[48]

---

prevention, detection, investigation and prosecution of terrorist offences and serious crime, SWD (2020) 128 final, 24 July 2020, p. 7.

[45]European Travel Information and Authorisation System (ETIAS). In: European Commission. https://home-affairs.ec.europa.eu/policies/schengen-borders-and-visa/smart-borders/european-travel-information-authorisation-system_en (accessed on 2 September 2022).

[46]Cf. Hildebrandt (2010), p. 125.

[47]Venice Commission, Report on the Rule of Law, 003rev-e, 2011, para 41(1).

[48]See Krygier (2021), p. 417.

Indeed, the disregard for the rule of law is one of the defining features of "illiberal democracies."[49] According to Jürgen Habermas, the rule of law and liberal democracy are interlinked and interdependent, as the rule of law is needed to have a functioning democracy and vice versa.[50] This connection however goes beyond laws being enacted by a duly elected parliament. The connection between clarity, foreseeability, and legality further implies that the democratic processes leading up to the finished legislative result can be subject to deliberations based on a reasonable understanding of what the law entails.[51] In other words, the clarity of laws that allows citizens to understand how such laws impact their freedom will also, ideally, allow lawmakers to understand what they are voting for. As Roger Brownsword notes, "[t]here needs to be systematic openness about the proposed use of technological management,"[52] as well as express authorization in law of its use, to live up to ideals of democratic deliberation.[53]

It thus may seem the increased, lawful use of automated decision-making would not necessarily carry implications for democratic legitimacy. However, the move towards automation implies that the law will become increasingly filtered through technological translations, where the definition of what the law entails for individuals, and the exercise of power, becomes shifted from the language of the law towards the translation of the law into technological processes in systems of automated decision-making.[54] Through this shift, the connection between administrative decisions and the democratic processes that legitimize those decisions may be weakened. Mistakes or translations in the code that depart from legal rules, or that misconstrue legal principles, may be perceived as "law" by individuals or even legal authorities, which could lead to a situation whereupon those involved in the development process become *ersatz* legislators.[55] Making legislation "digital-ready"—delivered by the legislator in a form fit for automation—is a way of keeping that connection,[56] but this process may give rise to another set of concerns. It can render legislation so complex as to challenge clarity and foreseeability, while blurring the line between making law and applying law.

[49] Zakaria (1997).

[50] Habermas (1996), p. 454.

[51] Naarttijärvi (2018).

[52] Brownsword (2016), p. 138.

[53] Brownsword (2016), p. 111.

[54] Waldman (2019), p. 627.

[55] Cf. Lessig (2006), p. 121.

[56] Mohun and Roberts (2020).

7 Conclusions and Implications: Normative Refraction and the Rule of Law

The intention of this chapter has not been to fully articulate what the rule of law is, or what the impacts of automated decision-making would be in that context. The previous sections have instead sought to illustrate the diversity of issues involved in situating the rule of law in a context of automated decision-making, and later chapters will further elaborate on this theme. I have thus attempted to show that, despite the differences in the definitions and discussions surrounding the rule of law, certain underlying values and aims are, if not agreed upon, at least not subject to rampant disagreement. In other words, there do appear to be some important points of consensus among significant international actors: the value of the rule of law for autonomy and dignity, the connected function of limiting or restraining arbitrariness in the exercise of power, and the modern understanding of the rule of law and democracy as interconnected.

I would like to conclude this chapter with an attempt to summarize some of the more salient implications of automated decision-making by talking about refraction. In physics, refraction is (simply put) the phenomenon of how light or radio waves, etc. are deflected when they pass obliquely through the interface between one medium and another.[57] A focused beam of light will refract when entering a lens or a prism, and then again when exiting, as illustrated on the iconic cover of Pink Floyd's 1973 album, *The Dark Side of the Moon*. I would argue that the clarity of law, conceived of here as a fixed expression of legislators' intent, displays a similar effect.

In law, scholars and practitioners are accustomed to the fact that political intent needs to be expressed through legal language. This language may or may not be an accurate reflection of the political intent, or it may contain vague terms or concepts which need interpretation.[58] As the intent of the legislature enters the language of law, some refraction occurs, as the capacity of an individual or group to translate this intent with exact precision is inherently limited. Once this language is interpreted (albeit imperfectly) and applied by courts and other legal actors, another refraction occurs, as the interpretation may stray further from the intent, and possibly from the language of the law as well. Still, these issues are ones which the law, and the rule of law, have mechanisms in place to manage. Legality as a component of the rule of law will help enforce the clarity and foreseeability of the language of the law, and enable subjects of the law to understand what it requires, thereby gaining a means to maximize their autonomy. The rule of law further allows those subjects under the law to challenge decisions (and laws) before independent courts. For example, one may challenge the application of law when it strays from its legal meaning as expressed in the language of the law.

---

[57] Park and Allaby (2013), p. 360.

[58] See Endicott (2000).

Fig. 1 Normative refraction

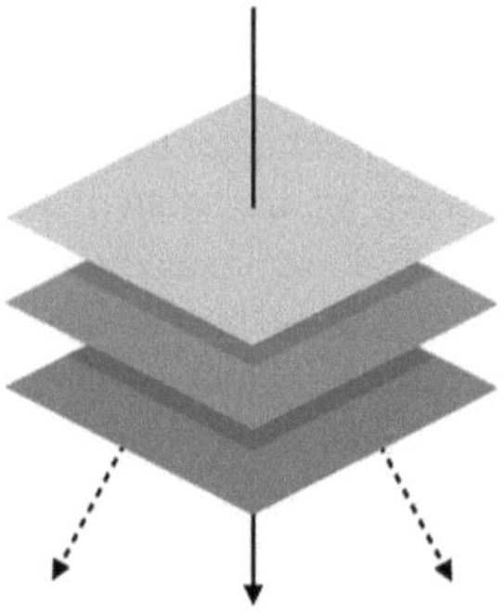

The language of statutory law is also imbued with democratic legitimacy, as it passes through the democratic process of lawmaking. Each word of statutes is, ideally, scrutinized in committees, by experts and lawyers, before being enacted by parliament and promulgated to the public. To allow subjects of the law to trust in the law as expressed in the language of statutory norms, independent courts are tasked under the rule of law with being the final arbiters of meaning in view of evolving circumstances, legal principles, and the interest of justice. In this way, the refraction implied by legislative intent passing through language is institutionally managed, if not fully, at least to a certain extent. The refraction is in fact expected, as legislative intent is only partially allowed to influence the interpretation of the language of the law, and the interpretation of legal norms in courts are open to being revisited as circumstances evolve.

Automated decision-making, as well as semi-automated decision-making, adds two more refractive layers: code and data. The code layer is added as legal norms are translated into code, possibly imperfectly, or with slight nuances, compared to the original legal meaning. Such imperfections further distance code from political intent.[59] It is also possible that the translation will capture a specific *momentary* state of what the law requires, but will not be able to replicate the open texture of the language of law, and the gradual development of that law occurring through adjudication, resulting in refraction occurring over time as the code is frozen while the law evolves (Fig. 1).[60]

In non-rule-based systems, such as those employing machine-learning technologies trained on or adapting to new data, another layer of refraction is added: data. This layer may shift the application of law not only away from the intent of the legislator, or the language of the law, but additionally away from the intent of those coding or implementing the decision-making system. This may, as mentioned above, be the result of norms or biases hidden in the datasets which produce unexpected or unintended results. Another example of how data can add a layer of refraction

[59] Mohun and Roberts (2020).

[60] See Kennedy (2020), pp. 226–227 describing similar concerns as unadaptive ambient law.

between legal intent and application would be if a machine-learning model produces seemingly accurate results, but that those results are based on extra-legal considerations which have no basis in the normative requirements of law. One other instance of refraction-through-data could come in the form of a machine-learning model producing results based on correlations that seem correct in average situations but which turn out to be faulty as the algorithm faces new circumstances or outlier situations.

Importantly, code and data are refractive layers that, unlike the language of the law, hold no innate democratic legitimacy.[61] The extent to which such legitimacy can be imbued into code depends on the extent to which legislators are prepared and able to articulate the specific requirements of such systems to create a democratic consensus about the standards such systems should meet. Data protection rules are examples of such standards, but these rules target only a smaller subset of concerns. Also, the extent to which the rule of law is equipped to manage these refractive layers is still a matter of debate.

One way of managing the impact of newly developing refractive layers would be to insist on the normativity of law—that the exercise of public power must be based on the law itself, rather than on its translation or approximation by other means, such as code or data. Another would be to insist on applying existing rule of law standards to these other layers of refraction as well, by forcing clarity and transparency of these layers to promote foreseeability, and to vigilantly guard against encroachments on equality or non-discrimination and attempt to democratize the design and application of code, bringing the use of data in public decision-making under the processes of democratic deliberation.

An alternative approach to managing new, added layers of refraction would be to adopt new rule of law components, or adapt existing components to face these challenges, to reimagine or bolster the rule of law to preserve autonomy, dignity, and democracy in the face of algorithmic models of governing.[62] Leading scholars in law and technology have suggested the need for such steps in light of the specific challenges society faces in this context.[63] But the warnings precede our current discussion surrounding automated decision-making as well. Hayek warned of the impact that technological developments are bound to have on individual liberty, stating: "Today we must be particularly aware that, as a result of technological change, which constantly creates new potential threats to individual liberty, no list of protected rights can be regarded as exhaustive."[64]

Given the historical difficulty of finding agreement on what the rule of law entails, the task of reaching a wider consensus remains daunting; however, this pursuit is

[61] Hildebrandt (2016a).

[62] Hildebrandt (2016a), pp. 28–29.

[63] Brownsword (2016); Hildebrandt (2016b), p. 226.

[64] Hayek (2011), pp. 324–325. Hayek imagined future possibilities of chemical alteration of opinions, but arguably algorithmic manipulation may carry similar implications.

increasingly necessary due to the profound impact that automation is sure to have on legal decision-making and many other facets of society in the years ahead.

References

Allan TRS (2016) The rule of law. In: Dyzenhaus D, Thorburn M (eds) Philosophical foundations of constitutional law. Oxford University Press, Oxford, pp 201–220

Bingham T (2011) The rule of law. Penguin Books, London

Binns R (2020) Human judgment in algorithmic loops: individual justice and automated decision-making. Regul Gov:197–211. https://doi.org/10.1111/rego.12358

Brayne S (2021) Predict and surveil: data, discretion, and the future of policing. Oxford University Press, New York

Brownsword R (2016) Technological management and the rule of law. Law Innov Technol 8:100–140. https://doi.org/10.1080/17579961.2016.1161891

Bullock JB (2019) Artificial intelligence, discretion, and bureaucracy. Am Rev Public Adm 49: 751–761. https://doi.org/10.1177/0275074019856123

Burrell J (2016) How the machine 'thinks': understanding opacity in machine learning algorithms. Big Data Soc 3:1–12. https://doi.org/10.1177/2053951715622512

Clayton R (2019) The Venice Commission and the rule of law crisis. Public Law, pp 450–460

Custers B (2018) Profiling as inferred data. Amplifier effects and positive feedback loops. In: Bayamlioğlu E, Baraliuc I, Janssens L, Hildebrandt M (eds) Being profiled: cogitas ergo sum: 10 years of profiling the European citizen. Amsterdam University Press, Amsterdam, pp 112–116

Dupré C (2014) Art 1 – human dignity. In: Peers S (ed) The EU Charter of Fundamental Rights: a commentary. Hart [u.a.], Oxford, pp 3–24

Endicott TAO (2000) Vagueness in law. Oxford University Press, Oxford

Fuller LL (1969) The morality of law. Yale University Press, New Haven

Goldstein J (1959) Police discretion not to invoke the criminal process: low-visibility decisions in the administration of justice. Yale Law J 69:543–594

Habermas J (1996) Between facts and norms: contributions to a discourse theory of law and democracy. Polity, London

Hayek FA (2011) The constitution of liberty: the definitive edition. University of Chicago Press, Chicago

Hildebrandt M (2010) Proactive forensic profiling: proactive criminalization? In: Duff RA, Farmer L, Marshall SE et al (eds) The boundaries of the criminal law. Oxford University Press, Oxford, pp 113–137

Hildebrandt M (2016a) Law as information in the era of data-driven agency. Mod Law Rev 79:1–30. https://doi.org/10.1111/1468-2230.12165

Hildebrandt M (2016b) Smart technologies and the end(s) of law: novel entanglements of law and technology, Paperback edition. Edward Elgar Publishing, Cheltenham, Northampton

Kennedy R (2020) The rule of law and algorithmic governance. In: Barfield W (ed) The Cambridge handbook of the law of algorithms, 1st edn. Cambridge University Press, Cambridge, pp 209–232

Krygier M (2009) The rule of law: legality, teleology, sociology. In: Palombella G, Walker N (eds) Relocating the rule of law. Bloomsbury Publishing Plc, London, pp 45–70

Krygier M (2021) Democracy and the rule of law. In: Meierhenrich J, Loughlin M (eds) The Cambridge companion to the rule of law, 1st edn. Cambridge University Press, Cambridge, pp 406–424

Lessig L (2006) Code: version 2.0. Basic Books, New York

Lipsky M (2010) Street-level bureaucracy: dilemmas of the individual in public services, 30th anniversary expanded edn. Russell Sage Foundation, New York
Meierhenrich J (2021a) Rechtsstaat versus the rule of law. In: Meierhenrich J, Loughlin M (eds) The Cambridge companion to the rule of law, 1st edn. Cambridge University Press, Cambridge, pp 39–67
Meierhenrich J (2021b) What the rule of law is...and is not. In: Meierhenrich J, Loughlin M (eds) The Cambridge companion to the rule of law, 1st edn. Cambridge University Press, Cambridge, pp 569–621
Mohun J, Roberts A (2020) Cracking the code: rulemaking for humans and machines. OECD Working Papers on Public Governance No. 42. https://doi.org/10.1787/3afe6ba5-en
Musco Eklund A (2022) Frontex and 'algorithmic discretion' (Part I): the ETIAS screening rules and the principle of legality. In: Verfassungsblog. https://verfassungsblog.de/frontex-and-algorithmic-discretion-part-i/
Naarttijärvi M (2018) Kvalitativ legalitet: ett demokratiskt perspektiv. Tidsskrift for Rettsvitenskap 131:206–234. https://doi.org/10.18261/issn.1504-3096-2018-02-03-02
Park CC, Allaby M (2013) A dictionary of environment and conservation, 2nd edn. Oxford University Press, Oxford
Plato (1995) The Statesman. Cambridge University Press, Cambridge
Plato (1997) Complete works. Hackett Pub, Indianapolis
Ranerup A, Henriksen HZ (2020) Digital discretion: unpacking human and technological agency in automated decision making in Sweden's social services. Soc Sci Comput Rev:1–17. https://doi.org/10.1177/0894439320980434
Raz J (2009) The authority of law: essays on law and morality. Oxford University Press, Oxford
Sandnes J (2006) Engi maðr skal atför at öðrum gera – noen merknader til motstandsbestemmelsene i Frostatingsloven. Historisk tidsskrift 85:289–298. https://doi.org/10.18261/ISSN1504-2944-2006-02-06
Sunde JØ (2019) Frostatingslova. In Store Norske Leksikon. https://snl.no/Frostatingslova
Tamanaha BZ (2004) On the rule of law: history, politics, theory. Cambridge University Press, Cambridge
Tamanaha BZ (2009) A concise guide to the rule of law. In: Palombella G, Walker N (eds) Relocating the rule of law. Bloomsbury Publishing Plc, London, pp 3–16
Tamanaha BZ (2021) Functions of the rule of law. In: Meierhenrich J, Loughlin M (eds) The Cambridge companion to the rule of law, 1st edn. Cambridge University Press, Cambridge, pp 221–236
Vinx L (2012) Hobbes on civic liberty and the rule of law. In: Dyzenhaus D, Poole T (eds) Hobbes and the law, 1st publ. Cambridge University Press, Cambridge, pp 145–164
Waldman E (2019) Power, process, and automated decision-making. Fordham Law Rev 88:613–632
Waldron J (2020) The rule of law. In: The Stanford encyclopedia of philosophy. Metaphysics Research Lab, Stanford University. https://plato.stanford.edu/archives/sum2020/entries/rule-of-law/
Waldron J (2021) The rule of law as an essentially contested concept. In: Meierhenrich J, Loughlin M (eds) The Cambridge companion to the rule of law, 1st edn. Cambridge University Press, Cambridge, pp 121–136
Zakaria F (1997) The rise of illiberal democracy. Foreign Aff 76:22–43

Legislating for Legal Certainty, with a Right to a Human Face, in an Automated Public Administration

Tuomas Pöysti

Abstract Administrative and constitutional law, as well as wider legal principles complement European Union data protection legislation in balancing various fundamental rights and interests in automated decision-making in public administration. This chapter will, from the administrative law perspective, with a *de lege ferenda* emphasis, further develop a legal-certainty-based framework on automated administrative decisions. Finland's legislative proposals and constitutional practice, complemented by comparative perspectives from legislation and doctrine in Germany, France, and Sweden, and U.S. Federal administrative law, will be used in the analyses. European law recognizes a right to human review. The role of legislation is to set general but sufficiently guiding requirements on the design of automated systems and procedures. The chapter concludes that legislators, system-developers, and those who apply the law have a common task to maintain human dignity and human agency in the face of automated public administration.

Keywords Digitalization · Automated decision-making · Artificial intelligence · Administrative law · Data protection · Legal certainty

1 Introduction

The use of automated decision-making in public administration has become an increasingly salient issue in the legislatures of the European Union (EU) and its Member States, but at the same time, it represents the return of an old topic. Throughout the 2020s, we have actually been witnessing not the first or even second wave of automation, but the fifth.[1] And to revisit some of the first proposals and analyses concerning automated decision-making and the law, we would need to

[1]From the Finnish perspective on the history of the reflections on the automation of public administration, see Hirvonen (2022), pp. 388–390. See, generally, Pohle (2021).

T. Pöysti (✉)
Chancellor of Justice, Helsinki, Finland
e-mail: Tuomas.Poysti@gov.fi

M. Suksi (ed.), *The Rule of Law and Automated Decision-Making*,
https://doi.org/10.1007/978-3-031-30142-1_3

return to Lee Loevinger's 1963 essay, "Jurimetrics: The Methodology of Legal Inquiry," in addition to Layman E. Allen's ideas on the computing of normalized legal drafting and on the logic of early legal artificial intelligence (AI).[2]

Legal and administrative informatics between the 1960s and 1990s in Germany and Scandinavia picked up on many of Loevinger's and Allen's themes and worked with similar ideas on the automation of administrative work in public administration.[3] French data protection law addressed automated decision-making in judicial, administrative, and private contexts as early as 1978. This entry into French law served as a legislative model for Article 15 of the European Community Personal Data Directive 95/46/EC.[4] In recent years, there has been a resurgence of efforts, philosophical and legal, to grapple with and manage the current practical advance of AI-related technologies, rule-based decision-making, and decision-support solutions, and the use of large data sets and data processing.[5]

Generally, horizontally-applicable principles and rules on automated decision-making follow from data protection law and principles of equality and non-discrimination.[6] Following French data protection law, the European Personal Data Directive 95/46/EC prohibited the subjection of natural persons to decision-making by solely automatic means, without specific protection measures. The directive also required the logic of automated decision-making to be made available.[7] The rationale of these provisions was to protect human autonomy and agency, as well as the legitimacy of and trust in legal and governmental decision-making.[8]

Currently, the European Union General Data Protection Regulation (EU) 2016/679 contains a similar kind of general prohibition against subjecting a natural person

---

[2] See Loevinger (1963) and Allen and Engholm (1978).

[3] See, for example, Magnusson-Sjöberg (1992), Wahlgren (1992), Wiese Schartum (1993), and Sartor (1993).

[4] See French loi n:o 78–17 du 6 janvier 1978 relative à l'informatique, aux fichiers et aux libertés art. 2, at: https://www.legifrance.gouv.fr/jorf/id/JORFTEXT000000886460. See Art. 15 of Directive 95/46/EC of the European Parliament and of the Council of 24 October 1995 on the protection of individuals with regard to the processing of personal data and on the free movement of such data, OJ L 281, 23.11.1995, pp. 31–50. See COM (90) 314 final, and COM (92) 422 final, p. 26. See Bygrave (2001), pp. 17–18.

[5] On the increased use of algorithmic decision-making in the public administration, see Rinta-Kahila et al. (2022) and Zalnieriute et al. (2020). On the use of automated decision-making and other automatic means in Finnish public administration, see the Ministry of Justice and Ministry of Finance, draft Proposal for the Acts on Automated Decision-making in Public Administration, public consultation VN/3071/2020, 25 March–6 May 2022. Documents available at: https://oikeusministerio.fi/hanke?tunnus=OM021:00/2020#lainvalmistelu (accessed on 9 June 2022). See also final Government Proposal for Acts on Automated Decision-making in Public Administration HE 145/2022 vp, pp. 25–30. On the increased automated data processing as underlying factor for regulatory and legislative needs, see Hirvonen (2022), p. 387.

[6] See Bibal et al. (2021), pp. 151–153; Wachter et al. (2017); Wachter (2020, 2022).

[7] Art. 15 and para 41 of the preamble of Directive 95/46/EC of the European Parliament and of the Council of 24 October 1995 on the protection of individuals with regard to the processing of personal data and on the free movement of such data, Official Journal L 281, 23.11.1995, pp. 31–50.

[8] See Bygrave (2001), p. 18.

to solely automatic processing of his or her personal data, except when explicitly allowed in an EU or Member State act.[9] The admissibility of automated decision-making is also an issue of formal, procedural, and substantive rule of law, criteria connected with the realization of fundamental and human rights, and administrative law.[10] Administrative and constitutional law, as well as wider legal principles, and a fundamental or human rights-centric approach, complement data protection legislation in balancing various fundamental rights and interests in automated decision-making.[11]

Sweden, France, and Germany, among other EU Member States, have recently passed noteworthy legislation on automated decision-making in public authorities, by means of general acts of administrative law. Sweden, in its Administrative Procedure Act, has included a concise, generic rule enabling automated decision-making in administrative matters.[12] Legislative activities still go on despite these generic provisions on automated decision-making in Sweden.[13] Germany has legislated, as part of the reform of the tax and social security administration, in the newly revised Section 35a to the Administrative Procedure Act (VwVfG), that automated decision-making can be carried out for administrative acts when such decision-making is explicitly authorized in a legal act and if there is no discretion in deciding the matter.[14] The German VwVfG also requires that there shall always be a specific authorizing legal rule in specific legislation to apply automated decision-making.[15]

France has more detailed horizontally applicable rules included in the administrative code and in other laws that create legal foundations for the use of automated decision-making.[16] Finland, like many other countries, already makes use of widely automated decision-making and decision-support. The Finnish legislator has been trying to keep pace with living law and administrative practice while regulating automated functions in a meaningful way in public administration and public service. In September 2022, the Government of Finland concluded a public

[9] Regulation (EU) 2016/679 of the European Parliament and of the Council of 27 April 2016 on the protection of natural persons with regard to the processing of personal data and on the free movement of such data, and repealing Directive 95/46/EC, OJ L 119, 4.5.2016, pp. 1–88.

[10] See Suksi (2020, 2022).

[11] See Enarsson et al. (2022), pp. 123–124 and 131.

[12] See Sweden's Administrative Procedure Act, SFS 2017:900, Sect. 28.

[13] See, for example, Swedish legislative initiatives in the municipal sector, SOU 2021:16.

[14] See German Administrative Procedure Act (Verwaltungsverfahrensgesetz, VwVfG), Sect. 35a. On the reform, see BR-Drs. 255/16, documents available at: https://dip.bundestag.de/vorgang/gesetz-zur-modernisierung-des-besteuerungsverfahrens/71245 (accessed on 9 August 2022). The law was published at BGBl. I 2016, S. 1679. For a short introductory commentary, see Braun Binder (2016), and for a commentary, Martini and Nink (2017).

[15] See Djeffal (2018), pp. 19–21 and Martini and Nink (2017), pp. 2–3.

[16] See French data protection act, loi n:o 78–17 du 6 janvier 1978 relative à l'informatique, aux fichiers et aux libertés, Art. 47. See also French administrative procedure act, Code des relations entre le public et l'administration, Art. L311-3-1 which shall be read together with the other subarticles in L311 and also with reference to data protection act, loi n:o 78–17.

consultation on a draft proposal for general provisions to be included in the Administrative Procedure Act (434/2003), the Act on Information Management in Public Administration (906/2019), the Act on the Provision of Digital Services (306/2019), and several other acts.[17] The Government presented the final legislative proposal to the Parliament on 19 September 2022. The Government's objective is to create generally applicable legal foundations for automated decision-making.[18]

Constitutional guardians—constitutional courts or other constitutional organs overseeing constitutionality—have taken positions on the proposed laws that relate to the use of AI and automation, as well as on the constitutional requirements concerning automated decision-making in government. For example, the French Constitutional Council (Conseil constitutionnel) gave a significant decision on automated decision-making (number 2018-765 DC) in June 2018. The following year, the Constitutional Council reached an additional decision (number 2019-796 DC), which concerns tax control in digital platforms. These decisions display legal reasoning that has several commonalities with the Finnish constitutional doctrine.[19]

Finland has a parliament-centric prior constitutionality review of draft legislation pursuant to Section 74 of the Constitution of Finland, where the Constitutional Law Committee of the Parliament has the primary role in the assessment of constitutionality of legislation. The courts and the constitutional supreme guardians of the law, the Chancellor of Justice and the Parliamentary Ombudsman, also have significant roles in constitutionality review, including systematic *ex ante* opinions and constitutionality reviews by the Chancellor of Justice for government legislative initiatives and for laws to be promulgated.[20] Finland's Constitutional Law Committee has given several review opinions and statements that call for guaranteeing the principles and rights of good administration in automated decision-making, via rules in

---

[17] General acts to be amended are Act on the Processing of Personal Data in Criminal Matters and in Connection with Maintaining National Security (1054/2018) and Code of Real Estate (540/1995).

[18] See Government Proposal to Parliament for Acts on Automated Decision-making in Public Administration, HE 145/2022 vp. For legislative drafting history, see draft Proposal for the Acts on Automated Decision-making in Public Administration, Ministry of Justice and Ministry of Finance, public consultation VN/3071/2020, 25 March–6 May 2022. See Government legislative project, Preparation of general legislation concerning automated decision-making in the public administration, OM021:00/2020 and Government legislative project, Working group for review of general legislation on public administration information systems, VM059:00/2021. The draft Government Proposal was subject to the prior constitutional review by the Chancellor of Justice, see prior constitutional review OKV/2162/23/2022.

[19] See Conseil constitutionnelle, décision n:o 2018-765 DC du 12 juin 2018, Loi relative à la protection des données personnelles, at: https://www.conseil-constitutionnel.fr/decision/2018/2018765DC.htm; Conseil constitutionnelle décision N:o 2019-796 DC, 27.12.2019 paras 77–96, at: https://www.conseil-constitutionnel.fr/decision/2019/2019796DC.htm.

[20] For a short overview of Finland's arrangements on constitutionality control and checks and balances, see the European Union Rule of Law Report 2021, Country Chapter on the Rule of Law Situation in Finland, SWD (2021) 711 final. See also Organisation for Economic Co-operation and Development (OECD) (2021), Civic Space Scan of Finland, Chap. 3 (Key role of oversight mechanisms).

generally applicable Acts of Parliament.[21] The Chancellor of Justice and the Parliamentary Ombudsman have given several decisions on the conditions of the use of automated decision-making as well.[22]

I will continue from the administrative law perspective with a *de lege ferenda* emphasis on the analyses developed by Dag Wiese Schartum on the rule of law and the legal-certainty-based framework on automated administrative decisions, and use Finland's legislative proposals and constitutional practice to make a case study of administrative law doctrine on automated decision-making.[23] I will focus on legal certainty as a principle guiding the design of automated decision-making systems, and on the eventual right to human decision-making, or at least a right to review by humans, which are two inter-related and very topical issues related to automated decision-making.

As the current Chancellor of Justice in Finland, I am also the author of the decisions and constitutional reviews of the Chancellor of Justice cited in this chapter. In addition, under the new Act on the Division of Tasks between the Chancellor of Justice of the Government and the Parliamentary Ombudsman (330/2022), systemic oversight of the development and maintenance of the automatic systems in public administration is in the specific remit of the Chancellor of Justice. This chapter is a legal actor's internal account on legislative developments. I balance this lack of distance from my research topic by anchoring my argument carefully in other sources of law, and I also engage in self-reflection, examining my argument in light of doctrinal positions in legal literature and international comparison.

[21] See, particularly, Constitutional Law Committee Opinions PeVL 7/2019 vp, PeVL 78/2018 vp, PeVL 70/2018 vp, PeVL 62/2018 vp, PeVL 49/2017 vp, PeVL 35/2005 vp.

[22] See Chancellor of Justice Decision concerning automated decision-making in the Finnish Social Insurance Institution (OKV/131/70/2020, 20 April 2021) and Chancellor of Justice Decision concerning automatic generation of legally binding opinion concerning the status in the labour market defining the eligibility on unemployment benefit (OKV/138/10/2020, 29 October 2020). See Deputy Parliamentary Ombudsman Decision concerning automation in the Finnish Tax Administration, EOAK/3379/2018, 20 November 2019. In addition the Chancellor of Justice has given several prior constitutionality review opinions on the draft Government proposals. See Suksi (2022), for a thorough analysis of these decisions from formal, procedural and material rule of law perspectives.

[23] See Wiese Schartum (2020). See also Dag Wiese Schartum's pioneering work on legal certainty in the public sector system's development, Wiese Schartum (1993), which contains topical insights to the question of designing legal certainty to automated decision-making systems. By doing so I will also comment Markku Suksi's analysis, in Suksi (2020), of the needs for rule-of-law-based approach to administrative procedure in automated decision-making.

2 Automation and Automated Decision-Making as a Specific Context in European Law and the Right to Human Review

Legal principles and doctrines of administrative law cover automated decision-making like any other procedure or method of decision-making and service delivery. We could even wonder if a truly technologically neutral approach would suffice, and if there are any needs for specific acts related to automated decision-making.[24] Wider questions concerning digitalization are nevertheless relevant.[25] Henry Praekken and Giovanni Sartor argue that law and legal decision-making are natural fields of application for AI, since legal decision-making is rich in information processing and involves argumentation, decision-making, and communication, all of which can be greatly assisted and partly performed by machines.[26] Concerning U.S. Federal administrative law, Gary Coglianese and David Lehr assess that automated decision-making would pass the test of general principles and doctrines of administrative law. Coglianese and Lehr furthermore caution against extensive skepticism, or alarmism, on the use of algorithmic decision-making.[27] Thus, according to Coglianese and his colleague Steven M. Appel, the application of the general principles of administrative law could guide the use of machine learning and other algorithmic decision-making processes in a lawful, responsible, and a societally beneficial way.[28]

The legitimacy of automated decision-making, and the alignment of automated decision-making with administrative law principles, seems to depend on the design choices.[29] The law establishes a process through which design and its values are realized in systems, as well as in the social processes related to technological design. The design of algorithms used in automated decision-making is no different from this general process of setting values and limits. Enacted law can therefore provide legitimacy for technological designs.[30]

Furthermore, the law not only guides legal and administrative reasoning and decision-rules, but the law also places acceptable limits upon such reasoning and decision-rules.[31] Automation-friendly legislation contains legal rules formulated in a way that make legally correct and sustainable automation possible. For example,

[24] More specific rule-based approach may not necessarily cover by its scope of application all the phenomena which need to be covered whereas general principles can reach them. A good example is non-discrimination in the affinity profiling in online advertising, which is not easily within the scope of application of the GDPR. See Wachter (2020).

[25] Wiese Schartum (2021), pp. 92–93.

[26] Praekken and Sartor (2015), pp. 214–215.

[27] Coglianese and Lehr (2017).

[28] Appel and Coglianese (2020).

[29] Zalnieriute et al. (2019).

[30] See Koulu (2021). Koulu ends her argument with optimism: "law can constrain and support societally sustainable technological design," p. 99.

[31] Verheij (2020), p. 187.

clear rules on standard cases are formulated within such legal rules.[32] An automation-friendly legal perspective would cover the significant aspects of the use of AI, including insights gleaned via mathematics, logic, technology, psychology, sociology, and other related fields of study.[33] Clarity, predictability, comprehensibility, and the democratic legitimacy of the fundamental design and value choices call upon the legislator to set general rules on automated decision-making in the public sector.

The European Union General Data Protection Regulation (GDPR) sets a framework for automated decision-making through its risk-centric approach, the data protection principles, and explicit provisions in Article 22 concerning solely automated decision-making and profiling.[34] Provisions of the GDPR have had a quasi-constitutional impact on the national laws of EU Member States, as the GDPR directly connects to Article 8 of the Charter of Fundamental Rights of the European Union.

In Finland, the Constitutional Law Committee has, since the entry into force of the GDPR, systematically held that compliance with the Constitution of Finland's Section 10 on the protection of private life and personal data is maintained through the protection of personal data by compliance with the GDPR and its risk-centric and risk-based view. The GDPR's risk-centric and risk-based approach defines the need for additional protection measures either in the EU law or within the national law of Member States. Finland's constitutional tradition emphasizes the relatively detailed and careful management of the risks to rights through clearly formulated rules contained in the acts of parliament.[35] Automated decision-making in the public sector thus creates a specific family of contexts for the application of the GDPR.[36]

Similarly to its predecessor, Article 15 of the Personal Data Directive, Article 22 of the GDPR creates a relative right of individuals not to be subject to *solely* automated decision-making in the public or the private sector, without appropriate and specific protection measures. Furthermore, Article 22 requires a specific legal basis for processing and a specific legal basis in the EU or Member State law,

[32] Wiese Schartum (2021), p. 94.

[33] Verheij (2020), pp. 189–191.

[34] European Union data protection law is one of the drivers for legislating in the field of automated decision-making. See Hirvonen (2022), p. 387; Koivisto and Koulu (2020), pp. 805–807. Data protection law generally encounters new digital phenomena and balances between various interests and fundamental rights. See Greenstein (2021), Chap. 5.2.

[35] See Constitutional Law Committee Opinions PeVL 14/2018 vp, pp. 2–5; PeVL 15/2018 vp, pp. 36–38 and PeVL 62/2018 vp, pp. 2–4.

[36] Helen Nissenbaum's account of the contextuality of privacy and personal integrity is highly relevant for the GDPR and the European data protection law in general, particularly in capturing some of the philosophy behind European Court of Human Rights jurisprudence on privacy. Many of the broad and open-ended principles of data protection written into Article 5 of the GDPR gain their flesh and bone contextually, on Nissenbaum's theory. See Nissenbaum (2010), pp. 129–139 and 190. For my analysis for the general relevance and accuracy of Nissenbaum's approach to improve also understanding of core elements of European data protection and privacy law, see Pöysti (2019), pp. 195–197.

particularly in the public sector context where explicit informed consent, performance of a contract, and legitimate expectations have little to no space for application as legal bases for processing.[37] In Article 22, profiling and automated decision-making are two different but partly overlapping phenomena. Profiling is an example of automated decision-making, but the GDPR recognizes other forms of automated decision-making as well.[38]

Article 22's scope of application, and the expression "solely by automatic processing" contained therein, have created confusion over whether or not automated administrative procedures are covered under the GDPR. "Solely automated decision-making" is when technological means have the ability to make decisions without human involvement. The human participation in decision-making should thus be effective and real to remain in compliance with Article 22 of the GDPR.[39]

The GDPR seems, when Article 22 is read together with paragraph 71 of the Preamble, to establish at least a right to human review.[40] The GDPR is hence a legal foundation for a relatively strong constitutional argument for a specific kind of human oversight. Paragraph 71 of the GDPR's Preamble states that data processing leading to automated decisions should be subject to suitable safeguards, which should include furnishing specific information to the data subject, and the right to obtain human intervention, to express his or her point of view, to obtain an explanation of the decision reached after such assessment, and to challenge the decision.

Article 11 of the Law Enforcement Data Protection Directive (EU) 2016/680, applicable to processing of personal data by competent authorities in the prevention of crime and criminal law enforcement, is clearer than Article 22 of the GDPR and requires that the safeguards for the rights and freedoms of the data subject in automated decision-making shall contain at least the right to obtain human intervention on the part of the controller.[41] The intention of the European legislator is to place specific requirements on the protection of the legal rights of the data subject

[37] See paras 43 and 47 of the preamble of the GDPR and Art. 6(1) GDPR. See European Data Protection Board Guidelines 05/2020 on consent under Regulation 2016/679, paras 16–24.

[38] See Guidelines on Automated Individual Decision-making and Profiling for the Purposes of Regulation 2016/679, WP251rev.01, adopted by the Article 29 Data Protection Working Party, now European Data Protection Board.

[39] See Guidelines on Automated Individual Decision-making and Profiling for the Purposes of Regulation 2016/679, p. 8 and Chancellor of Justice Decision OKV/131/70/2020, 20 April 2021, pp. 16–17. See also Bygrave (2001), p. 20, on the interpretation of the relatively similar provisions in Article 15 of the Personal Data Directive 95/46/EC in a way that gives effect on the rights of the data subject.

[40] This interpretation seems to be in line with the legislative history and the preceding provisions in the Personal Data Directive 95/46/EC. See Bygrave (2001).

[41] Art. 11(1) of Directive (EU) 2016/680 of the European Parliament and of the Council of 27 April 2016 on the protection of natural persons with regard to the processing of personal data by competent authorities for the purposes of the prevention, investigation, detection or prosecution of criminal offences or the execution of criminal penalties, and on the free movement of such data, and repealing Council Framework Decision 2008/977/JHA, OJ L 119, 4.5.2016, pp. 89–131.

and, following the principle of data protection by design and default in Article 25 of the GDPR, build these requirements into the systems used for automated decisions. These requirements concur with and influence the manner in which automated decision-making shall be organized in administrative law.[42] Particularly, the requirement of explainability under the GDPR partly concurs with the duty of reasoning and requirements of transparency and access to public service in administrative law.[43] Explainability and duty of reasoning enable data subjects to understand what the authorities do, and how and why they exercise public power. Explainability and duty of reasoning also enable review and control of public administration.[44] However, actual pragmatic explanation and reasoning in a user-centric way seeking to provide understandable information to specific users or stakeholders in a concrete context are different from the general concept of explainability seeking to provide abstract explicability by theoretical, often one-model-fits-all approaches.[45]

In a Finnish constitutional and legal-certainty-based reading, the right to human review serves two different objectives. First, the right to human review would be a remedy to eventual appreciation errors in complex situations where formalistic applications of norms, and lack of individual discretion based on legal principles, would conflict with fundamental requirements of justice, such as fairness and reasonableness.[46] An old general problem of automated legal reasoning would be, namely, the context-dependent nature of legal argumentation and the resulting complexity and modeling of the strategic choices where the whole line and logic of reasoning in a case is decided.[47] Second, the right to human review would support the claim derived from the Preamble of the GDPR that information and communications technology (ICT) systems and data processing should serve humans, and the right to human review would also support Section 1(2) of the Constitution of Finland, which establishes the protection of the inviolability of human individuals, and thereby the protection of human dignity, among the ultimate tasks of all public

---

[42] Chancellor of Justice Decision OKV/131/70/2020, 20 April 2021, pp. 16–17 and 19–23.

[43] Chancellor of Justice's established interpretation in case law is that the service principle and access to service include also the individual right to know how and by whom the service is delivered and what are the requirements for such service delivery.

[44] On the functions of explainability in the machine learning context, see Bibal et al. (2021), pp. 155–156.

[45] See Sovrano et al. (2021). The Chancellor of Justice has required recognition of the needs, situation, and cognitive context of the actual target group and consideration of the users and users' needs in pragmatic contexts concerning the information provided on automated decisions and automated public services. See Chancellor of Justice Decision OKV/2674/10/2020, 7 June 2020, concerning terms of use and information to be given to the users on the AI-powered OmaOlo – health care services platform and Decision of the Deputy Chancellor of Justice OKV/1418/10/2020, 1 November 2021, on the web-services provided by Public Economic and Employment Offices and the misunderstandings the interface design could lead to.

[46] See Enarsson et al. (2022), pp. 128–129.

[47] See Praekken and Sartor (2015), particularly pp. 214–215, 223–234 and 240–242. See also Ashley (2019).

powers and the constitutional order.[48] Beyond the protection of human dignity, the rule of law should allow human beings to flourish.[49] The GDPR-based principle of transparency and the related right to reasonable explanation also intersect with other legal requirements including the administrative law-based requirements on transparency and right to reasoning, and access both to service and understanding.[50]

To safeguard fundamental rights and human rights within a context of automated systems, the rights need to be translated into contextual design solutions in system architectures and designs.[51] Due process and the right to contest and appeal are even more important in the complex realities of automated decision-making.[52] The role of legislation is to set general but sufficiently guiding principles in the design of automated systems, and to inform the design, procurement, testing, training, quality assurance, and quality control processes related to the systems and the applications used in them. Also, more generically, the role of legislation is to set guiding principles for the functioning of automated systems and for the procedures and resources of such systems and for the organization of handling of matters generally.[53] The legislator's role is therefore ideally somewhat similar to the role played by practically-oriented academic legal research, that is, to set well-founded general conditions for the secure and durable digitalization of legal and administrative processes and for the application of automated decision-making in them.[54]

---

[48] On this radical rule of law based humanistic principle, see Pöysti (2018).

[49] Greenstein (2021), Chap. 6.

[50] See, for example, Wachter et al. (2017). For a more positive account based on systemic interpretation, see Malgieri and Comandé (2017). See also Wachter et al. (2018), for an account for ensuring comprehensibility of algorithmic decision-making. Generally on the automated decision-making under Art. 22 GDPR, see, for example, Brkan and Bonnet (2020) and Brkan (2019).

[51] See Aizenberg and van den Hoven (2020), where both substantive principles and procedural consultation requirements are seen as parts of the design process. See also Larsson (2020) and the contribution by Riku Sarlin in this volume.

[52] See contributions in Hildebrandt and de Vries (2013), particularly de Vries (2013), pp. 17–19 and Koops (2013), pp. 202–203.

[53] More concretely, the principles concerning the content of the legislation can be analyzed by focusing on each stage of the creation of automated systems and their maintenance and the lifecycle of data and knowledge in systems. See Koulu et al. (2019), pp. 18–20.

[54] See Koivisto and Koulu (2020), p. 800; Koulu (2020); Djeffal (2018), pp. 18–19. See Wiese Schartum (2021), passim., on the broad impacts of digitalization and the role of legislation in enabling automated decision-making and the benefits it entails.

3 A Right to Legal Certainty and Human Dignity: What Is the Stance of Administrative Law Toward Automated Decision-Making?

3.1 Legal Certainty, with Respect for the Inviolability of Human Dignity

European regulation of AI and automated functions in public administration contain a mix of arguments concerning trust, trustworthiness, and legality connected with a human-centric approach and protection of fundamental rights.[55] Specific formal', procedural, and material rule-of-law-based requirements concern governmental use of power and technology, including the use of algorithmic decision-making.[56] Administrative law focuses on principles such as the acting within conferred powers (legality), the delegation of powers within the limits of law, due process, fairness of the procedure, transparency, and, under that broad and ambiguous concept of transparency, the reasoning of administrative decisions and the general right and means of citizens to know what the government is doing on their behalf.[57] European legal literature and constitutional practice emphasize the right of appeal and the contestability of decisions in all exercises of public power by automated systems.[58] In addition to formal appeal possibilities, well-thought-out and adapted preventive and reactive guarantees, and their coherent interplay, should exist in a context of automated decision-making.[59] Trust is more a sociological phenomenon, and comes as a result of legislation, and the consistent and fair application of law, in addition to other empiric conditions. Social proof seems to play a role in individual decisions to trust algorithms and other forms of automated systems.[60]

Legal certainty refers to multiple qualities, including accessibility of law, that result from transparent and fair procedures, relative stability of the law, and decisions strictly based on the law; as well as foreseeability, intelligibility, and understandability of the law and its application, so that persons subject to the law can align their activities in accordance with the law. Legal certainty also depends upon the absence of erratic and arbitrary power, the absence of errors, and upon a general

[55] See European Commission, White Paper on AI – A European Approach to excellence and trust, COM (2020) 65 final and COM (2020) 206 final on the Artificial Intelligence Act. See OECD, Recommendation of the Council on Artificial Intelligence, 22 May 2019, OECD/LEGAL/0449.

[56] See Bibal et al. (2021), pp. 153–155. On the formal, procedural and material rule of law requirements on automated decision-making in the light of the practice of Finland's Chancellor of Justice, Parliamentary Ombudsman and Constitutional Law Committee, see Suksi (2022).

[57] Coglianese and Lehr (2017), p. 1259.

[58] See Koulu (2020) and Greenstein (2021), Chap. 5.1. On constitutional jurisprudence, see French Conseil constitutionnel, Décision 2018-765, para 70.

[59] Suksi (2020), pp. 94–97.

[60] See, for example, Alexander et al. (2018). On the trust in Finnish administrative law, see Pöysti (2020).

absence of legal uncertainty.[61] For the legislator to assure legal certainty, a wide understanding of possible difficulties and sources of error in digital administration and automated decision-making is needed. This includes the modeling of decision-making with argumentation in the law, about the law, and about the facts pertaining to, as well as the appropriate contextualization of, each decision.[62] Legal certainty requires accountability for legislation and for the use of legal powers and decisions.[63] In administrative law, legal certainty is connected to the principle of legitimate expectations, which also requires equal treatment in equal cases, and which builds upon the idea of consistency of case application, and to a certain extent the consistency of policies. Legitimate expectation is the absence of the arbitrary use of power, and the existence of predictability: consistency in policies can support legitimate expectation, and automated decision-making can improve a jurisdiction's level of legitimate expectation.[64] Good government and good administration as it is defined in Article 41 of the Charter of Fundamental Rights of the European Union extends to the skillful application of legal principles and to the skillful application of discretion in individual cases, to ensure fairness in decision-making.[65] The Chancellor of Justice in Finland has required remedial action in cases where the service of clients of government unemployment services has been reduced to a rule-based treatment of typical cases, without due consideration of the individual and his or her specific service needs.[66]

The essential elements of legal certainty concerning automated public administration are: (1) reliability and trustworthiness of public administration following from a strict observance of the law; (2) equal treatment in processing and decision-making; (3) objectivity, impartiality, and non-discriminatory quality of all

[61] See Eckhoff (1958) and Eckhoff (1989), pp. 85–86.

[62] On the review of modelling of argumentation in the law, about the facts and about the law for artificial intelligence, see Praekken and Sartor (2015), pp. 223–240. On the difficulties of modelling legal argumentation in AI, see Ashley (2019), particularly pp. 1123–1124, on the specific problem of successful predictability in machine learning based modelling without consideration of substantive features of legal texts and hence without robust causality in modelling of legal reasoning. For a still informative account on the likely sources of errors in modelling of legal argumentation for automation, see de Bruin et al. (2002).

[63] See Council of Europe (2016), Venice Commission, Rule of Law Checklist, CDL-AD(2016)007rev.

[64] See Pöysti (2020). On the Finnish concept of the principle of legitimate expectations in administrative law and its intersection with constitutional law, see Koillinen (2012). On the judicial review of the consistency of policies and the impact of the automated decision-making to policy consistency, see Cobbe (2019).

[65] Charter of Fundamental Rights of the European Union, OJ C 202, 7 June 2016, pp. 401–402.

[66] Chancellor of Justice Decision on the automatic issuance of statement on applicant's position in labor markets (OKV/138/10/2020, 29 October 2020). In that case, problems emerged from the oversimplifying assumption in the procedure and information system design that all clients of government unemployment services are seeking social security contributions. This was not the case of the individual concerned and he got a negative opinion (which was correct in his situation) without reason and hence his data was automatically processed without any justifiable reason.

public action and (4) control and controllability of all public functions consisting of public access to documents, party access to his or her own file, and the control of administration by courts and general legal oversight from authorities. In Sweden and Finland, "control and oversight by oversight authorities" refers to the general oversight by the Chancellor of Justice, the Parliamentary Ombudsman, and, in addition, oversight by the data protection authorities and authorities for the protection of equality.[67] The realization of legal certainty allows automated systems to achieve a good level of quality and trustworthiness, which contributes to citizens' trust toward public administration.[68]

Recital 4 of the GDPR restates an important general legal principle derived from the Personal Data Directive 95/46/EU, which states that the processing of personal data should be designed to serve humanity. In Recital 2 of the Personal Data Directive of 1995, this aim was stated in more detail: "data-processing systems are designed to serve man; whereas they must, whatever the nationality or residence of natural persons, respect their fundamental rights and freedoms, notably the right to privacy, and contribute to economic and social progress, trade expansion and the well-being of individuals." ICT and all automation should serve this purpose.

A proper legal basis to support this aim requires legislative measures that are clear and precise, and the application of such measures should be foreseeable to persons subject to it, in accordance with the case law of the Court of Justice of the European Union and the European Court of Human Rights.[69] The realization of the aims laid out in Recital 2 can also be regarded as elements of material legal certainty, and these aims extend beyond data protection law, to the administrative law that determines digital administration. The constitutional and data protection law-based requirement to form a proper legal basis is not simply a formal one: this requirement provides a legitimate process by which public authorities can adapt legislation to respond to current needs and to better protect individuals and other private parties vis-à-vis public authorities. The requirement to form a proper legal basis thus creates an opportunity to consider form, substance, and mutual relations of legislation, as well as the protection measures that should be included in such legislation.[70]

A fundamental problem in the automated decision-making and hybrid systems combining automation and human work is that the human being is part of a technological system. The human actor engages in far-reaching interactions with the system, and the system in turn steers human cognition and attention. This increases the capacity of problem solving and data processing by combining

[67] See Magnusson-Sjöberg (1992), pp. 75–76.

[68] Pöysti (2020), pp. 349–350.

[69] See Recital 41 GDPR.

[70] See Suksi (2018), pp. 369–371, where Suksi concludes a general mapping of legal questions arising from automated decision-making that proper legal grounds and sufficiently reflected legislation are a way to consider the constitutional and administrative law impacts and implications of automated decision-making. See also Suksi (2019), pp. 270–271 and 289–295. Suksi underlines the dialectic impact of both preventive and reactive safeguards of legality and good administration. Similarly Djeffal (2018), pp. 18–19.

operations where humans and machines are at their best.[71] Normative ethical and legal requirements cover this human-machine interaction as part of a socio-technical system.[72] Good design and architecture cover widely technical, organizational, procedural, and human aspects, including a cognitive environment for human actors, one that factors emotional and social intelligence, and possible sources of error.[73]

In the prior constitutional review of Finland's legislative white paper concerning rules of automated decision-making, the Chancellor of Justice raised the issue that background automation and automation-assisted decision-making were in need of some guiding principles of a legal nature. Such principles may also need clarification in legislative acts.[74] ICT systems and the data processing within such systems increasingly impact the realization of fundamental rights, and other rights; therefore, the infrastructure, information management, ICT systems, and applications, as well as the fundamental principles on the organization of work and procedures in public authorities and services, need to be governed through law and by law.[75] Human control and effective legal control should cover the whole lifecycle of automated systems and the entire path of data and information in data processing systems.[76] Concerning automated decision-making and the processing of personal data under the GDPR, the data protection principles and requirements of Article 25 of the GDPR pertain to background automation by design and default.[77]

[71] See Akata et al. (2020). For a legal analysis for this kind of hybrid form, see Enarsson et al. (2022).

[72] Sartor (2020), p. 706.

[73] See Ashley (2019), where Kevin Ashley underlines significance of the understanding of the origins of errors for legal certainty. On the sources of errors in practice, see de Bruin et al. (2002) which is still topical and relevant. On the hybrid environment and architecture as challenge for AI and law research and development, see Rodríguez-Doncel et al. (2021), pp. 3–6, and on education, emotional intelligence and holistic governance of automation from a legal profession's perspective, Carrel (2019).

[74] See Chancellor of Justice Opinion on the Ministry of Justice evaluation memorandum (white paper) on the need for legislation concerning automated decision-making, OKV/1348/21/2020, 27 August 2020.

[75] See Chancellor of Justice Opinion on the Ministry of Finance memorandum (white paper) on evaluation on the needs to develop legislation concerning public sector ICT-systems, OKV/2005/21/2021, 1 September 2021.

[76] Consistent functioning over the lifecycle of the systems over time is an important quality factor of AI tools. See preambular para 49 of the Commission Proposal for Artificial Intelligence Act, COM (2021) 206 final, concerning high-risk systems, and see Rodríguez-Doncel et al. (2021), pp. 2–3. Consistent functioning can be regarded as a general quality and robustness criteria, which is not limited to high-risk systems. However, the Commission proposal considers all systems with user interaction with AI as high-risk systems and the Commission proposal also requires state of the accuracy, robustness and cybersecurity for high-risk systems. See also Koulu et al. (2019), pp. 18–20.

[77] See European Data Protection Board, Guidelines 4/2019 on Article 25 Data Protection by Design and Default, where the key ideas behind Article 25 GDPR are explained to be effectiveness of data protection principles defined in Article 5 GDPR and considering them at all stages of processing

In automation, humans become part of a technological system. There is therefore a need to make interaction between humans and technical systems subject to legislation and regulation through law.[78] For example, this interaction, and how it has been defined in information and communication systems, determines the conditions for the realization of the service principle, which is one of the core principles of administrative law in Finland.[79]

The realization of legal certainty typically involves complexity created by multiple layers and actors participating in the development, design, and implementation of automated decision-making systems, processes, and training data used in such systems.[80] Unprecedented, thorny moral and legal questions and conflicts are bound to emerge.[81] These questions and conflicts are however unavoidable, and the solutions they require need to be carefully addressed by legal, moral, and ethical reasoning.[82]

3.2 *Systemic-Level Conditions for Legal Certainty*

Nordic legal literature, as well as legislation concerning public sector information and communication processes and ICT systems, already distinguishes the systemic quality of infrastructure and information management, legal certainty, and other aspects of good government at the level of individual decisions. In Finland, the Public Information Management Act (906/2019) applies to public sector information management and leadership responsibilities in relation to effectiveness of certain

---

including planning of the processing and constant evaluation of the risks and effectiveness of data protection principles.

[78] See Koulu (2020), pp. 18–24.

[79] See, for example, Chancellor of Justice Decision concerning comprehensibility, transparency and user-friendliness of the user conditions concerning OwnHealth –family of health and health self-help and analyses applications provided by the Finnish Government, which are also based on AI tools (OKV/2674/10/2020, 7 June 2022). See also Chancellor of Justice Decision on how equality would be enhanced by technology-neutral and access-device independent digital services, where the problem was the barriers and error possibilities authorities' information and communication systems created for a considerable clientele of public employment services (OKV/338/1/2018, 26 March 2019).

[80] This complexity is a point of departure in the Council of Europe Recommendation CM/Rec (2020)1 on the human rights impacts of algorithmic systems and in the European Commission proposal for Artificial Intelligence Act. Complexity is recognised in academic and legislative discourses as a significant challenge to liability rules applicable to artificial intelligence. Complexity with several actors involved in the design, training, maintenance and running of the AI systems leads to the need of layered liability rules. Consequently, there is need to reconsider some liability arrangements to maintain the functions and applicability of liability regime. On the problem of complexity and allocation of responsibilities, see Suksi (2019) and Hirvonen (2022).

[81] Elish (2019), p. 41.

[82] See Dahaher (2022).

information rights, and the Act applies to information security, information systems, and infrastructure generally. The traditional legal approach focuses on the moments of power, decisions when public power is exercised. In more complex contexts of digitalization, systemic power becomes weightier. Systemic power is inherent in the societal, administrative, and technological structures and networks.[83]

Similarly, legal guarantees of legality and good government include individual decision-related and general systemic guarantees. Part of the unwritten principles of administrative law is that all activities of public administration shall be based on explicit and legitimate reasons, and that alignment of all activities of administration with the principles and requirements of good government can be shown by documents (justifiability). Systemic guarantees of good government and legal certainty include proper organization, education and training, external steering and stewardship, internal leadership and management, possibilities for critical evaluation and correction, dialogic and open leadership, systematic assessment, and the consideration of service needs of public administration clients. Such guarantees also cover internal quality assurance, quality management, and risk management measures needed to secure good government. In addition, systemic controls include independent, external oversight and internal control focusing on structural and systemic issues.[84] Systemic controls include preventive, corrective, and reactive mechanisms and guarantees.[85]

Systemic issues of legal certainty entail correctness and quality of data in the databases and information systems. Systemic issues of legal certainty also entail the compliance of information and communication systems with requirements set for them, in addition to the general correctness and robustness of the functioning of such systems.[86]

Ideas of systemic-level aspects of legal certainty and systemic guarantees of good government have been developed in the Nordic literature on legal and administrative informatics. The task now is to determine how good government and legal certainty shall and can be secured by design and implementation in the information systems of public administration.[87] A simple error in system operations and systems design can produce repeatedly erroneous decisions, which may be costly or difficult to rectify. The complexity of systems leads to difficulties in observing errors in individual decisions, and this creates a number of challenges for legal certainty and may limit

[83] On the networks of power as a challenge of digital administrative law, see Pöysti (2018), p. 900.

[84] Boe (1993a), pp. 885–887.

[85] On the preventive, corrective and reactive guarantees in automated decision-making in Finnish law, see Suksi (2019), pp. 279–285, and Suksi (2020).

[86] Boe (1993b), pp. 271–274 and Boe (2018), pp. 151–185, on the quality assurance of ICT-systems and software and on the controls and procedures designed and coded into software to prevent errors and abuse. For an updated and expanded discussion on the systemic errors and controls in public administration, see Boe (2020).

[87] See Bing (1977). Wiese Schartum (1993, 2020).

the effectiveness of judicial review and other controls on individual decisions.[88] In Finnish legal literature, the need for strengthening the systemic and structural guarantees was recognized by Jorma Kuopus, back in 1988.[89] However, doctrinal solutions have been slow.

The legislation of Finland contains several explicit provisions, in addition to the GDPR, focusing on the systemic aspects of digital public administration. Finland's Public Information Management Act sets significant systemic requirements to plan information management in a systematically documented manner. The Act also defines detailed responsibilities for the maintenance of good information management and information security, as well as requirements to facilitate access to information covered by freedom of information rules. The new Act on the Division of Tasks between the Chancellor of Justice of the Government and the Parliamentary Ombudsman (330/2022) recognizes the need for systemic external control of automated systems. The Act therefore delegates the task of general oversight of the development and maintenance of automated systems in public administration, and the performance of public tasks, to the Chancellor of Justice.[90]

4 Finnish Law and Legislative Initiatives on Automated Decision-Making

4.1 Constitutional Points of Departure and Ratio of Digital Administrative Law

The legislation in force in Sweden, France, Germany, and Finland, together with other ongoing legislative activities, suggest that there is generally nothing in automated decision-making which could not be accommodated into current systems of administrative law.[91] However, such integration requires sufficiently profound and

[88] See Chauhan (2020). Concerning Finland, see Government Proposal to Parliament for an Act on the Division of Tasks between the Chancellor of Justice of the Government and the Parliamentary Ombudsman, HE 179/2021 vp, pp. 26–27 and 50. The Deputy Parliamentary Ombudsman Decision on automated decisions in the Finnish Tax Administration showed the realization of the multiplication of error, error in program produced erroneous letter with initiation of administrative sanctions procedure to 11 000 taxpayers (EOAK/3379/2018, 20 November 2019).

[89] See Kuopus (1988), pp. 486 and 544, concerning individual case officer's accountability and liability. Similar call has now been repeated by a group of researchers studying the constitutional official liability in Finland in the context of digitalization and other changes in the working environment of public administration. See Mäntylä et al. (2022).

[90] On the Act, see Government Proposal to Parliament for an Act on the Division of Tasks between the Chancellor of Justice of the Government and the Parliamentary Ombudsman, HE 179/2021 vp, and the Constitutional Law Committee Report PeVM 3/2022 vp.

[91] See Coglianese and Lehr (2017), p. 1147, and Appel and Coglianese (2020). On Finnish law, see Voutilainen (2009), particularly p. 345.

open-minded consideration to recognize the sometimes far-reaching legal impacts and implications that automation creates.[92]

The Finnish Parliament has already passed one narrowly defined specific act authorizing the use of fully-automatized administrative decision-making concerning financial assistance to sustainable forestry.[93] Automated decision-making is, however, used in several contexts without explicit support in legislation. In the case of natural persons, the use of automated decision-making immediately raises issues of legal basis in light of Article 22 of the GDPR and in all situations in the light of Section 2(3) of the Constitution of Finland, which requires that all exercise of public powers shall ultimately be based on, and thereby derive democratic legitimacy from, an Act of Parliament. Administrative and legal practice, the living law, is often ahead of legislators' activities as well as laws on the books.

A specific issue to be addressed is how to legislate for comprehensibility for humans, the principle of decision-automation under human control, and the auxiliary right incorporated in the GDPR, expressed in paragraph 71 of the Preamble, that there is a general right to have one's case reviewed by a human. In the light of the legislative history of Article 22 of the GDPR, the *ratio* of this principle is connected to moral principles on the fundamental value and uniqueness of each individual. The *ratio* is to protect the uniqueness, autonomy, and agency of each human being as a legal and legally powerful actor, and the *ratio* is intended to protect the human dignity of each individual and to prevent individuals from being reduced to objects of policy-making, both of which are derived from fundamental republican values protected by the rule of law and liberal democracy.[94]

One of the societal dangers of digitalization in general, and with automated decision-making and artificial intelligence-powered prediction and other decision-support tools in particular, is that these digital tools enable what the French sociologist Michel Foucault called "bio-politics." Bio-politics refers to the capacity of public power to influence and manipulate large masses of society for well-intentioned or evil purposes, and to wield the enormous power of governance over society and in all aspects of the lives of its members.[95] A specific challenge to human control by users of AI systems and the right to human review in automated decision-making follows from the fact that current law and the doctrine of administrative law is mainly concerned with natural and legal persons. There is an assumption that administrative decisions are made by humans and not by systems, or by humans and systems together.[96] In automated decision-making this assumption does not

---

[92] See Hirvonen (2022), pp. 410–411 and 416–417, concerning official accountability; Suksi (2018); and Suksi (2019), on the rule of law and legislation of automated decision-making in general.

[93] Temporary Act on the Financing of Sustainable Forestry (Kestävän metsätalouden määräaikainen rahoituslaki) (34/2015), Sect. 31 a.

[94] See Fleury (2015), pp. 12–13, 148, 190–193, 224–225, 291 and 310.

[95] See Foucault (2004), where bio-politics was a central theme. On a possible interpretation of Foucault for administrative law of a digital society, see Pöysti (2018), pp. 872–874.

[96] See Cobbe (2019), p. 639, and Zalnieriute et al. (2020), p. 261.

correspond with the reality and this failure to account for empiric reality may lead administrative law to fail in its fundamental functions. However, a shift toward a broader realm of law, and the protection of human autonomy, is increasingly present in the practice of the Chancellor of Justice.[97]

In the spring of 2022, Finland had a public consultation concerning amendments to the Administrative Procedure Act to provide a foundation for the use of automated decision-making. The legislative proposal submitted to Finnish Parliament in September 2022 broadly follows wording similar to that of the German Administrative Procedure Act Section 35a, but the Finnish proposal holds the more ambitious aim of creating a generic, primary norm to allow automated decision-making in its own right. Section 35a of the German Administrative Procedure Act is a secondary norm, making the legal basis and the use of the automated decision-making subject to additional legislative provisions (*Normvorbehalt*). The German Act requires that automated decision-making be specifically accepted by a legal provision (*Rechtsvorschrift*).[98]

Compared to Sweden, Finland's proposed rules are more detailed and restrictive than the Swedish Administrative Procedure Act. Sweden's revised Administrative Procedure Act, which authorizes automated decisions through a short provision, represents a minimalist authorizing rule.[99] Finnish legislative drafts and thinking instead go further, moving in a similar direction as the French Constitutional Council in its 2018 decision, by setting some significant limits to automated decision-making, as is the case with the current French legislation.

The point of departure for legislative work in Finland, as well as for the Parliamentary Ombudsman's and Chancellor of Justice's decisions on automated decision-making, has been Section 2(3) of the Constitution of Finland on the rule of law and the legality principle, which requires that all exercise of public powers be based on an Act and principles of good government, and that other fundamental rights need to be protected through provisions in the Acts of Parliament. Section 2(3) further stipulates that in all public activity, the law shall be strictly observed. From this perspective, the existing legal foundations in Finland, as they concern automated decision-making in public administration, are not sufficient.[100]

These existing formal, procedural, and material rules for legal provisions provide the democratic foundation and legitimacy for the exercise of all forms of public

[97] See Chancellor of Justice Decision on the digital net services of the Finnish public employment services (OKV/338/1/2018, 27 March 2019) and Decision on the user-centric digital services and terms of use (OKV/2674/10/2020, 7 June 2022).

[98] Martini and Nink (2017), pp. 2–3. Djeffal (2018), pp. 19–22.

[99] For comparison with Finland, see Pöysti (2018).

[100] See Deputy Parliamentary Ombudsman Decision concerning automation in tax administration (EOAK/3379/2018, 20 November 2019); Chancellor of Justice Decision concerning automated decision-making in the Finnish Social Insurance Institution (OKV/131/70/2020, 20 April 2021) and Chancellor of Justice Decision on the automated opinions of the Employment Office in public employment services and unemployment insurance (OKV/138/10/2020, 29 October 2020). See also the contribution of Riku Sarlin in this volume.

power.[101] Concurrently, such rules cultivate trust in public administration through legitimacy and the avoidance of the arbitrary use of power, ultimately by preventing excesses of power (*ultra vires*, or disproportional or unreasonable use of power) and government intrusion without proper legal basis and authorization, in violation of the liberties of individuals. In line with this, the Parliament should approve the use of automated decision-making in an Act of Parliament as a minimum precondition for automation. In contrast with Germany, this may happen in Finland in a general Act with sufficiently precise rules.

The legislator's role thus extends to safeguard good government and proper realization of fundamental rights in a wider manner, and to resolve value-conflicts and perform societal weighting and balancing related to automated administration and public services. Both supreme guardians of law in Finland, the Chancellor of Justice and the Parliamentary Ombudsman, have essentially argued for wider, sufficiently detailed, and more concrete *ex ante* protection, provided by legislation, when automated decision-making is used. The Chancellor of Justice has argued that general legislation is necessary to secure (1) good government and transparency under Section 21 of the Constitution of Finland, and (2) the correct application of Article 22 of the GDPR and additional safeguards and protection measures this Regulation requires.[102]

The GDPR itself represents a risk-centric view and requires that the relative risks to the protection of personal data as a human right are addressed in the complementary EU and Member State legislation. Finland's Constitutional Law Committee applies a distinctively risk-centric approach to legislation. Within that approach, risks related to the realization of fundamental rights and freedoms shall be managed by explicit, exact, and clearly-drafted rules in law.[103]

4.2 Finland's Acts on Automated Decision-Making in Public Administration: A Viable Solution or Just a Very Cautious Beginning?

The Government has responded to the opinions of the Constitutional Law Committee, and to the decisions of the Deputy Parliamentary Ombudsman and the Chancellor of Justice, by initiating a drafting of general provisions concerning automated decision-making in public administration. These general provisions are slated for inclusion in the Administrative Procedure Act and the Public Information

[101] See Suksi (2022).

[102] Chancellor of Justice Decision concerning automated decision-making in the Finnish Social Insurance Institution (OKV/131/70/2020, 20 April 2021).

[103] See Constitutional Law Committee Opinions PeVL 14/2018 vp, PeVL 15/2018 vp and PeVL 62/2018 vp.

Management Act.[104] A legislative proposal was submitted to the Parliament in September 2022.[105]

According to the Government Proposal, there will be general rules permitting, narrowing, and setting conditions for the use of automated decision-making in the public sector in the new sections, 53e and 53f of the Administrative Procedure Act, together with the rules on a general duty to inform about automated decision-making in a new section, 53g of the Administrative Procedure Act. Amendments to the Public Information Management Act would contain rules concerning design and approval for the purpose, quality testing, and quality control of the automated procedures in decision-making and of the technical systems used in those procedures.[106] The new provisions of the Public Information Management Act in Chapter 6a would further require comprehensive documentation of, and publication of, decisions concerning the use of automated decision-making. If enacted into law, the revised Acts would require authorities to communicate to the public about matters to be decided automatically, about the grounds and foundations of the use of automated processes, as well as about all essential information related to safeguarding the rights of those interacting with public administration in such automated processes.

These revised laws would provide a prudent point of departure for a wider use of automated decision-making. Similar to Section 35a of the German Administrative Procedure Act, Finland's new legislation would allow automated decision-making in situations that require little to no discretion, and in situations that do require some discretion, those matters would be decided by humans. To ensure such ideal functioning, arguments about the law should be settled before coding the decision-rules.

And while they urge caution, the Acts do display the need to harness the benefits of automation. For example, automated decision-making can be very useful for

[104] See Government Proposal for Acts on Automated Decision-making in Public Administration HE 145/2022 vp. For the drafting history of the Proposal see Ministry of Justice (2020), Evaluation memorandum on the needs for general legislation on automated decision-making in public administration; Ministry of Finance (2021), Evaluation memorandum on the needs for further development of legislation on public administration information management, Ministry of Finance public consultation, VN/4400/2021, 12 July 2021; and the Chancellor of Justice Opinion OKV/2005/21/2021, 1 September 2021. See draft Government Proposal for the Acts on Automated Decision-making in Public Administration, Ministry of Justice and Ministry of Finance, public consultation VN/3071/2020, 25 March–6 May 2022; and the Chancellor of Justice prior constitutionality review opinion on the draft Government Proposal OKV/984/21/2022, 4 May 2022.

[105] Government Proposal for Acts on Automated Decision-making in Public Administration HE 145/2022 vp.

[106] Government Proposal HE 145/2022 vp. For the drafting history see Ministry of Justice law drafting project OM021:00/2020, at: https://oikeusministerio.fi/hanke?tunnus=OM021:00/2020 and draft Government Proposal for the Acts on Automated Decision-making in Public Administration, Ministry of Justice and Ministry of Finance public consultation VN/3071/2020, 25 March–6 May 2022. A Draft Government Bill to final prior constitutional review by the Chancellor of Justice, OKV/2162/23/2022.

keeping handling and response times short. Automation can also help fulfil the constitutional requirement to handle matters without unnecessary delay; additionally, automation can improve legal certainty and reduce errors. In the Chancellor of Justice's assessment of automated decision-making used by the Finnish Social Insurance Institution, the error rate in automatically-treated applications for study subsidy presented via a webform was documented to be 0.0654%, while in the manual handling of applications, this error rate reached 3%.[107]

Furthermore, a properly designed automated system has the ability to function faster and better than human decision-making. Good automated decision-making can improve legal certainty by reducing errors, allowing for faster, more accurate handling, and by making more consistent decisions, while enabling human decision-making and interaction to take place in situations in which it is needed. Although with such constructive possibilities, it is worth bearing in mind that, in actual practice, automated systems do still produce mistakes. For example, the Deputy Parliamentary Ombudsman's decision included mention of a situation in which defective automated procedures had caused errors in tax administration documents. In the first case, an unnecessary administrative penalty fee concerning taxes which were already duly paid was imposed, and in the second case, 11,000 unnecessary inquiries on the application of administrative sanctions against taxpayers were initiated.[108]

Automation in administrative law is not always limited to automatically-decided administrative decisions. Automation in administrative law covers (1) automated decision-making where an administrative decision is issued solely by automatic means through a computer system, (2) automation of the underlying preparation, investigation, and analysis of a particular matter, including background automation, where the final decision is made by a human, and (3) automation of advice and guidance on services.[109] The new Finnish legislation covers aspects of (1) and (3), whereas background automation is regulated by general provisions in the Public Information Management Act, the GDPR, and the national data protection legislation complementing the GDPR. Planned changes to the Act on the Provision of Digital Services introduce a duty to inform that communication takes place with a robot or another type of automated system. In other words, there would be a right to know when one is communicating with a machine, rather than a human.

In some academic contributions, and in Council of Europe and EU regulatory documents, including the proposed Artificial Intelligence Act of the EU, algorithmic decision-making is considered distinctively from the point of view of general legal

---

[107] Chancellor of Justice Decision concerning automated decision-making in the Finnish Social Insurance Institution (OKV/131/70/2020, 20 April 2021), p. 5.

[108] See Deputy Parliamentary Ombudsman Decision EOAK/3379/2018, 20 November 2019.

[109] On the concept of automation of public administration, see Magnusson-Sjöberg (1992), p. 34; Kuopus (1988), pp. 123–143; Voutilainen (2009), p. 262; Hakapää (2009), pp. 3–4. See Chancellor of Justice Decision concerning automated decision-making in the Finnish Social Insurance Institution (OKV/131/70/2020, 20 April 2021), pp. 2–9 based on the report and statement by the Social Insurance Institution on its use of automation.

issues related to automated decision-making.[110] In the Artificial Intelligence Act of the EU, there exist both general questions related to different forms of automated decision-making, and some specific issues related to self-learning algorithmic decision-making.[111] In practice, it may be hard to distinguish problems of self-learning systems from general legal issues of digital administration.

AI can refer to many different techniques and things. According to a definition from the Organisation for Economic Co-operation and Development (OECD), an AI system is a machine-learning-based system that can, for a given set of human-defined objectives, make predictions, recommendations, or decisions that influence real or virtual environments. AI systems are designed to operate with varying levels of autonomy.[112]

In the Artificial Intelligence Act of the EU, the European Commission aims to include a definition of AI that is as technologically neutral as possible. In Article 3 of the Commission proposal for the Act, "artificial intelligence system" (AI system) is defined as software that is developed with one or more of the techniques and approaches listed in the Annex, and can, for a given set of human-defined objectives, generate outputs such as content, predictions, recommendations, or decisions that influence the environments with which the system interacts. The examples of AI systems in the Commission proposal include machine learning, and statistical and Bayesian approaches.[113] The text of the Artificial Intelligence Act, however, is bound to change in the European legislative procedure. The Council of the European Union considers, for example, that a more precise definition of AI be included in the text of the Regulation, and that a distinction be made between rule-based and machine-learning systems.[114]

Generally, algorithmic systems imply applications that, often by using mathematical optimization techniques, perform one or more tasks such as gathering, combining, cleaning, sorting, classifying, and inferring data, as well as selection, prioritization, the making of recommendations, and the execution of decision-making.[115] Mathematical optimization and statistical reasoning with probabilities can be somewhat intimidating to many lawyers because these methods add a quantitative dimension to otherwise qualitative and logical reasoning, the latter being areas in

[110] See, for example, Zalnieriute et al. (2019), p. 448, and for a mapping of the fairly broad concept of automated decision-making from the perspective of the application of the GDPR, Brkan (2019), pp. 93–95.

[111] Zalnieriute et al. (2020).

[112] OECD Recommendation on Artificial Intelligence, OECD/LEGAL/0449, 22 May 2019, para 1.

[113] COM (2021) 206 final.

[114] See Council of the European Union, Second Presidency compromise text of 15 July 2022, Interinstitutional file 2021/0106 COD, document 11124/22, https://data.consilium.europa.eu/doc/document/ST-11124-2022-INIT/en/pdf (accessed on 2 September 2022).

[115] See Appendix to Recommendation CM/Rec(2020)1, Sect. A Scope and context. See, for example, Zalnieriute et al. (2019), p. 448, and, for a mapping of the fairly broad concept of automated decision-making from the perspective of the application of the GDPR, see Brkan (2019), pp. 93–95.

which lawyers tend to be better versed.[116] The original insight by Lee Loevinger and his jurimetrics, calling for science-based, formal, and mathematically quantitative analyses to enrich legal methods, is hence very topical, although statistical models and software solutions are very different from one another.[117] From this perspective, algorithmic decision-making has indeed gained some specific attention in recent years.[118]

The new Finnish legislation does not include any explicit definitions of "automated decision-making" or "algorithm." The French Constitutional Council, and Finland's draft legislation on automated decision-making in the public sector, each draw a distinction between machine learning and other technologies where the algorithm is capable of modifying itself on the one hand, and on the other hand, pre-programmed rules, which are simply run on data. The French Constitutional Council reasoned that French administration could not rely upon an algorithm as the sole foundation of a decision if the algorithm modifies itself in a way that renders its functioning unexplainable, making it so the decision-rule cannot be validated in advance. Because the French legislation included a guarantee not to rely upon self-modifying algorithms, and because the legislation met other essential rule of law requirements, the legislation has not, as of yet, caused any constitutional problems.[119] Explainability remains a principal criterion for approval of algorithmic decision-systems.

The French Constitutional Council set the criteria of validation, controllability, explainability, and contestability in appeal. Finnish law-drafters have effectively followed the same line. The idea in the Finnish draft provisions, in Section 53e to the Administrative Procedure Act, is that automated decision-making can be used if a matter can be resolved by applying decision-rules defined in advance, if such decision-rules can be effectively programmed into the system. The rationale is that automated decision systems would remain under human control and would ultimately depend on human-accepted decisions. The proposed new Chapter 6a to the Public Information Management Act would require a prior decision approving an automated procedure with its systems for use, following a documented procedure. The new, planned legislation seeks to capture system design as a significant stage and instance of the use of public power.[120]

---

[116] On the indicators from the rule of law perspective and challenges legal thinking faces with statistically composed quantitative analyses extending beyond classic legal sociology and criminology, see Davis et al. (2015). On the challenges of the computational turn for law, see Hildebrandt and de Vries (2013).

[117] On the legacy of jurimetrics and Lee Loevinger, see Pohle (2021).

[118] Coglianese and Lehr (2017) and Zalnieriute et al. (2020).

[119] See French Constitutional Council, Conseil constitutionnel Décision n:o 2018-765, paras 65–72, where the key point is at para 71.

[120] See Chancellor of Justice prior constitutionality review opinion on draft Government Proposal for Acts on Automated Decision-making in Public Administration, OKV/984/21/2022. See also the contribution by Riku Sarlin in this volume.

The dichotomy between rule-based and self-learning systems applied in the proposed Finnish legislation, as well as in the French constitutional thinking and legislation, is intuitively appealing to lawyers. The inclusion of this dichotomy seems to offer a way to use automated decision-making in a manner that ensures human control and transparency.

This dichotomy has, however, been subject to serious theoretical and practical criticism. First, many ICT systems contain, and may increasingly contain, both types of elements, and the distinction itself is technology-dependent. Second, even rule-based systems can be very complex; a decision tree may contain thousands of choices and long lines of programming code, so the transparency and human review is a bit of a fallacy, or a nice objective but more difficult to achieve in practice. Third, there are also mechanisms of control and oversight that concern even the reasoning produced by self-learning systems, although the control of complex and adaptive systems is difficult. In practice, effective control and quality assurance requires computer-based monitoring systems.[121] Finally, the limitation of solely using rule-based systems may give a false sense of certainty, and at the same time, human control faces expectations that are too great to adequately manage. Such a limitation is neither efficient, nor sufficient, for the protection of human autonomy and ultimately human dignity.[122]

The pursuit of general, technology-neutral rules with sufficient durability over time should extend beyond rule-based/self-learning dichotomies. Durable legislation builds upon systematic knowledge of automation and digitalization and upon the impacts such systems have on public administration. Durable legislation also builds upon a balanced realization of fundamental and human rights, as well as principles of administrative law.[123] While Finland's new, proposed legislation repeats the old legislative model, which focuses only on human actors and individual decision-makers,[124] it does however contain some features of durable law. For example, there is the legislation's explicit connection to Articles 22, 25, and 35 of the GDPR, and to the right to human review by means of an internal complaint and appeal procedure. These safeguards, together with the systemic review capacity, constitute durable features of the new legislation. These features furthermore provide at least the initial potential to provide efficient protection of the individual, and maintain the inviolability of human dignity, as required by Section 1 of the Constitution of Finland.

---

[121] See Wachter et al. (2018).

[122] See Koulu (2020).

[123] See Pohle (2021), pp. 286–287, where he sees the systematic and disciplined common interface and communication between legal science and information and common sciences and the disciplined and methodical study on the informationalization of society and its structures among the enduring legacies of previous generations' work in legal informatics. Similar systematic and disciplined approach also informs lawmaking for enduring laws.

[124] See Hirvonen (2022).

5 Conclusions

Finland's proposed new legislation concerning general rules of administrative law for automated decision-making in public administration reflects the legislative and regulatory dilemmas in the concretization of general principles and other doctrines of administrative law. The new legislation also reflects the debates over how best to adhere to principles of efficient personal data protection, and how best to maintain other fundamental rights. And Finland is not alone. These are debates that other liberal democracies are facing as well. Solving these dilemmas requires deep reflection upon legislative strategies, structures, and content, as lawmakers and citizens alike encounter and grapple with rapidly developing technologies.

Legislators, systems-developers, and those who apply the law have a common task to maintain human dignity and human agency in the face of automated public administration. They all have a common mission to ensure that such systems remain at the service of humanity and individuals, and that a fair balance of all fundamental rights and interests is optimally maintained and optimally built into the system architectures, software, algorithms, and data flows. The new legislation proposed in Finland takes small and cautious steps in that direction. It explicitly covers individual administrative decisions, as well as requirements and controls at the systemic level. The steps are cautious, although the objective is to create a more intra-contextual framework than that of the German Administrative Procedure Act. Due to the fact that the new Acts still maintain the idea of individual official liability as a fundamental rule of law criteria, and, the fact that machine-learning vs. rule-based automated decision-making distinction can be problematic in practice, and, the fact that explicability and transparency are highly contextual issues, it seems evident that a more comprehensive review of legislation may be needed in the future. The proposed legislation is, hence, just the beginning in a long journey of creating digital administrative law.

Automated decision-making calls for a human-centric approach to administrative systems and applications. A human-centric approach means ensuring that fundamental legal principles and quality criteria are designed and coded into automated systems. It also means ensuring that automated systems are reviewed and controlled, so that fundamental legal principles are realized in practice. Legal certainty can thus result from automation, but legal certainty is also a fundamental *requirement* for systems of automation. Built-in legal certainty is a necessary condition for trustworthiness, and it creates founded trust. Rights-friendly infrastructure and systems are then needed, beyond legal certainty. Built-in and constantly supervised and enforced observance of the material principles of law is also needed to ensure a human-centric approach.

In design, and beyond design, legal guidance on the foundations of human-computer interaction is furthermore needed to ensure a human-centric approach. Such an approach implies that the right to appeal and the right to remedies—which are constitutional requirements of good government—include at least a right to a review by a human. Future digital administrative law should arise as the result of a collaborative and multi-disciplinary dialogue. The position of the human beings, working and living together with computer and data processing systems, deserves specific attention in law, and in the application of the law, both with regard to individual decisions and to processes, applications, and organization on the systemic level. Finnish law and legal institutions are taking steps toward strengthened systemic guarantees of good government.

Recent efforts in Finland show that Finnish law has been developing in dialogue with thinkers representing law, computer science, and information technology; all of these three areas have informed the legislature's analyses of social and legal processes. But the law around digital administration is far from mature. Systematic, collaborative, disciplined analyses that lead to durable developments in digital administration and digital administrative law will be crucial in the days and years ahead.

References

Aizenberg E, van den Hoven J (2020) Designing for human rights in AI. Big Data Soc 2020:1–14

Akata Z et al (2020) A research agenda for hybrid intelligence: augmenting human intellect with collaborative, adaptive, responsible, and explainable artificial intelligence. IEEE Comput 28: 281–326

Alexander V et al (2018) Why trust an algorithm? Performance, cognition, and neurophysiology. Comput Hum Behav 89:279–288. https://doi.org/10.1016/j.chb.2018.07.026

Allen LE, Engholm CR (1978) Normalized legal drafting and the query method. J Leg Educ 29: 380–412

Appel SM, Coglianese C (2020) Algorithmic governance and administrative law. In: Barfield W (ed) The Cambridge handbook of the law of algorithms. Cambridge University Press, Cambridge, pp 162–181

Ashley KD (2019) Automatically extracting meaning from legal texts: opportunities and challenges. Ga State Univ Law Rev 35(4):1117–1151

Bibal A et al (2021) Legal requirements on explainability in machine learning. Artif Intell Law 29: 149–169

Bing J (1977) Automatiseringsvennlig lovgivning. Tidsskrift for rettsvitenskap 91:1995–2229

Boe E (1993a) Innføring i juss. 2, Statsrett og forvaltningsrett. Tano, Oslo

Boe E (1993b) Oversikt over forvaltningsretten. NKS-Forlaget, Oslo

Boe E (2018) Forsvarlig forvaltning. Universitetsforlaget, Oslo

Boe E (2020) Forsvarlig systeminnretning i forvaltningen. Lov og rett 59(3):129–140

Braun Binder N (2016) Weg frei für vollautomatisierte Verwaltungsverfahren in Deutschland. Jusletter IT 22. September 2016

Brkan M (2019) Do algorithms rule the world? Algorithmic decision-making and data protection in the framework of the GDPR and beyond. Int J Law Inf Technol 27(2):91–121

Brkan M, Bonnet G (2020) Legal and technical feasibility of the GDPR's quest for explanation of algorithmic decisions: of black boxes, white boxes and fata morganas. Eur J Risk Regul 11:18–50

Bygrave L (2001) Automated profiling. Minding the machine: Article 15 of the EC Data Protection Directive and automated profiling. Comput Law Secur Rep 17:17–24

Carrel A (2019) Legal intelligence through artificial intelligence requires emotional intelligence: new competency model for the 21st century legal professional. Ga State Univ Law Rev 35(4): 1153–1184

Chauhan A (2020) Towards the systemic review of automated decision-making systems. Judic Rev 25(4):285–295. https://doi.org/10.1080/10854681.2020.1871714

Cobbe J (2019) Administrative law and the machines of government: judicial review of automated public-sector decision-making. Leg Stud (Soc Leg Sch) 39:636–655

Coglianese C, Lehr D (2017) Regulating by robot: administrative decision making in the machine-learning era. Geo Law J 105:1147–1223

Council of Europe (2016) Venice Commission, Rule of Law Checklist, CDL-AD(2016)007rev. https://www.venice.coe.int/webforms/documents/default.aspx?pdffile=CDL-AD(2016)007-e

Dahaher J (2022) Tragic choices and the virtue of techno-responsibility gaps. Philos Technol 35, Article no. 26. https://doi.org/10.1007/s13347-022-00519-1

Davis KE et al (2015) The quiet power of indicators: measuring governance, corruption, and the rule of law. Cambridge University Press, New York

de Bruin H et al (2002) The use of legal knowledge-based systems in public administration: what can go wrong? In: Bench-Capon TJM et al (eds) Legal knowledge and information systems. IOS Press, pp 123–132

de Vries K (2013) Privacy, due process and the computational turn: a parable and a first analysis. In: Hildebrandt M, de Vries K (eds) Privacy, due process and the computational turn: the philosophy of law meets the philosophy of technology. Taylor and Francis, pp 9–38

Djeffal C (2018) Künstliche Intelligenz in der öffentlichen Verwaltung. Berichte des NEGZ, Nr. 3: 1–32. SSRN: https://ssrn.com/abstract=3289109. Accessed 10 Aug 2022

Eckhoff T (1958) Effektivitet og rettssikkerhet i den offentlige forvaltning. I. Nordisk Administrativt Tidskrift 1958:15–27

Eckhoff T (1989) Forvaltningsrett. 3. utgave. Tano, Oslo

Elish M (2019) Moral crumple zones: cautionary tales in human-robot interaction. Engag Sci Technol Soc 5:40–60

Enarsson T, Enqvist L, Naarttijärvi M (2022) Approaching the human in the loop: legal perspectives on hybrid human/algorithmic decision-making in three contexts. Inf Commun Technol Law 31:123–153

European Union Rule of Law Report (2021) Country chapter on the rule of law situation in Finland, SWD (2021) 711 final. https://eur-lex.europa.eu/legal-content/EN/TXT/?uri=CELEX:52021SC0711

Fleury C (2015) Les Irremplacables. Gallimard, Paris

Foucault M (2004) Sécurité, territoire, population. Cours au Collége de France, 1977–1978. Gallimard, Paris

Government legislative project (2020) Preparation of general legislation concerning automated decision-making in the public administration (Automaattista päätöksentekoa koskevan hallinnon yleislainsäädännön valmistelu) OM021:00/2020. https://oikeusministerio.fi/hanke?tunnus=OM021:00/2020. Accessed 31 Aug 2022

Government legislative project (2021) Working group for review of general legislation on public administration information systems (Julkisen hallinnon tietojärjestelmiä koskevan yleislainsäädännön tarkistamista valmisteleva työryhmä) VM059:00/2021. https://vm.fi/hanke?tunnus=VM059:00/2021. Accessed 31 Aug 2022

Government Proposal to Parliament for an Act on the Division of Tasks between the Chancellor of Justice of the Government and the Parliamentary Ombudsman (2021) (Hallituksen esitys eduskunnalle laiksi valtioneuvoston oikeuskanslerin ja eduskunnan oikeusasiamiehen tehtävien jaosta), HE 179/2021 vp. https://www.eduskunta.fi/FI/vaski/HallituksenEsitys/Documents/HE_179+2021.pdf

Government Proposal to Parliament for Acts on Automated Decision-making in Public Administration (2022) (Hallituksen esitys eduskunnalle julkisen hallinnon automaattista päätöksentekoa koskevaksi lainsäädännöksi), HE 145/2022 vp. https://www.eduskunta.fi/FI/vaski/HallituksenEsitys/Documents/HE_145+2022.pdf

Greenstein S (2021) Preserving the rule of law in the era of artificial intelligence (AI). Artif Intell Law. https://doi.org/10.1007/s10506-021-09294-4

Hakapää S (2009) Hallintosovellusten hyödyntäminen arvonlisäverotusmenettelyssä. Online. Edilex, Helsinki

Hildebrandt M, de Vries K (eds) (2013) Privacy, due process and the computational turn: the philosophy of law meets the philosophy of technology. Taylor and Francis

Hirvonen H (2022) Virkavastuu ja päätösautomaatio: vastuun henkilökohtaisuus kriisissä. Lakimies 120(3–4):386–418

Koillinen M (2012) Luottamuksensuoja eurooppalaisena oikeusperiaatteena. Suomalainen lakimiesyhdistys, Helsinki

Koivisto I, Koulu R (2020) Miten hyvä hallinto digitalisoidaan? Haaste oikeustieteelliselle tutkimukselle. Lakimies 118(6):798–821

Koops BJ (2013) On decision transparency, or how to enhance data protection after the computational turn. In: Hildebrandt M, de Vries K (eds) Privacy, due process and the computational turn: the philosophy of law meets the philosophy of technology. Taylor and Francis, pp 196–220

Koulu R (2020) Proceduralizing control and discretion: human oversight in artificial intelligence policy. Maastricht J Eur Comp Law 27(6):720–735

Koulu R (2021) Crafting digital transparency: implementing legal values into algorithmic design. Crit Anal Law 8:81–100

Koulu R et al (2019) Algoritmi päätöksentekijänä?: tekoälyn hyödyntämisen mahdollisuudet ja haasteet kansallisessa sääntely-ympäristössä. Valtioneuvoston kanslia, Helsinki. http://urn.fi/URN:ISBN:978-952-287-764-2

Kuopus J (1988) Hallinnon lainalaisuus ja automatisoitu verohallinto. Lakimiesliiton Kustannus, Helsinki

Larsson S (2020) On the governance of artificial intelligence through ethics guidelines. Asian J Law Soc 7:437–451

Loevinger L (1963) Jurimetrics: the methodology of legal inquiry. Law Contemp Probs 28:5–35

Magnusson-Sjöberg C (1992) Rättsautomation: särskilt om statsförvaltningens datorisering. Norstedt, Stockholm

Malgieri G, Comandé G (2017) Why a right to legibility of automated decision-making exists in the General Data Protection Regulation. Int Data Priv Law 7(4):243–265

Mäntylä N et al (2022) Virkavastuu julkishallinnon muuttuvassa toimintaympäristössä. Valtioneuvoston tutkimus- ja selvitystoiminnan julkaisusarja 2022:14. Valtioneuvoston kanslia, Helsinki. http://urn.fi/URN:ISBN:978-952-383-237-4

Martini M, Nink D (2017) Wenn Maschinen entscheiden ... : vollautomatisierte Verwaltungsverfahren und der Persönlichkeitsschutz. Neue Zeitschrift für Verwaltungsrecht – Extra 36(10/2017):1–14

Ministry of Finance (2021) Evaluation memorandum on the needs for further development of legislation on public administration information management (Arviomuistio julkisen hallinnon tietojärjestelmiä koskevan sääntelyn kehittämistarpeista), public consultation (lausuntopyyntö), VN/4400/2021, 12 July 2021. https://www.lausuntopalvelu.fi/FI/Proposal/Participation?proposalId=40ebb45b-c282-4ba7-b5e4-0c8b390038cc

Ministry of Justice (2020) Evaluation memorandum of the Ministry of Justice on the needs for general legislation on automated decision-making in public administration (Arviomuistio hallinnon automaattiseen päätöksentekoon liittyvistä yleislainsäädännön sääntelytarpeista), Oikeusministeriön selvityksiä ja ohjeita 2020:14. https://julkaisut.valtioneuvosto.fi/handle/10024/162355

Ministry of Justice and Ministry of Finance (2022) Draft proposal for the Acts on automated decision-making in public administration (luonnos julkisen hallinnon automaattista päätöksentekoa koskevaksi lainsäädännöksi), public consultation VN/3071/2020, 25 March–6 May 2022. https://www.lausuntopalvelu.fi/FI/Proposal/Participation?proposalId=4dfeb6d1-afc5-4f21-a931-9764eacd42cb

Nissenbaum H (2010) Privacy in context: technology, policy, and the integrity of social life. Online, Stanford California

OECD (2021) Civic space scan of Finland, OECD Public Governance Reviews. OECD Publishing, Paris. https://doi.org/10.1787/f9e971bd-en
Pohle J (2021) Eine juristische Disziplin der Zukunft: An der Schnittstelle von Recht und Infomatik. In: Pohle J, Lenk K (eds) Der Weg in die "Digitalisierung" der Gesellschaft: Was können wir aus der Geschichte der Informatik lernen? Metropolis-Verlag, Marburg, pp 263–294
Pöysti T (2018) Kohti digitaalisen ajan hallinto-oikeutta. Lakimies 116(7–8):868–903
Pöysti T (2019) The IIoT and design for contextually relevant data protection. In: Ballardini RM et al (eds) Regulating industrial internet through IPR, data protection and competition law. Wolters Kluwer, Alpen aan den Rijn, pp 183–206
Pöysti T (2020) Luottamuksesta hallinnon automaattiseen päätöksentekoon. In: Juhlajulkaisu Pekka Vihervuori, Suomalainen lakimiesyhdistys C 44, Helsinki, pp 345–360
Praekken H, Sartor G (2015) Law and logic: a review from an argumentation perspective. Artif Intell 227:214–245
Rinta-Kahila T et al (2022) Algorithmic decision-making and system destructiveness: a case of automatic debt recovery. Eur J Inf Syst 31(3):313–338
Rodríguez-Doncel V et al (2021) Introduction. In: Rodríguez-Doncel V et al (eds) AI approaches to the complexity of legal systems XI-XII: AICOL international workshops 2018 and 2020: AICOL-XI@JURIX 2018, AICOL-XII@JURIX 2020, XAILA@JURIX 2020, revised selected papers. Springer International Publishing AG
Sartor G (1993) Artificial intelligence and law: legal philosophy and legal theory. Tano, Oslo
Sartor G (2020) Artificial intelligence and human rights: between law and ethics. Maastricht J Eur Comp Law 27(6):705–719
SOU (2021) En väl fungerande ordning för val och beslutsfattande i kommuner och regioner [A well-functioning order for elections and decision-making in municipalities and regions], Swedish Government Official Report SOU 2021:16
Sovrano F et al (2021) Making things explainable vs explaining: requirements and challenges under the GDPR. In: Rodríguez-Doncel V et al (eds) AI approaches to the complexity of legal systems XI-XII: AICOL international workshops 2018 and 2020: AICOL-XI@JURIX 2018, AICOL-XII@JURIX 2020, XAILA@JURIX 2020, revised selected papers. Springer International Publishing AG, pp 169–182
Suksi M (2018) Förvaltningsbeslut genom automatiserat beslutsfattande: statsförfattnings- och förvaltningsrättsliga frågor i en digitaliserad myndighetsmiljö. JFT 154(5):329–371
Suksi M (2019) Rättsstatlighet, god förvaltning och ämbetsansvar vid automatiserat beslutsfattande. JFT 155(5–6):267–302
Suksi M (2020) Administrative due process when using automated decision-making in public administration: some notes from a Finnish perspective. Artif Intell Law 29:87–110
Suksi M (2022) Lagbundenhetskravet vid automatiserat beslutsfattande i myndighetsverksamhet enligt finsk rätt. In: de Vries K, Dahlberg M (eds) Law, AI and digitalisation. De lege, juridiska fakulteten i Uppsala, Årsbok 2021. Iustus, Uppsala, pp 157–178
Verheij B (2020) Artificial intelligence as law. Artif Intell Law 28:181–206
Voutilainen T (2009) ICT-oikeus sähköisessä hallinnossa: ICT-oikeudelliset periaatteet ja sähköinen hallintomenettely. Edilex/Edita Publishing Oy, Helsinki
Wachter S (2020) Affinity profiling and discrimination by association in online behavioural advertising. Berkeley Technol Law J 35:367–430
Wachter S (2022) The theory of artificial immutability: protecting algorithmic groups under anti-discrimination law. Tul Law Rev 97. https://doi.org/10.2139/ssrn.4099100
Wachter S et al (2017) Why a right to explanation of automated decision-making does not exist in the General Data Protection Regulation. Int Data Priv Law 7:76–99
Wachter S et al (2018) Counterfactual explanations without opening the black box: automated decisions and the GDPR. Harv J Law Technol 31:841–887
Wahlgren P (1992) Automation of legal reasoning: a study of artificial intelligence and law. Juristförlaget, Stockholm

Wiese Schartum D (1993) Rettssikkerhet og systemutvikling i offentlig forvaltning. Universitetsforlaget, Oslo

Wiese Schartum D (2020) From legal sources to programming code: automatic individual decisions in public administration and computers under the rule of law. In: Barfield W (ed) The Cambridge handbook of the law of algorithms. Cambridge University Press, Cambridge, pp 301–336

Wiese Schartum D (2021) Jus og digitalisering. Lov og Rett 60:92–109

Zalnieriute M et al (2019) The rule of law and automation of government decision-making. Mod Law Rev 82(3):425–455

Zalnieriute M et al (2020) From rule of law to statute drafting: legal issues for algorithms in government decision-making. In: Barfield W (ed) The Cambridge handbook of the law of algorithms. Cambridge University Press, Cambridge, pp 251–272

Formal, Procedural, and Material Requirements of the Rule of Law in the Context of Automated Decision-Making

Markku Suksi

Abstract The rule of law requirements concerning automated decision-making are approached from the viewpoint of formal, procedural, and material requirements. The chapter argues that in addition to a clear legal basis for automated decision-making, formal rule of law also contains the requirement that automated decision-making should be based on legal reasoning, that is, subsumption of legal facts under a norm. This impacts the choice of technology for the system of automated decision-making by expecting that only such techniques are used which can reproduce subsumption. This means that rule-based solutions are possible for automated decision-making, while machine-learning-based applications, which are based on statistical inferences leading to predictions, are normally not. Procedural rule of law requires that good government, such as the right of motivation, right of an individual to be heard, and transparency of decision-making should be guaranteed. Material rule of law requires that aspects of substantive law, such as different benefit levels and conditions for granting benefits, are properly considered when the algorithm and the source code are developed. These requirements are relevant for all situations where automated decision-making is used, exemplified in this context by practice from the Finnish supervisors of legality and the Constitutional Law Committee of the Finnish Parliament.

Keywords Automated decision-making · Subsumption · Legal reasoning · Rule-based systems · Machine learning

1 Introduction

To a significant degree, the principle of the rule of law, which in continental Europe normally assumes the form of *Rechtsstaat* known from German law, or the French *l'État de droit*, or from the civil law tradition in general, constitutes a corner-stone

M. Suksi (✉)
School of Law, Åbo Akademi University, Turku/Åbo, Finland
e-mail: markku.suksi@abo.fi

M. Suksi (ed.), *The Rule of Law and Automated Decision-Making*,
https://doi.org/10.1007/978-3-031-30142-1_4

for all activities carried out by public authorities in a state,[1] including Finland and Sweden. This principle of the rule of law, as established in, for instance, Section 2, subsection 3 of the Constitution of Finland, implies that all exercises of public power by public authorities must be based on an Act, and that the law shall be strictly observed in all public activity. In Sweden, the principle of the rule of law is found in the principle of legality in Chapter 1, Section 1(3) of the Instrument of Government (Constitution) Act. The constitutions of Finland and Sweden additionally contain other provisions that are strongly related to the principle of legality and the rule of law. The principle of the rule of law is embedded in the constitutional fabrics of many other European countries in a relatively similar way.[2]

Although the legislation that regulates the procedural and material activities of public authorities is, in principle, technology-neutral, this legislation is nevertheless, and until now, generally enacted under the presumption that the decisions of public authorities will be made by physical decision-makers, that is, by civil servants and collective bodies of elected or appointed persons. The requirement of the rule of law in the exercise of public authority has therefore mainly focused on decision-making by individual civil servants or by collegial bodies against the background of the principle of administration through public servants. With the increasing use of automated decision-making by governmental authorities, the requirements set by the rule of law must now be considered when public authorities create and use automated systems of decision-making.

Currently, there are legal provisions that explicitly require that decisions made by public authorities be made by physical civil servants, or appointed representatives. An example of such a legal provision would be the Finnish Local Government Act (410/2015) Section 91, subsection 1, first sentence. Under this provision, the municipal council may transfer, through provisions in the by-law, decision-making authority to the other organs of the municipality and to appointed representatives and civil servants. The provision can be understood so that it requires a human decision-maker and thus precludes the use of automated decision-making procedures. The provisions concerning the transfer of public authority in the corresponding Swedish Municipalities Act (2017:725) formerly contained similar rules about the delegation of decision-making authority to committees, boards, and civil servants, that is, to physical decision-makers in a municipality, but the Act was amended on 1 July 2022 to make possible the delegation of decision-making competence to automated procedures, except in some explicitly-mentioned decisions.

Since 2018, Section 28 of the Swedish Administrative Procedure Act (2017:900) has contained a general permission for public authorities to use automated

[1] In its Anglo-American fashion, the rule of law is often constructed based on three dimensions: (1) the law is public and knowable for all; (2) the law is general and binds everyone, even the state and its civil servants; and (3) the law is interpreted by independent courts. For an account of automated decision-making from the point of view of British administrative law, see Williams (2022) and the case examples mentioned therein. On the different facets of the rule of law, see also Raitio et al. (2022).

[2] Concerning Norway, see Wiese Schartum (2020).

decision-making; it was this general provision that created the impetus to change the above-mentioned Municipalities Act (2017:725). In principle, therefore, the legal order of a state may display various levels of openness to automated decision-making by public authorities: the law may be entirely open to the use of automated decision-making by public authorities, it may be indifferent to the method of decision-making, it may be negatively predisposed to such decision-making, or it may contain *prima facie* prohibitions or limitations of the use of automated decision-making by public authorities.

Simultaneous with the increasing automatization of decision-making by public authorities,[3] problematizing questions about the appropriate legal basis for algorithmic decision-making have started to arise,[4] questions about automated decision-making that takes place without the participation of any physical public servant or organ with physical representatives. Obviously, one would be hard-pressed to find an advocate for the notion that the constitutional principle of the rule of law would not or should not apply to automated decision-making, that is, that a public entity could set aside or bypass the principle of the rule of law by transferring decision-making capabilities from humans to machines. On the contrary, the expectation should be that the rule of law applies in all stages and forms of public decision-making, whether carried out by automated systems or by humans.

Some of the key questions that have arisen about the appropriate legal basis for algorithmic decision-making grapple with the continued applicability of the principle of the rule of law in an increasingly automated decision-making environment: how should the principle of the rule of law apply within the area of automated decision-making, and how should automated decision-making be regulated so that it satisfies the requirements created by the principle of the rule of law? Because automated decision-making must take place within the constitutional requirement of the rule of law, the question is also, how should the principle of the rule of law be made concrete in decision-making that is based on algorithms? Against the background of the proposal for an Artificial Intelligence Act (AI Act) launched by the European Commission in April 2021,[5] including an identification of high-risk uses and prohibited uses of algorithmic techniques, a further question would be: considering Finnish legal interpretations, should the emerging Finnish practices around algorithmic techniques be qualified as high risk, or even, should such practices be considered among the prohibited uses of algorithmic techniques?

[3] For a general overview of the developments in various countries and for a short description of the plans in Hungary, see Csótó et al. (2021).

[4] See, e.g., Williams (2022), p. 474: "The conclusion, therefore, is that if public authorities wish to rely wholly on ADM they will require some kind of specific legal basis to do so, which must lay down protections for the DS." The use of automated decision-making (ADM) in public authorities thus also impacts the data subject (DS).

[5] Proposal for a Regulation of the European Parliament and of the Council laying down Harmonised Rules on Artificial Intelligence (Artificial Intelligence Act) and Amending certain Union Legislative Acts, Brussels, 21.4.2021, COM(2021) 206 final, 2021/0106 (COD).

The role of the rule of law and of *Rechtsstaat* in the area of administrative law is a theme that has been discussed in many contexts, by many authors.[6] Alexander Pezcenik has emphasized that a state based on the rule of law proceeds, in its ideal form, from the maxim that public powers should be exercised within a legal frame that makes the exercise of such powers foreseeable in light of legal norms.[7] According to Pezcenik, a state based on the rule of law requires that the contents of the exercise of public powers is regulated by legal norms, which means that citizens must be able to know everything that is relevant about *how* public powers will be exercised, beyond simply knowing *who* is exercising such powers.[8] Rules and principles of this kind prevent the exercise of public powers from becoming arbitrary.

From this vantage point, different categorizations of the rule of law have been presented, such as formal and substantive elements of the rule of law, as well as procedural and substantive elements of the rule of law, as pointed out in the checklist for the rule of law developed by the European Commission for Democracy through Law (Venice Commission).[9] These categorizations, as presented for the context of automated decision-making by Monika Zalnieriute, Lyria Bennett Moses, and George Williams,[10] emphasize the role(s) of procedural elements of the rule of law, such as transparency, accountability, predictability, consistency, and equality before the law. In addition, as pointed out by Mireille Hildebrandt, "contestability is at the heart of the rule of law, notably its procedural core,"[11] which means that the right to appeal an automated decision must be afforded to the affected party.

A summary of these different facets of the rule of law by Ida Asplund furthermore holds that the rule of law may consist of three different dimensions: formal rule of law, procedural rule of law, and material rule of law. Formal rule of law may be understood as a system where the decision-making is based on a law enacted by the

[6]For a useful summary of arguments, see Greenstein (2022), pp. 293–297, particularly the definitions by Fuller on p. 293.

[7]Peczenik (1995), p. 50.

[8]Peczenik (1995), p. 50.

[9]See, particularly, the Rule of Law Checklist, European Commission for Democracy through Law (Venice Commission). Strasbourg, 18 March 2016, at https://www.venice.coe.int/webforms/documents/default.aspx?pdffile=CDL-AD(2016)007-e (accessed on 1 November 2022). The checklist identifies legality, legal certainty, prohibition of arbitrariness, access to justice before independent and impartial courts, including judicial review of administrative acts, respect for human rights, and non-discrimination and equality before the law as core elements of the rule of law. These elements and a number of more specific dimensions of the rule of law may apply to automated decision-making by public authorities in the same manner as to human decision-making. Automated decision-making was not included as a potential challenge to the rule of law at the time of the adoption of the checklist, but collection of data and surveillance is identified as a particular challenge for the rule of law in a manner that approaches issues of automated decision-making. It may become necessary for the Venice Commission to re-visit the checklist on automated decision-making.

[10]Zalnieriute et al. (2019), p. 3.

[11]Hildebrandt (2018), p. 8.

parliament. Procedural rule of law may be understood as procedural guarantees that surround decision-making by public authorities. And finally, material rule of law may be understood as legal norms that establish the substantive features of a legal decision.[12] This categorization will be used here for analytical purposes to give a nuanced picture of the implications of the rule of law when attempting to legislate on automated decision-making by public authorities.

The intention of this chapter is to present a number of general observations concerning automated decision-making, and also to analyze the manner in which the Finnish practice of the Parliamentary Ombudsman, the Chancellor of Justice, and the Constitutional Law Committee of the Parliament of Finland has evolved in the area of automated decision-making. Furthermore, this chapter attempts to characterize Finnish practice concerning automated decision-making in terms of the three categories mentioned above—formal, procedural and material rule of law—before (re)connecting Finnish experiences to a more general perspective, including to some dimensions of the EU proposal for an AI Act. The focus is on fully automated decision-making, that is, on such decision-making where the administrative decision is issued by an algorithmic decision-maker without the involvement of any civil servant or other person, but occasional references may be made to automation in supporting functions. The author hopes that the issues brought up by means of the analysis of constitutional requirements in one country will be of a general nature and of general interest, because each state will need to consider a similar set of issues related to the rule of law when establishing systems of automated decision-making.

2 The Legal Method of Decision-Making in an AI Context

2.1 Legal Reasoning (Subsumption) Based on Law

Every sovereign legal order is naturally interested in maintaining power over individuals within its territory. Until this point, the powers of the state have virtually always been legitimized by means of physical decision-makers, public servants. The legitimacy of algorithmic decision-making by public authorities depends to a large extent on the way the algorithmic systems can be successfully tied to existing concepts and requirements concerning the exercise of public powers, such as the rule of law and the fulfilment of constitutional rights of individuals. This section will focus on two fundamental features of the formal aspect of the rule of law; namely, the legal basis required for the exercise of public powers, and legal reasoning as a method of making administrative decisions.

The exercise of public powers takes place in a vertical dimension between public authorities and the individual. The law determines the competences of the public authorities and gives them a unilateral position in the decision-making process. A

[12] Asplund (2021), pp. 81, 102–103.

characteristic of such government-to-citizen relationships is that the recipient of a legal decision cannot "vote with their feet" and "change administration or judge when dissatisfied with the criteria used by the public authority, but [they] can always contest the legality of the decision before a superior judge."[13] A compulsory jurisdiction exists between the public authority and the individual and that relationship, based on the law, is non-negotiable.

Each decision of a legal nature in the vertical dimension, including an administrative decision of a public authority, is expected to follow in a logical manner from at least one general rule and some additional premises. Such a general rule can be a written legal rule, a rule defined in precedence, or another rule that is supported by another source of law.[14] What is produced based on the legal subsumption of this kind is an argument that expresses the general nature of the decision in the individual case. This argument will be presented in a manner that fulfils the expectation of a coherent motivation, normally expressed as a sentence "if..., then..." (or IFTTT; if this, then that).[15] Subsumption thus denotes a syllogism between two propositions, one which identifies the norm that is appropriate for the case and another which identifies the facts that exist. The task of the decision-maker is to place the facts in relation to the norm and then draw a conclusion in the form of a decision in an individual case.[16] For that reason, the rule of law can, in this context, be understood as a requirement that a legal consequence in the form of an administrative decision can only arise when the law has formulated a norm and described the requisite facts.

Subsumption is a technique that is used in systems of the rule of law, characterized thusly by a high level of abstraction of legal rules, the autonomy of the law, and the existence of particular legal concepts and methods of argumentation.[17] In a state based on the rule of law, all decisions of a legal nature must be subsumed under general legal rules, that is, the decisions must be understood as the application of legal rules in a manner where the practice of public authorities furthers legal certainty.[18] Subsumption, that is, legal reasoning, denotes, in this context, the application of a rule on facts in what are sometimes easy and straightforward cases, but sometimes difficult cases.[19]

This method of legal decision-making, until now mainly performed by human public servants, can be transformed into the algorithmic form and carried out in a rule-based system, leading to an outcome of automated decision-making by public

[13] Bibal et al. (2021), p. 156.

[14] See Peczenik (1995), pp. 333, 620.

[15] On the IFTTT, see also Hildebrandt (2018), pp. 2–3; Williams (2022), p. 470.

[16] See Aarnio (1989), pp. 156–157, 174. For different ways to deliver facts for subsumption in automated decision-making, see Wiese Schartum (2020), pp. 323–326.

[17] Peczenik (1995), p. 88.

[18] Peczenik (1995), p. 53.

[19] See Peczenik (1995), pp. 290–291, where difficult cases of subsumption involve a legal rule, a description of fact and a value-based proposition or other addition that is reasonable but that may be questioned. See also Klami (1987), pp. 63–67, and Hildebrandt (2020), pp. 28–30.

authorities. However, different kinds of constitutional requirements would have to be considered when rule-based automated decision-making is used. These requirements will be discussed in subsequent sections of this chapter.

2.2 *The Distinction Between Rule-Based and Machine-Learning-Based Algorithmic Systems*

It can be argued that automated decision-making based on machine learning departs from the above-mentioned subsumption-based legal decision-making, and from legal reasoning, in manners that bring machine-learning techniques at odds with the rule of law. When using machine-learning for the purposes of public administration, a shift from the realm of law to the realm of statistics occurs: machine-learning is used to extract, from a pool of materials, a prediction of how a new case might be resolved by the decision-making system.[20] As stated by Williams, "where [machine learning] is used, it relies on statistical inferences, not reasoning, so when such a system uses a particular factor it is not identifying that factor as relevant to the decision it is making in the way that a human would, but merely recognising that, statistically, that factor often correlates with the relevant outcome."[21] As pointed out by Zalnieriute, Bennett Moses, and Williams, "[r]ules derived from data raise more complex challenges, particularly in ensuring predictability and consistency with the 'law on the books'."[22] Automated decision-making based on machine-learning thus appears to compound a number of problematic issues.

Because of that shift from law to statistics, automated decision-making operating based on machine-learning algorithms produces decisions that lose their immediate contact with the law. At its best, the connection to the law is indirect, because the

[20] See also Williams (2022), p. 470.

[21] Williams (2022), p. 487. Also Greenstein (2022), p. 308, makes the distinction between the rules of the AI, which are "the rules of mathematics and statistics. To exacerbate matters, these rules are hidden either in the proprietary 'black box' or hidden also to the extent that they cannot be understood—they cannot be read, they cannot be discussed, they cannot be analysed and they cannot be reasoned. The rule of law up until now has been dependent on its form being in the format of natural language—it entails a governance by natural language as compared to the governance of the algorithm." See also Greenstein (2022), p. 313, making the point that "the existence of the prerequisites demanded by a traditional law may be difficult to identify within the complex mathematical processes of AI. Compounding the situation is the notion that the mathematical rules of the decision-making models have not necessarily been exposed to traditional law-making procedures, but rather are 'promulgated' by private corporations." Greenstein arrives at the following conclusion on p. 319: "A challenge will be to determine which values to balance technology against. In this regard, it is argued that the values enshrined in the rule of law operate as a good starting point in determining the fabric of any society. Herein lies the value of protecting the rule of law from technologies incorporating AI." This conclusion appears to point at the necessity to rule out machine-learning applications from automated decision-making in public authorities.

[22] Zalnieriute et al. (2019), p. 20.

training data used to train the machine-learning system uses previous decisions as the point of departure for producing decisions.[23] While those previous decisions may have a provision in the law as the point of departure, the new decision made based on a machine-learning algorithm has the pool of previous decisions as the point of departure, rather than the legal norm. Hildebrandt makes an important point about explainability, a feature of procedural rule of law, that is relevant also in the context of subsumption and of formal rule of law: "knowing how the algorithm came to its conclusion does not imply that the conclusion is 'in accordance with the law'."[24] This means that knowing the logic, or even the source code, of a machine learning algorithm does not suffice to explain the reasons behind or give the legal motivations of such a decision in an individual case in a manner that is expected under the administrative law in most countries.[25]

Therefore, the right to an explanation or a right to know the logic of a machine-learning-based automated decision-making system, as established in Article 22 of the General Data Protection Regulation (GDPR), is probably not sufficient as a legal justification of a decision from the perspective of administrative law. For instance, Section 44(1), paragraph 3, of the Administrative Procedure Act of Finland states that a written decision shall indicate clearly "the reasons for the decision and specific information about what a party is entitled or obliged to do or how the matter was otherwise decided," while Section 45 requires that the reasons for a decision be stated: "The reasons shall indicate the circumstances and evidence that influenced the decision and specify the provisions applied." The Section also contains exceptions to the requirement of a justification, inter alia, when the decision approves a claim that does not concern any other party and others do not have the right to request a review of the decision. This might relax, to some extent, the requirement of legal justification for positive decisions where the legal effects are limited to the applicant, but this exception would not erase the fundamental complications associated with the use of machine-learning-based applications for making administrative decisions. Therefore, even for positive decisions, only rule-based applications of algorithmic decision-making appear to be possible from a legal point of view.

Adrien Bibal, Michael Lognoul, Alexandre de Streel, and Benoît Frénay correctly conclude that requirements concerning explainability in business to business (B2B) and business to customer (B2C) relationships are lower than in government to citizen (G2C) relationships. For the B2B and B2C relationships, it would be sufficient under Article 22 of the GDPR to be able to demonstrate the logic of a machine-learning-based application, but that is quite another matter for administrative decision-making in the G2C relationship. The authors nevertheless appear to consider it possible to

[23] For illustrations of how machine-learning systems are operated in administrative structures in the UK, see Williams (2022), pp. 476–479, and for the US, see Appel and Coglianese (2020), pp. 163–167.

[24] Hildebrandt (2018), p. 3.

[25] For six types of explanation of which only one, the rationale or the reasons leading to a decision, appears to qualify as a legal justification for an automated decision in an individual case, see Williams (2022), p. 475.

develop, at least in the future, machine learning applications that may fulfil the requirements of explainability in G2C contexts, which at the same time might mean that some rule-of-law problems with machine learning could be overcome.[26] Until such a capability has been reached, however, it is submitted here that the ability to produce a legal justification for an administrative decision is confined to rule-based applications of automated decision-making.

As explained above, legal subsumption and legal reasoning cannot and should not be replaced by predictions based on previous cases, because the direct link to the law is broken. The rule of law requires a direct link from the decision to the legal rule, not an indirect one. As a consequence, it appears to be against the rule of law to use machine-learning for automated decision-making in administrative contexts.[27] Another complication is that machine-learning for automated decision-making could evolve into a very rigid system of a *stare decisis* kind, because the machine learning would continue to reproduce the structures of the training data in future decisions.[28]

For at least these reasons, the choice to set up a system of automated decision-making either as a rule-based system ("if..., then..."), or as a system based on machine learning, should, at this moment in time, take the form of a rule-based system, sometimes also termed "expert system." There is hence a crucial methodological difference between rule-based (code-driven) automated decision-making and automated decision-making that is operating based on machine learning (data-driven),[29] and that difference leads to the conclusion that only the rule-based alternative is compliant or compatible with the formal rule of law, that is, with the

[26] Bibal et al. (2021), p. 156. For observations concerning public administration, see pp. 153–155, 164–165, and for illustrations of how algorithms are constructed, see pp. 157–160.

[27] Machine-learning applications may also be viewed as posing different kinds of threats to the rule of law. See Greenstein (2022), p. 292, who points out that "[t]he threat to the rule of law lies in the fact that most of these decision-making systems are 'black boxes' because they incorporate extremely complex technology that is essentially beyond the cognitive capacities of humans and the law too inhibits transparency to a certain degree. It is here that the demands of the rule of law, such as insight, transparency, fairness and explainability, are almost impossible to achieve, which in turn raises questions concerning the extent to which the rule of law is a viable concept in the technocratic society." What may loom ahead of us from this is a rule of algorithm instead of a rule of law.

[28] Suksi (2021), p. 101. See also Hildebrandt (2018), pp. 2–3, where distinction is made between code-driven (IFTTT; "if this then that") and data-driven systems (the code is informed by the data on which it has been trained, not by legal experts that have translated their insights into code). See also Williams (2022), p. 470. According to Greenstein (2022), p. 303, "distinction must be made between rule-based systems and ML systems. The former can be described as static systems, with stand-alone characteristics, where the rules are determined by humans," while machine-learning systems "are dynamic and heavily integrated with other systems."

[29] See also Hildebrandt (2018), pp. 2–4; Zalnieriute et al. (2019), pp. 8–9. As pointed out by the Social Insurance Institution of Finland in the opinion the Chancellor of Justice about automated decision-making at the SII (see below), the algorithmic systems in use are rule-based. See also the chapter by Riku Sarlin in this volume.

requirement that a decision is based on an Act.[30] Zalnieriute, Bennett Moses, and Williams also operate with this main distinction between rule-based and machine-learning-based automated decision-making, but they make the point that the distinction between the two categories is not always clear, and that the two categories may sometimes display a mix where it is difficult to separate between the two.[31] However, in this context, it is submitted that there is a principal difference between the two methods of automated decision-making, and that only rule-based automated decision-making is capable of producing subsumption that is compatible with the rule of law.

Interestingly, a description of subsumption is included in Annex III of the EU's proposed AI Act. In the listing of Annex III covering high-risk uses of AI, there is a particular paragraph, 8(a), that connects to our discussion of subsumption, because it identifies, within the title "Administration of justice and democratic processes," high-risk uses of AI, such as AI systems that are intended to assist a judicial authority in researching and interpreting facts and the law, and AI systems that are intended to assist a judicial authority in applying the law to a concrete set of facts.[32] This description of subsumption in Annex III is thus relevant for assisting functions in

---

[30] As required in the recently adopted Section 53 e, subsection 2, of the Finnish Administrative Procedure Act (434/2003), in force from 1 May 2023, automated decision-making must be based on pre-determined rules, which according to Government Bill 145/2022 and the specific justification for Section 53 e means that automated decision-making systems has to be rule-based. As pointed out in Suksi (2021), p. 102, development work is being done to create machine-learning where modifications in the training data are facilitated depending on changes introduced through amendments of the legal rules or interpretations of them by means of court decisions. Currently, it is not possible to change training data in such a manner that it would instantaneously reflect changes in law or court praxis in a satisfactory way.

[31] Zalnieriute et al. (2019), pp. 9, 24. They also think that it is not so that machine learning can never be used by public authorities, but the examples given, such as traffic flow management and interventions in economy, fall outside of the area of automated decision-making in individual administrative matters. However, they appear to associate more risks to applications based on machine learning, such as the COMPAS system for recidivism used in the USA, which would mean that the rule-based systems they are reviewing are to be preferred from a legal point of view. They make the point on p. 20 that "[s]upervised machine learning and other iterative systems also struggle with consistency over time. However, these are matters that can be controlled from the perspective of predictability and consistency, in the first case through design of the system as well as independent testing and evaluation, and in the latter by moderating continual learning. Hence, a system that combines both types of automation by using explicit programming to automate the application of a fixed rule (originally derived from data, for example through machine learning) can ensure consistency over time. Automation can thus prove beneficial for predictability and consistency, *although the evidence suggests that may not be achieved in practice*" [italics by MS]. See also Koulu et al. (2019), pp. 132-133, who make the point that the distinction between rule-based systems and machine learning systems should not entirely exclude the possibility of using machine learning systems in automated decision-making, inter alia, for the reason that automated decision-making may combine different techniques, that is, the rule-based and the machine-learning-based ones.

[32] However, para 8 of Annex III makes no corresponding specification about the use of AI in the democratic process.

the administration of justice, although the presumption seems to be that actual judicial decision-making, that is, the actual subsumption in the court case, would be carried out by physical persons. If assisting in judicial decision-making is high-risk, it can be asked, why would the deciding in administrative matters by means of automated decision-making also not belong among the high-risk uses of AI, because the technique of subsumption is the same?

That only rule-based systems would be compatible with the formal rule of law in a manner that makes it possible to use them for automated decision-making by public authorities does not normally prevent the use of machine-learning applications for assisting functions in decision-making by physical public servants. In such cases, the machine-learning application is not charged with making the final decision, which is still a task for the physical public servant or a collegial body of appointed decision-makers. Therefore, the machine-learning application can, in such assisting functions, be given a role, smaller or larger, in the preparation of the final decision made by physical decision-makers. Such use of machine-learning applications is clearly less problematic from the point of view of the formal rule of law, in comparison with giving machine-learning applications actual decision-making functions. However, and as indicated by Annex III of the proposed AI Act, the use of machine learning applications in courts would be a high-risk activity, even when performing assisting functions.

2.3 *Reflections and Interpretations Concerning Algorithmic Techniques*

Giving a philosophical point of view, Hildebrandt has commented on the distinction between rule-based and machine-learning-based algorithmic systems, asserting that "cybernetic understanding of regulation [machine-learning-based—MS] makes a lot of sense, but [...] it takes an external perspective on law, missing out on the domain specificity of law and the force of law." She continues by saying that the "fact that lawyers may take such an external perspective does not turn it into an internal perspective; it rather means that such lawyers fail to distinguish between a sociological or cybernetic account of law and the domain-specific operations of legal normativity which is closely aligned with the concept and the rule of law."[33] From our vantage point of the rule of law in automated decision-making in public authorities, this appears to confirm what was said above about the inability of machine-learning (data-driven) algorithmic systems to perform subsumption, and thus to comply with the rule of law.

The distinction Hildebrandt makes is that data-driven applications are not deterministic in the sense that IFTTT or rule-based applications are.[34] The implication of

[33] Hildebrandt (2018), p. 5.

[34] Hildebrandt (2018), p. 3.

this distinction is that rule-based automated decision-making is, at least currently, the only acceptable option for the use of algorithmic systems in public administration, in situations of fully automated decision-making. However, as Hildebrandt points out, machine-learning applications may well be used in semi-automated contexts, where the application has the function of decision-support.[35] In such situations, the final human decision-maker must, however, remember to exercise the consideration that human decision-making requires,[36] because in such semi-automated contexts, the human decision-maker is (or at least should be) directly responsible for the individual decision.

Therefore, the general view appears to be that rule-based solutions for automated decision-making are in harmony with the rule of law. This appears to be the understanding in France, where, as explained by David Restrepo Amariles, the Conseil Constitutionnel held in its decision no. 2018–765 on the constitutionality of the 2018 French Data Protection Law that, "in order to fulfill the requirements of the Law for a Digital Republic, the administration cannot use machine learning algorithms for automated decision-making." According to the Court, machine learning algorithms hinder "the administration knowing the rules on the basis of which administrative decisions have essentially been made," as they are able to autonomously "revise the rules that they apply."[37] Restrepo Amariles thinks that the complication follows from "how rules are produced; they are drawn continuously from data flows and, thus, are hardly identifiable and recognizable to both the administration and the citizen."[38] In fact, rules in the data program "may differ substantially from the legal rules in the books."[39]

Reliance on rule-based systems would seem to exist also in Norway, as is evident based on an analysis by Dag Wiese Schartum, where the examples are all drawn from a rule-based environment of automated decision-making.[40] Wiese Schartum

[35] Hildebrandt (2018), p. 1. Hildebrandt also appears to consider it possible that code-driven applications of machine learning could be used in actual decision-making contexts, that is, in fully automated decision-making, when concluding that instead of taking the output of data-driven applications for granted, "we—the lawyers—and us—the people—must learn to *speak law to statistics*." See Hildebrandt (2018), p. 9. However, such a development could result in a stark deviation in decision-making from subsumption and thus from the rule of law.

[36] On human consideration as a requirement in semi-automated contexts, see Williams (2022), pp. 486, 488, 489.

[37] Conseil Constitutionnel (Constitutional Court), Decision no. 2018–765 DC, June 12, 2018, at https://www.conseil-constitutionnel.fr/decision/2018/2018765DC.htm (accessed on 5 September 2022), para 66, where the Court notes that on the one hand, it is not guaranteed that the rules applied by the algorithms stand in conformity with the law, and that on the other hand, the government has handed over its regulatory power to algorithms that define their own rules. See comments in Restrepo Amariles (2020), p. 286.

[38] Restrepo Amariles (2020), p. 287.

[39] Restrepo Amariles (2020), p. 299.

[40] Wiese Schartum (2020), pp. 304–305, 307, 312–314, 317–318, 326–327. He thus thinks (p. 303) that formal representation based on "fixed rules" is the standard method but makes the point that the possibility of applying statistical methods and machine learning is of special interest. While this is

does, however, consider statistical methods with machine learning as a (theoretically) possible alternative to rule-based applications,[41] something he thinks has not been adequately attempted in Norwegian public administration. Therefore, because jurisdictional differences might result in a different view on the conformity of machine-learning techniques to the rule of law, the possibility should not be ruled out that such techniques might be acceptable elsewhere.

The Court of Justice of the European Union (CJEU) appears to take a negative stance toward machine-learning applications in the case of *Ligue des droits humains v Conseil des ministres*,[42] which is a preliminary ruling dealing with automated processing of personal data in passenger name records based on, inter alia, Directive (EU) 2016/681 of the European Parliament and of the Council of 27 April 2016 on the use of passenger name record (PNR) data for the prevention, detection, investigation and prosecution of terrorist offences and serious crime. The CJEU notes that the criteria used in the processing of PNR data must be pre-determined. Citing the Opinion of the Advocate General in the matter, saying that the requirement of pre-determined criteria precludes the use of AI technology in self-learning systems, the CJEU does not appear to rule out all possible forms of machine learning, only such applications that are capable of modifying without human intervention or review such matters as the assessment process and, particularly, the assessment criteria on which the result of the application of that process is based, as well as the weighting of those criteria (para 194).

However, the requirement of pre-determined data in combination of the opacity of machine learning techniques should, based on what the CJEU is expressing in paragraph 195, preclude the use of machine learning techniques in automated decision-making:

> It is important to add that use of such technology would be liable to render redundant the individual review of positive matches and monitoring of lawfulness required by the provisions of the PNR Directive. As observed, in essence, by the Advocate General in point 228 of his Opinion, given the opacity which characterises the way in which artificial intelligence technology works, it might be impossible to understand the reason why a given program arrived at a positive match. In those circumstances, use of such technology may deprive the data subjects also of their right to an effective judicial remedy enshrined in Article 47 of the Charter, for which the PNR Directive, according to recital 28 thereof, seeks to ensure a high level of protection, in particular in order to challenge the non-discriminatory nature of the results obtained.

---

so on statistical methods, the position taken in this chapter is that such methods are not in conformity with the rule of law.

[41] According to Wiese Schartum (2020), p. 316, "unless compensating routines are introduced, machine learning will only reinforce previous practice." See also Suksi (2021), p. 101, where the point is made that the use of machine learning for individual decision-making may lead to a situation of a strong *stare decisis* effect and an ultimate inflexibility in the administrative decisions.

[42] Case C-817/19 *Ligue des droits humains v Conseil des ministres*, Judgment of 21 June 2022, ECLI:EU:C:2022:491.

What the CJEU concludes here is that the difficulty for machine learning applications to produce reasons that justify a positive match, and the consequence that this might deprive the individual the right to an effective judicial remedy under the Charter of Fundamental Rights of the European Union, speaks against using machine-learning applications of any kind in the context of making PNR-decisions. Such a conclusion is in consonance with our findings and with the understanding that only rule-based solutions can be compatible with the rule of law.

From what has been said above, in Norway, Finland, and perhaps in European jurisdictions in general, which are of the civil law kind, the requirement of the rule of law might limit the use of available techniques to rule-based automated decision-making only. As explained by Steven M. Appel and Cary Coglianese, the rule of law in the legal order of the United States would also accept machine-learning techniques for automated decision-making in the functions of governmental entities.[43] In fact, Appel and Coglianese appear to encourage the use of machine-learning applications and appear not to be bothered by the predictive and forecasting nature of machine-learning tools in the context of individual decision-making. Their conclusion is that the "responsible use of machine-learning tools by government agencies can fit comfortably within prevailing administrative law doctrines" to the extent that such use can even substitute for human decision-making.[44] Their review of "major administrative law doctrines indicates that current law will not stand in the way of widespread use of machine learning within the administrative state,"[45] that "learning algorithms will sufficiently satisfy due process concerns,"[46] and that administrative agencies "should aim to use machine learning when it performs better, all things considered, than the status quo."[47]

From the perspective of this chapter, it is problematic that the ordinary technique of administrative decision-making in individual cases, subsumption or legal reasoning, could be replaced by statistical inferences.[48] Therefore, what has been presented above in this section can also be understood as a problematization of the position of

---

[43] See Appel and Coglianese (2020). However, most of the examples presented on pp. 165–166 are not on use of automated decision-making in individual cases, but on how algorithmic solutions can support public authorities in other matters, such as placing of rodent bait, ranking potentially unsafe buildings for fire inspection, prioritizing drinking water pipelines for replacement, optimizing traffic patterns in streets, deciphering handwritten zip codes on envelopes, forecasting catastrophic weather events, predicting toxicity of certain chemical compounds, detecting fraudulent securities transactions in need of further investigation and identifying man-made structures that have been consumed by lava flow. For examples of and ideas for machine-learning in government, see Raymond and Connelly (2020).

[44] Appel and Coglianese (2020), p. 168. They give a somewhat hesitant negative answer to the question of whether using data in federal agency algorithms (probably of a machine learning type) would violate equal protection because of the possibility of bias. See pp. 170–171.

[45] Appel and Coglianese (2020), p. 179.

[46] Appel and Coglianese (2020), p. 170.

[47] Appel and Coglianese (2020), p. 181.

[48] In the same vein, it would be problematic to suggest that a human decision-maker would be entitled to make decisions, e.g., about social benefits for an individual based on statistical

administrative law in the United States.[49] It is submitted here that the conclusion by Appel and Coglianese, that under the US legal system, machine-learning applications can and should be used, is probably not acceptable from the point of view of the rule of law, at least if the normative recommendations of Appel and Coglianese are intended to cover administrative decision-making concerning individuals, and if this means that administrative agencies would generally be free to choose between rule-based and machine-learning-based technologies when establishing fully automated decision-making systems.[50]

3 Some Notes Concerning the Draft of the AI Act of the EU

Because of the rapid development of algorithmic decision-making in all quarters of society, in public spheres as well as private, law-drafting projects on the use of algorithmic techniques by public authorities are pending or becoming completed in many countries, such as Finland and Sweden. Law-drafting and legislative activities are also taking place in the EU. The proposal for EU-wide general rules on the use of AI attempts to harness a technology that has been developing for quite some time, when considering the use of algorithms in robotics, private business, and society in general. Rules about AI appear necessary for different reasons, such as complications that increasingly common and broadly-used, advanced algorithmic systems may create. The European Commission has proposed that a regulation of AI, an Artificial Intelligence Act, should be adopted based on Article 114 in the Treaty on the Functioning of the European Union (TFEU).[51] The reason for the adoption of such an AI Act would thus be business-oriented, in a manner that could activate Article 114 TFEU as the legal basis, which provides for the adoption of measures to ensure the establishment and functioning of the internal market.

Rule-making in the area of AI has other implications, too, such as the potential shift of law-making authority from Member States to the EU, particularly because many of the high-risk uses of AI that are proposed to be regulated deal with core procedures and powers of public authorities in Member States. The proposed

calculation of probabilities that are based on earlier cases of a similar nature. It should be equally problematic to suggest that an algorithmic application could do so.

[49] See also Suksi (2021), pp. 103–104, and references mentioned therein.

[50] However, the possibility should not be ruled out that the legislator could, by means of explicit provisions in an Act, mandate machine-learning-based use of automated decision-making in particular situations, provided that applicable constitutional requirements are fulfilled. Also, it should not be ruled out that technological development surrounding machine learning results in solutions that may overcome the problems currently attached to the use of machine learning for automated decision-making. See Suksi (2021), pp. 102–105.

[51] Proposal for a Regulation of the European Parliament and of the Council laying down Harmonised Rules on Artificial Intelligence (Artificial Intelligence Act) and Amending certain Union Legislative Acts, Brussels, 21.4.2021, COM(2021) 206 final, 2021/0106 (COD).

regulation also contains an attempt to control the impact of AI in society in relation to individuals, not only in relation to business enterprises and other market actors. One possible way administrative authorities in Member States might attempt to avoid the constraints of the AI Act would be to produce the algorithmic systems by means of in-house procedures, because such in-house systems would not, or are at least not intended to, ever reach the market.

The proposed AI Act contains, in Annex I, a definition of various AI techniques.[52] According to the listing of techniques, the understanding of what AI is, and the area that the AI Act should cover under Article 3, Point 1, appears to be broad, albeit somewhat confusing:

(a) Machine learning approaches, including supervised, unsupervised and reinforcement learning, using a wide variety of methods including deep learning;
(b) Logic- and knowledge-based approaches, including knowledge representation, inductive (logic) programming, knowledge bases, inference and deductive engines, (symbolic) reasoning and expert systems;
(c) Statistical approaches, Bayesian estimation, search and optimization methods.

The basic distinction within the AI field between rule-based techniques and machine-learning techniques is not clearly visible in this proposed definition, but the distinction can be construed based on this proposed definition, so that rule-based techniques are mainly found in section (b) of the definition, while machine-learning applications are featured in a combination of sections (a) and (c).

Among these categories and methods, sections (a) and (c) appear to contain techniques and methods for the use of algorithms which may be characterized broadly as “machine-learning applications,” and which may be regarded as problematic in relation to the rule of law when used in administrative decision-making, while section (b) appears to cover such rule-based methods and techniques that, at least in principle, can be combined with the rule of law and with the subsumption-based manner of decision-making within law, including in public administration. The draft of the EU AI Act also seems to cover machine-learning applications used for assisting in human decision-making.

It is likely that the original proposal by the European Commission will change in several ways during the EU legislative process. The Presidency of the EU presented a compromise text in November of 2021,[53] with specifications in the preamble of the draft and in the contents of the proposed AI Act. The Presidency presented a second compromise text in July of 2022, according to which the definition of AI would be moved from Annex I to the text of the regulation. Furthermore, the criteria for defining high-risk activities would be modified at the same time as the methods for

[52] Annexes to the Proposal for a Regulation of the European Parliament and of the Council Laying Down Harmonised Rules on Artificial Intelligence (Artificial Intelligence Act) and Amending certain Union Legislative Acts, Annexes 1–9, Brussels, 21.4.2021, COM(2021) 206 final. It is estimated that the lawmaker of the EU might pass the AI Act before the end of 2023.

[53] Presidency compromise text of 29 November 2021, https://data.consilium.europa.eu/doc/document/ST-14278-2021-INIT/en/pdf (accessed on 22 August 2022).

dealing with high-risk activities would be changed.[54] It appears that the main thrust of the AI Act will be to regulate different machine-learning applications, but the AI Act would continue to cover both rule-based and machine-learning-based applications of algorithmic decision-making. In contrast, Annex III concerning the high-risk use of AI would be changed in several ways, inter alia, by classifying legal subsumption by judicial authorities, or legal subsumption made on behalf of judicial authorities, as a high-risk use of algorithms. If the Commission draft would have placed "the use of AI as decision-support by judicial authorities" in the high-risk category, then by inference, outright decision-making functions in the administration of justice would have constituted a prohibited use of AI. This does not seem to be the case in the compromise texts of the Presidency, however, because ordinary subsumption in the administration of justice has been placed in the category of high-risk uses of AI and is thus not understood as being among the prohibited uses of AI.

One essential feature of the proposed AI Act is the definition of high-risk uses of artificial intelligence.[55] In Sect. 4.3, below, we will try to indicate how the characterization of AI-use as high risk corresponds to the selection of draft legislation for review of constitutionality in Finland. It appears that the draft legislation in Finland deemed to be constitutionally problematic displays high-risk uses of algorithmic systems according to the draft of the AI Act. It is therefore likely that similar legislative initiatives on automated decision-making in other EU Member States will land in the category of high-risk uses of AI.

4 Different Categories of the Rule of Law in Light of Automated Decision-Making: Global and Finnish Examples

4.1 Legal Basis

Because machine-learning systems are not performing the legal operation of subsumption, they appear to be incompatible with the rule of law. This means that rule-based systems of automated decision-making are the ones that could, from a rule of law perspective, be taken into operation by public authorities. This does not mean that the rule-based systems could be taken into use without limitations. As stated in the introduction of this chapter, the constitution of a country places requirements of different kinds on administrative decision-making. Some constitutions are more demanding in that respect, while other constitutions may be less so. However, it is not only constitutions that require the observance of different facets of the rule of

[54] Second Presidency compromise text of 15 July 2022 (11124/22; Interinstitutional File: 2021/0106(COD), at https://artificialintelligenceact.eu/wp-content/uploads/2022/07/AIA-CZ-1st-Proposal-15-July.pdf (accessed on 25 August 2022).

[55] Annex III: High-Risk AI Systems Referred to in Article 6(2).

law, but the GDPR also carries such requirements in a comprehensive manner, at least on certain formal and procedural aspects of the rule of law. Article 22 of the GDPR grants individuals the right to opt out of such automated decision-making processes that are not grounded in law, while at the same time extending certain procedural protections to individuals in relation to automated decision-making procedures that are grounded in provisions of the law, whether European law or the law of a particular Member State.

By way of examples of legal bases that would exclude the opt-out possibility for an individual, reference could be made to Article 6(1) in Regulation (EU) No 952/2013 of the European Parliament, and of the Council of 9 October 2013, laying down the Union Customs Code and Section 31a concerning automated decision-making, as outlined in the Finnish Temporary Act on the Financing of Sustainable Forestry (34/2015). According to the former, "[a]ll exchanges of information, such as declarations, applications or *decisions* [emphasis mine], between customs authorities and between economic operators and customs authorities, and the storage of such information, as required under the customs legislation, shall be made using electronic data-processing techniques." According to the latter, by way of exception to Section 14(3) of the Act on the Forestry Centre of Finland (418/2011), decisions on granting subsidies for early tending of seedling stands, management of young stands and remedial fertilization, and for the final amount of subsidies can be made in an automated manner. Section 31a of the Finnish Act also contains some substantive conditions for utilizing automated decision-making in these contexts. The legal basis for automated decision-making is very clear in these examples of material legislation and would correspond well with the expectations from the point of view of the material rule of law.

The direct procedural rights mentioned in the GDPR contain meaningful information about the logic involved, as well as the significance and the envisaged consequences of such processing for the data subject in Article 13(2)f. These procedural rights also touch on the existence of automated decision-making, including profiling, in Articles 14(2)g and 15(2)h, and additionally, the GDPR requires that Member States establish legal protections for the use of automated procedures. In fact, the rules and requirements in the GDPR cover only a relatively narrow part of the procedural law to which an individual would normally be entitled, according to the administrative law of a Member State. The EU Customs Code contains legal protections of its own, but these legal protections are complemented by additional legal protections in the legislation of Member States. Those national legal protections would normally involve provisions of administrative law enacted under the respective constitutions of the Member States, and these additional legal protections might obviously vary according to the requirements of each Member State. The constitutions of some Member States require that more of the provisions be included in national law, while other Member States might require less. A common feature for all of the countries and legal orders is that the different facets of the rule of law—formal, procedural, and material—need to be considered when systems of automated decision-making are designed.[56] It is at the moment of design of the system for automated decision-making that the requirements of national law and the GDPR need to be implemented. What those requirements are in Finnish law will be covered below.

Some legal analyses of automated decision-making systems, from the point of view of administrative law, do exist. For instance, in Australia, some "legislation specifically authorizes the use of software within the decision-making system otherwise established by legislation," which means that an explicit legal basis for automated decision-making exists. As pointed out by Monika Zalnieriute, Lisa Burton Crawford, Janina Boughey, Lyria Bennett Moses, and Sarah Logan, "in Australia, there are at least 29 Commonwealth Acts and instruments that specifically authorize automated decision-making," such as Section 6A of the Social Security (Administration) Act, according to which the "Secretary may arrange for the use, under the Secretary's control, of computer programs for any purposes for which the Secretary may make decisions under social security law."[57] This means that at least there is a legal basis for the formal rule of law, and probably also the material rule of law. Zalnieriute, Bennett Moses, and Williams cover four different applications from an Australian and general point of view,[58] while Williams considers systems of automated decision-making mainly from a British perspective.[59] Restrepo Amariles reports on a French software used for allocation of applicants to universities. In this software, used for non-selective training programs, a procedure for drawing lots in certain situations of the automated application process lacked a legal basis.[60] Contributions to this volume also contain several analyses of automated decision-making systems used by public authorities.[61]

At the same time as the EU is activating itself in the regulation of various AI-related issues in a comprehensive manner, some Member States such as Sweden,

---

[56] Zalnieriute et al. (2019), pp. 16–17, 26.

[57] Zalnieriute et al. (2020), p. 270. According to the same authors, "there is also an Australian law that authorizes some data matching, which is often a step taken as preliminary to automated decision-making."

[58] See Zalnieriute et al. (2019), pp. 10–13, for analysis of the "Robo-debt" system in Australia (cross-checking income data for issuing tax debt decisions for individuals), COMPAS in the US (data-driven risk-assessment for recidivism in some jurisdictions in the US; see also below, fn. 58), student benefits in Sweden (a rule-based system operated by the Central Board of Student Support) and the Social Credit System in China (apparently a rule-based system for scoring individuals in some cities). For a development of the argumentation, see also Zalnieriute et al. (2020).

[59] See Williams (2022), pp. 476–478, 482, 490, for analysis of AFR Locate system in Britain (automated facial recognition system, developed by a private corporation and used as a decision-support by police for crowd control at football matches), EVAAS in the US (a privately developed algorithmic system for calculating and assessing teacher performance in Houston, Texas) and COMPAS in the US (a tool designed by the Northpointe corporation and used to assess the risk of recidivism among persons with a criminal background).

[60] Restrepo Amariles (2020), pp. 283–284, 285.

[61] See, particularly, the contributions of Yannick Meneceur (e.g., the SyRI in the Netherlands), Riku Sarlin (the SII in Finland), and Tuomas Pöysti (the SII and the Tax Administration in Finland).

Germany, and France have already passed legislation on the use of automated decision-making, while legislative projects that aim to regulate similar issues are pending in various other Member States. In Finland, discussions have been taking place over the past five years on the issue of how public authorities might use automated decision-making for administrative decisions. That discussion has been promoted by a number of important interpretations by the highest supervisors of legality, which are the Parliamentary Ombudsman and the Chancellor of Justice, as well as the Constitutional Law Committee of the Parliament of Finland. The Constitutional Law Committee is, under Section 74 of the Constitution of Finland, the authoritative body for interpreting the contents of the Constitution in relation to legislative proposals taken up by the Parliament of Finland.

The two supervisors of legality, and the Constitutional Law Committee, have given their interpretations on the relationship between the rule of law and automated decision-making from the point of view of provisions in the Finnish Constitution. The interpretations of the Constitutional Law Committee are furthermore relevant to the proposed EU AI Act, with regard to matters in the proposed Finnish legislation that the Constitutional Law Committee has identified as problematic from the point of view of constitutional provisions, because the same subject matters indicate "high-risk uses of AI" according to the classification of the proposed AI Act.

4.2 Automated Decision-Making at the Social Insurance Institution and at the Tax Administration

A number of Finnish public authorities already use automated decision-making for a variety of tasks. These processes of automated decision-making used by the Finnish Tax Administration and the Social Insurance Institution have already led to some complications that have resulted in complaints to the Parliamentary Ombudsman and the Chancellor of Justice.

The Deputy Parliamentary Ombudsman reviewed two rule-based automated procedures among several procedures of that kind at the Tax Administration, procedures concerning types of tax that require a self-initiated declaration of taxes by the individual.[62] Because of inconsistent responses from the automated system of the Tax Administration, which resulted in confusion about individual replies, and whether those replies had been received in good order, the automated decisions that were made included a mistaken 20% tax increase, and an additional late fee. In another situation, the automated procedure mistakenly sent letters to 11,000 farmers. The letters contained groundless requests, combined with threats of increased

[62] Avgörande av biträdande justitieombudsman Maija Sakslin, 20.11.2019, EOAK/3379/2018: Skatteförvaltningens automatiserade beslutsförfarande uppfyller inte grundlagens krav, https://www.oikeusasiamies.fi/r/fi/ratkaisut/-/eoar/3379/2018 (accessed on 1 November 2022).

taxation based on estimations and upcoming tax increases.[63] According to the Tax Administration, the farmers did not experience any negative consequences as a result of these erroneously sent letters, because the underlying errors were corrected. In the first case, the Tax Administration failed to provide adequate service, advice, and information about the grounds of the decision, and in the second case, the additional information requested by the Tax Administration, and filed by the individual, was not processed in the manner intended.

The Deputy Ombudsman stated that taxation involves a significant exercise of public powers, including some discretion and intrusion into the rights and duties of individuals. The Deputy Ombudsman continued by saying that Section 2 of the Constitution contains the principle of the rule of law (*Rechtsstaat*), where subsection 3 requires that public powers must be grounded in the law and that the law must be closely observed in all public activities. She went on to conclude that the principle of the rule of law in the Constitution, in combination with the provisions in the Constitution on the liability of public servants, is an expression of the principle of administration by civil servants. The main point in the Deputy Ombudsman's opinion is that the provisions that already exist in the taxation legislation concerning automatization regard the manner in which the facts are to be established, not the actual decision-making. The Deputy Ombudsman concluded that the automated procedures of decision-making by the Tax Administration did not meet the requirements set forth in the Constitution.[64]

Although most of the legal provisions referenced in the Deputy Ombudsman's opinion pertains to matters other than the principle of the rule of law, it is evident that the Deputy Ombudsman's conclusion is closely related to the rule of law. Because the automated procedures of the Tax Administration, on taxation and decision-making, were not based on a proper and exact regulation in the law—regulation that considers the proper fulfilment of the principle of good government, the protection of rights under the law, and the liability of the civil servant—the automated taxation and decision-making in this situation was found to be illegal.

It is possible to argue that the opinion contains elements of both formal and procedural rule of law, because the Deputy Ombudsman makes reference to Section 2, subsection 3 of the Constitution, to Section 21 of the Constitution on the right to good government and legal protection, to Section 118 of the Constitution, which concerns criminal and tort liability of the civil servant, and to Section 81 of the Constitution, which pertains to taxes and charges.[65] Another key observation made by the Deputy Ombudsman is that automated decision-making has evolved within

[63]The use of automated decision-making in the tax administration of Finland is comprehensive, as is evident based on the Annual Report 2019 of the Parliamentary Ombudsman, Riksdagens justitieombudsmans berättelse år 2019, p. 352.

[64]Riksdagens justitieombudsmans berättelse (2019), p. 351. For two other cases, see Riksdagens justitieombudsmans berättelse (2019), pp. 352–353.

[65]Section 81(1): "The state tax is governed by an Act, which shall contain provisions on the grounds for tax liability and the amount of the tax, as well as on the legal remedies available to the persons or entities liable to taxation."

the Tax Administration without sufficient consideration of the need for legal provisions to establish procedures that would have considered the Constitutional Law Committee viewpoints (see below). According to the Deputy Ombudsman, the automated procedures of taxation and decision-making of the Tax Administration must be regulated by means of precise and exact provisions in the law. These provisions should, inter alia, define how cases are selected for the automated procedure, and how the transparency of the algorithms underlying the procedures are guaranteed. In addition, the law should define exactly, and in a manner comprehensible to the common person, what is meant by an algorithm in automated decision-making.[66]

In 2021, the Chancellor of Justice presented an opinion about automated decision-making in the Social Insurance Institution (SII), echoing several points made by the Deputy Ombudsman.[67] The Chancellor of Justice discussed the legal basis of automated decision-making and concluded that such a basis is yet to be adequately established. The SII has the task of implementing legislation within the area of social security, as established in Section 19 of the Constitution. In the decision-making concerning this legislation, the SII should follow various procedural rules about good government and about managing administrative matters and guaranteeing the rights of its clients. Parts of the SII's decisions are made by means of rule-based automated processing of personal information of the clients, although the legal basis for such processing, required by Section 80 of the Constitution (and Article 22[2] of the GDPR), is lacking.

The Chancellor of Justice does not appear to believe that the SII failed to uphold the rights of its clients (although the clients should have been made aware when decisions had been made via an automated process). The Chancellor thinks that the procedure is not sufficiently regulated, not only as regards general legislation about automated decision-making,[68] but also as regards such provisions that might be needed in special legislation. The Chancellor thinks that well-functioning and sufficient legislation is the way in which good government and the legal protection of the clients in relation to automated decision-making can be established. The Chancellor's proposal is thus to carry out a comprehensive review of the need of

[66] Riksdagens justitieombudsmans berättelse (2019), pp. 351–352.

[67] The Chancellor of Justice Decision OKV/131/70/2020, 20 April 2021, https://oikeuskansleri.fi/documents/1428954/105838907/ratkaisu_kelan_automaattinen_paatoksenteko_okv_131_70_2020.pdf/49ec0071-558d-2bed-9afe-1d4012f4b84a/ratkaisu_kelan_automaattinen_paatoksenteko_okv_131_70_2020.pdf?t=1642143574123 (accessed on 1 November 2022).

[68] In the decision by the Acting Assistant Chancellor of Justice Petri Martikainen of 4 September 2019, OKV/868/1/2018, it is, however, concluded that automating decision-making functions does not justify steps away from the requirements that the Administrative Procedure Act places on administration. Under Section 44(1) of the Administrative Procedure Act on the contents of a decision, a written administrative decision must contain clear information, such as the name and contact details of the person from whom a party may request further information on the decision. The decision of the SII that had been communicated to the complainant did not fulfil these requirements.

legislation, with particular attention to the special legislation that the SII needs for its automated decision-making.

If a legal basis for automated decision-making, required under Section 80 of the Constitution (and by Article 22[2] of the GDPR)[69] is lacking, there would at least exist an indirect constitutional problem related to the principle of rule of law in Section 2, subsection 3, of the Constitution. The Chancellor of Justice has given the opinion that the general legislation concerning automated decision-making—in force since 1 May 2023—will solve some of the problems concerning automated decision-making. This view can be interpreted as a reference to procedural rule of law. The Chancellor is not, however, convinced that general legislation alone is sufficient to deal with the problems surrounding automated decision-making at the SII; therefore, the Chancellor has proposed an investigation into the need for special legislation for the SII. In this respect, the Chancellor of Justice appears to think in terms of material rule of law, that is, that the substance legislation applied by the SII should be furnished with special provisions concerning automated decision-making. Consequently, that could mean that the substance legislation should include provisions that authorize automated decision-making for use in those categories of decisions where such decision-making procedures are possible.

It is not easy to place the opinions of the two supervisors of legality in the three categories of the rule of law, but at the same time, their opinions also appear to display somewhat different profiles. The opinion of the Deputy Ombudsman connects mainly with formal and procedural rule of law, while the opinion of the Chancellor of Justice links into procedural and material rule of law. The common feature is that they state illegalities of different sorts in the use of automated decision-making and that each supervisor of legality requires legislation about automated decision-making. Both supervisors of legality are furthermore aware of the opinions of the Constitutional Law Committee concerning automated decision-making (see below), which means that their opinions are, in part, parallel to those of the Constitutional Law Committee, expressed during legislative processes concerning a number of Government Bills. The opinions of the supervisors of legality have thus been produced in an active phase of the attempt to grasp the legal issues and problems involved in the use of automated decision-making, which means that there is a great degree of urgency and topicality in their opinions.

[69] Section 80 in the Constitution of Finland contains the rule that "principles governing the rights and obligations of private individuals and the other matters that under this Constitution are of a legislative nature shall be governed by Acts." This means that an explicit legal basis is required for a relatively great number of phenomena in the government of the country without there being a possibility to expect that the Government or its ministries would have the authority to issue rules concerning, for instance, automated decision-making. On the GDPR; see Williams (2022), pp. 473–476.

4.3 *Automated Decision-Making in the Interpretations of the Constitutional Law Committee*

The Constitutional Law Committee of the Parliament of Finland is the authoritative body under Section 74 of the Constitution which performs controls of constitutionality of legislative proposals during the legislation's process of enactment. Unlike many other countries, the control of constitutionality is therefore, in Finland, a matter of *ex ante* determination by a standing committee of the Parliament—one that decides whether a piece of draft law is constitutional (in most cases, such draft laws will consist of Government proposals). If a draft law is deemed by the Committee to be constitutional, it can be passed by a simple majority in the Parliament, but if the draft law is deemed unconstitutional, the Constitutional Law Committee will set the threshold of decision-making at two-thirds of the Members of Parliament present. Such a qualified majority would make an exception to the Constitution possible, but such exceptions are best avoided, and therefore, the Parliament will avoid situations of unconstitutionality by amending the draft law to conform it to the opinion of the Constitutional Law Committee, and thus to the requirements of the Constitution. However, not all draft laws are reviewed by the Committee; only those draft laws where constitutional complications might be expected, which may amount annually to some 25–30% of the legislative proposals brought by the Government.

Over the past five years, the Parliament has dealt with at least six Government Bills on substantive legislation with provisions on automated decision-making at different public authorities, one of which was not referred to the Constitutional Law Committee. The Government Bills (GBs) and the Opinions of the Constitutional Law Committee (CC) are as follows, including indications of whether the Bills might be considered to contain high-risk uses of AI under the proposed AI Act of the EU (with the observation that the AI Act proposal of the Commission is likely to be amended before the legislative procedure is completed):

(1) GB 215/2016 on an experiment with basic income (CC Opinion 51/2016); potentially high-risk use of AI according to para. 5(a) of Annex III (evaluation of the eligibility of natural persons for public assistance benefits and services, as well as to grant, reduce, revoke, or reclaim such benefits and services),
(2) GB 153/2018 for amending the temporary act on the financing of sustainable forestry (no CC Opinion); *not* high-risk,
(3) GB 52/2018 for amendments in legislation concerning social security and insurance because of the GDPR (CC Opinion 78/2018); high-risk use of AI according to paragraph 5(a) of Annex III (see above, paragraph 1),
(4) GB 298/2018 for an act on insurance for patients (CC Opinion 70/2018); probably high-risk use of AI according to paragraph 5(a) of Annex III (see above, paragraph 1),
(5) GB 224/2018 for an act on processing of personal data in the migration administration (CC Opinion 62/2018); high-risk use of AI according to paragraph 7

(d) of Annex III even if only used in assisting functions (examination of applications for asylum, visa and residence permits and associated complaints on the eligibility of the natural persons applying for a status),

(6) GB 18/2019 for an act on processing of personal data in the migration administration (CC Opinion 7/2019); high-risk use of AI according to paragraph 7 (d) of Annex III even if only used in assisting functions, let alone in decision-making (see above, paragraph 5).

It appears, from the listing, that out of the six Government Bills with automated decision-making content, the Constitutional Law Committee has dealt with five. Of the two migration-related Bills, the first one lapsed because of the resignation of the Government, but only after the opinion of the Constitutional Law Committee had been given, so the new government re-submitted the Bill, but with changes to the provision on the use of automated decision-making, which means that the two Bills are actually dealing with the same matter (Bill No. 3 lapsed for the same reason but was not re-introduced). For two of the Government Bills, numbers 4 and 6, the final legislative decisions were made by the Parliament, so that the provisions on automated decision-making were excluded from the Act as enacted by the Parliament. This shows that the criticism of the Constitutional Law Committee concerning the proposed regulation of automated decision-making was very effective.

In terms of Annex III of the draft AI Act of the EU (as proposed by the Commission in April 2021; see above, Sect. 3), all Bills but one (No. 2) could be understood as subject matter entailing high-risk uses of AI. This is very interesting, because the Bills brought to review by the Constitutional Law Committee are exactly the same. Perhaps there is an incidental common ground here for the Finnish review of constitutionality, on the one hand, and the proposed definition of areas of high-risk use of algorithmic systems, on the other: identifying constitutionally problematic cases of proposed use of automated decision-making appears, at the same time, to qualify these uses as high-risk under the proposed AI Act.

The understanding of the constitutional requirements on the use of automated decision-making by public authorities when individual administrative decisions are made started to be formulated towards the end of the 2010s. This understanding has displayed, over the years, an increasing level of requirements that contain different dimensions of the rule of law. The formal rule of law is continuously present through the emphasis in the Constitutional Law Committee Opinions that automated decision-making by public authorities must be regulated on the basis of an Act because such decision-making equals an exercise of public powers, in the manner covered by Section 2, subsection 3, of the Constitution. This category of the rule of law is not, however, very prominent in the interpretations of the Constitutional Law Committee.

The main thrust of the Constitutional Law Committee's argumentation that has links to the rule of law can be found within the category of procedural rule of law. In this category, the principles of good government in Section 21 of the Constitution are emphasized. In addition, the material rule of law is an important area of argumentation, where the Committee's recommendations address the substantive grounds that provisions within an Act on automated decision-making should contain. The rule of law in relation to automated decision-making is thus, according to the Constitutional Law Committee, promoted from the point of view of procedural and material considerations.

At the same time, it is clear that the Constitutional Law Committee wishes that there would exist a more holistic approach to this new technique of decision-making. It is not considered sufficient by the Committee that varying provisions about automated decision-making are introduced in different parts of relevant substance legislation. Instead, it appears that the Constitutional Law Committee requires elaboration of general administrative legislation about automated decision-making—general legislation that guarantees good government and defines the liability of civil servants, as well as general legislation that provides for transparency when automated decision-making is in use. The right and only time to introduce provisions into substance legislation about the use of automated decision-making would be *after* the enactment of the general legislation, when the parameters for the use of automated decision-making have been determined and identified. Because of this general holding in the interpretations of the Constitutional Law Committee, the drafting of general legislation about automated decision-making—and amendments in the legislation concerning the public nature of documents, and concerning the provisions of liability of civil servants for automated decision-making—was started at the Ministry of Justice and the Ministry of Finance. The law-drafting resulted in the submission by the Government of Government Bill 145/2022 to the Parliament with proposals for legislation on automated decision-making within the public administration,[70] with adoption in February of 2023 and entry into force on 1 May 2023.

The strict interpretations of the Constitutional Law Committee concerning the requirements for provisions on automated decision-making, in practice, brought to a

[70] Government Bill 145/2022 to the Parliament with proposals for legislation on automated decision-making within the public administration, submitted in September 2022. The Bill, adopted into law in February 2023 and in force from 1 May 2023, contains proposals to amend several pieces of law. For the Administrative Procedure Act, the provisions concern the prerequisites for automated decision-making, enhancement of legal protection, and obligation of public authorities to notify a party that a case has been decided automatically. In the Act on Information Management in Public Administration, provisions deal with issues such as how service responsibility is distributed in the context of automated decision-making and how compliance with the principle of good administration will be promoted with regard to, inter alia, documentation of development, quality assurance, quality control and the introduction of automated processes, as well as the obligation to inform about automated processes. Notably, a formal administrative decision must be made on the basis of Section 28 d of the Act on Information Management in Public Administration (906/2019) before an application for automated decisions is taken into use, and the requirement of pre-determined rules in Section 53 e, subsection 2, of the Administrative Procedure Act (434/2003) rules out machine-learning applications, that is, applications where the decision is based on statistical probability, from the range of techniques that could be used for automated decision-making. Decision-making applications would thus be rule-based.

halt the preparation of all such separate Government Bills that might amend substance legislation to make automated decision-making possible. The development of legislation about the concrete use of automated decision-making by public authorities was therefore pending the adoption of the above-mentioned general legislation, including provisions on civil service liability and transparency that the Constitutional Law Committee has required before the step of furnishing substance legislation with particular and contextualized provisions about automated decision-making. In its Opinion 81/2022, the Constitutional Committee appears to have been generally satisfied with the safeguards for constitutional rights that the above-mentioned Government Bill was proposing, although it required more exactness and clarity in some parts of the proposed legislation.

Because the Constitutional Law Committee does not review each legislative proposal, it may happen that the Parliament passes a law with provisions concerning automated decision-making—without having that law reviewed by the Constitutional Law Committee. This has happened in at least one case, Government Bill 153/2018 for amending the temporary act on the financing of sustainable forestry (Act No. 34/2015), an Act that will remain in force until the end of 2023 (proposal No. 2 in the above list). The Government proposed that the Act be furnished with a new Section 31a that makes automated decision-making possible, concerning subsidies for early tending of seedling stands and management of young stands. The Parliament enacted the law with minor changes, but the constitutionality was not reviewed by the Constitutional Law Committee.

In Government Bill 153/2018, the Government had, to some extent, considered the relationship between the proposal and the Constitution, and the Government also mentioned the principle of good government in relation to the provisions in the Administrative Procedure Act. The enacted provision was included in the relevant Act of Parliament, which means that the minimum requirements of the formal rule of law had been fulfilled. However, the provision, in the fashion in which it was passed into an Act, lacked all those dimensions of procedural rule of law that the Constitutional Law Committee has considered essential for the constitutionality of such legislation that deals with automated decision-making. It also appears, based on the provision, that the system of automated decision-making can, in this case, be expected to perform operations that may involve discretion, because some limited issues of feasibility may be included in the decision-making.

It is perhaps a mistake that a provision of this kind was enacted into law, but it was done only some months before the understanding emerged within the Constitutional Law Committee that the introduction of automated decision-making may involve various constitutional complications. Therefore, the drafters of the law, or the relevant standing committee of the Parliament, were not alerted to the need to request an opinion from the Constitutional Law Committee. It is, of course, also possible that the temporary nature of the entire act diminished the need for a review of constitutionality by the Constitutional Law Committee.

5 Conclusion

The law, including the Constitution of Finland, requires, in light of the interpretations we have reviewed here, a lot of the legal framework surrounding automated decision-making. From the point of the formal rule of law, automated decision-making in public authorities should be based on provisions in Acts of Parliament. Actually, the formal rule of law requires an even more fundamental feature of automated decision-making when used by public authorities, namely that it displays the normal mechanism of subsumption, that is, of legal reasoning. Procedural aspects of the rule of law require, inter alia, a regular motivation for administrative decisions and an indication of who is liable for automated decisions, and also that automated decisions can be reviewed by a court of law. The material aspects of the rule of law may introduce—by way of provisions in substantive law concerning, for instance, social benefits—different specifications on how the automated decision should be made in practice.

The interpretations that the supervisors of legality and, particularly, the Constitutional Law Committee of the Parliament of Finland, have given about automated decision-making in Finland have, in practice, and until the Fall of 2022, stopped almost all such draft legislation that could lead to the creation of separate provisions for automated decision-making in substance legislation.[71] Also, the review practice of the Constitutional Law Committee has resulted, at least twice, in the exclusion of a provision which would have allowed automated decision-making in the final Act adopted by Parliament.

Recently, the legislative process in Finland has produced general legislation about the use of automated decision-making in administration,[72] the liability of public servants when automated decisions are being made, the transparency around such automated decisions, the decision-making procedures when automated decision-making is used, and a preference for rule-based decision-making systems. From 1 May 2023, Finland has in place a set of provisions that defines the manner in which the legal order permits the use of automated decision-making and establishes a prior guarantee of legality of a procedural kind for such decision-making. It is also

[71] The Social Insurance Institution and the Finnish Tax Administration can nevertheless continue to use their existing automated systems of decision-making for making administrative decisions until general legislation enters into force on 1 May 2023. It appears, however, that these public authorities have already modified some of the problematic details in their automated case management.

[72] See Government Bill 145/2022 to the Parliament with proposals for legislation on automated decision-making within the public administration, submitted in September 2022. Government Bill 145/2022 contains proposals on amendments to, inter alia, the Administrative Procedure Act and to the Act on Information Management in Public Administration. For further details, see also the chapter by Tuomas Pöysti in this volume. This chapter is final as of 30 October 2022 and reflects the situation at that time, but the legislation adopted by the Parliament of Finland in February 2023 conforms to a large extent to the Bill, especially as concerns the amendments to the Administrative Procedure Act, and will strengthen especially the formal and procedural rule of law in the context of automated decision-making.

likely that substance legislation will include special provisions about automated decision-making within some branches of administration. Because the constitutional rules are different in each country, it is furthermore likely that the Finnish rules concerning automated decision-making will continue to be different from those in Sweden, Germany, and France. However, it appears that the level of detail in Finland displays an affinity with the French regulation of automated decision-making.

Formal, procedural, and material rule of law will guarantee that the principle of the rule of law is observed throughout, and at a high level, when automated decision-making becomes more widely-used by public authorities. It is essential that the principle of the rule of law is observed at least at the same level within automated decision-making as is the case within ordinary administrative decision-making by physical public servants. Against this background, it appears to be necessary to employ rule-based systems of automated decision-making because of the subsumption that the formal rule of law requires of a decision; this requirement means that an administrative decision must be based on an Act of Parliament.

An automated decision by public authorities should always maintain a direct link to the legal rule that provides a basis for the decision. At least for the time being, machine-learning applications cannot perform the operation of subsumption, that is, carry out legal reasoning, because machine learning relies on statistical inferences. At the same time, automated decision-making should produce the same kind of justifications for the decision as is required of human decision-makers, and automated decision-making should also fulfil other procedural requirements, such as protection of personal data. Finally, applications of automated decision-making should be designed so that the specific requirements for the decision, normally established in material law, can be traced back from the decision to substantive law. All these requirements seem to point to the necessity of regulating not only the formal aspects of the rule of law in Acts of Parliament, but also the procedural and material aspects of the issue. If done in a comprehensive manner, the individual will always know how the decision has been made and by "whom."

At the same time as legislative action is being taken in the EU Member States, the EU is proposing comprehensive legislation about AI. From the point of the administrative functions of the Member States, more particularly of Finland, it is illuminating to inquire into the scope of the high-risk uses of AI, as elaborated in the EU draft, and to assess the extent to which the Finnish proposals for substantive legislation concerning automated decision-making might fall under the umbrella of high-risk activities. It appears that, in those cases where the Constitutional Law Committee of Finland has found constitutional problems in relation to automated decision-making, the relevant provisions in Government Bills could, at the same time, be characterized as intending to legalize high-risk uses of AI, as defined in terms of Annex III of the EU's proposed AI Act. It also appears that the administrative structures of the Member States are very often using automated decision-making in areas that would constitute "high-risk uses of AI" under the EU's proposed AI Act. Consequently, this could mean that the AI Act of the EU, when adopted, might inadvertently also regulate administrative procedures that in principle belong to the legislative competence of the Member States.

References

Aarnio A (1989) Laintulkinnan teoria. Werner Söderström Osakeyhtiö, Porvoo

Appel SM, Coglianese C (2020) Algorithmic governance and administrative law. In: Barfield W (ed) The Cambridge handbook of the law of algorithms. Cambridge University Press, Cambridge, pp 162–181. https://doi.org/10.1017/9781108680844

Asplund I (2021) Den enskildes rättssäkerhet i individnära tillsyn. Umeå universitet, juridiska institutionen, Umeå

Bibal A, Lognoul M, de Streel A, Frénay B (2021) Legal requirements on explainability in machine learning. Artif Intell Law 29:149–169. https://doi.org/10.1007/s10506-020-09270-4

Csótó M, Rupp Z, Petényi S (2021) In the wake of algorithmic decision making: mapping AI related advancements in the Hungarian public sector. In: Hemker T, Müller-Török R, Prosser A, Sasvári P, Scola D, Urs N (eds) Central and Eastern European e|Dem and e|Gov Days 2021: conference proceedings. Facultas & Austrian Computer Society, Vienna, pp 273–284. https://doi.org/10.24989/ocg.v341.20

Greenstein S (2022) Preserving the rule of law in the era of artificial intelligence (AI). Artif Intell Law 30:291–323. https://doi.org/10.1007/s10506-021-09294-4

Hildebrandt M (2018) Algorithmic regulation and the rule of law. Philos Trans R Soc A 376: 20170355 – Mathematical, Physical and Engineering Sciences (published on 6 August 2018), 1–11. https://doi.org/10.1098/rsta.2017.0355

Hildebrandt M (2020) Law for computer scientists and other folk. Oxford University Press, Oxford. http://fdslive.oup.com/www.oup.com/academic/pdf/openaccess/9780198860884.pdf. Accessed 17 Aug 2022

Klami HT (1987) Introduktion till rättsteorin. Juristförbundets förlag, Helsingfors

Koulu R, Mäihäniemi B, Kyyrönen V, Hakkarainen J, Markkanen K (2019) Algoritmi päätöksentekijänä? Tekoälyn hyödyntämisen mahdollisuudet ja haasteet kansallisessa sääntely-ympäristössä. Valtioneuvoston selvitys- ja tutkimustoiminnan julkaisusarja 2019:44. Valtioneuvoston kanslia, Helsinki

Peczenik A (1995) Vad är rätt? Om demokrati, rättssäkerhet, etik och juridisk argumentation. Norstedts Juridik, Stockholm

Raitio J, Rosas A, Pohjankoski P (2022) Oikeusvaltiollisuus Euroopan unionissa ja Suomessa (The rule of law in the European Union and Finland). Prime Minister's Office, Helsinki. urn.fi/URN:ISBN:978-952-383-088-2

Raymond AH, Connelly C (2020) Governance of algorithms: rethinking public sector use of algorithms for predictive purposes. In: Barfield W (ed) The Cambridge handbook of the law of algorithms. Cambridge University Press, Cambridge, pp 233–250. https://doi.org/10.1017/9781108680844

Restrepo Amariles D (2020) Algorithmic decision systems: automation and machine learning in the public administration. In: Barfield W (ed) The Cambridge handbook of the law of algorithms. Cambridge University Press, Cambridge, pp 273–300. https://doi.org/10.1017/9781108680844

Suksi M (2021) Administrative due process when using automated decision-making in public administration: some notes from a Finnish perspective. Artif Intell Law 29:87–110. https://doi.org/10.1007/s10506-020-09269-x

Wiese Schartum D (2020) From legal sources to programming code: automatic individual decisions in public administration and computers under the rule of law. In: Barfield W (ed) The Cambridge handbook of the law of algorithms. Cambridge University Press, Cambridge, pp 301–335. https://doi.org/10.1017/9781108680844

Williams R (2022) Rethinking administrative law for algorithmic decision making. Oxford J Leg Stud 42(2):468–494. https://doi.org/10.1093/ojls/gqab032

Zalnieriute M, Bennett Moses L, Williams G (2019) The rule of law and automation of government decision-making. Mod Law Rev 82(3):1–26

Zalnieriute M, Burton Crawford L, Boughey J, Bennett Moses L, Logan S (2020) From rule of law to statute drafting: legal issues for algorithms in government decision-making. In: Barfield W (ed) The Cambridge handbook of the law of algorithms. Cambridge University Press, Cambridge, pp 251–272. https://doi.org/10.1017/9781108680844

Automation in Administrative Decision-Making Concerning Social Benefits

A Government Agency Perspective

Riku Sarlin

Abstract This chapter presents automated administrative decision-making from a practical perspective. The point of view is that of a government agency with a long history of automated decision-making concerning social benefits. Special emphasis is given to the actual process of constructing various kinds of information systems that make administrative decisions. Differences and similarities between manual and automated decisions are presented in a practical context. This includes a discussion on the possibilities of "fully automated" social benefit decision-making in Finnish legal environment, and the pivotal role of "partial" automation in effective public administration. The current and possible uses and challenges of applying artificial intelligence in administrative decision-making are also discussed.

The legal context of this chapter is the ongoing legislative process concerning automated administrative decisions in Finland. One of the main concerns has been the question of responsibility in automated decision-making, that is, who is or who are the person(s) legally responsible for the automatically made decision. The chapter argues that the responsibility should be divided among persons responsible for constructing the information system that makes the administrative decision in question. Lastly, the chapter argues that legislators should separate rule-based decision logic from decisions made using artificial intelligence.

Keywords Social benefits · Automated decision-making · GDPR · Artificial intelligence

---

R. Sarlin (✉)
Former Chief Architect of Social Benefit Systems, Social Insurance Institution of Finland, Helsinki, Finland

M. Suksi (ed.), *The Rule of Law and Automated Decision-Making*,
https://doi.org/10.1007/978-3-031-30142-1_5

Table 1 Recipients of the SII benefits at year's end (SII 2018, 2019a, 2021)

	2017	2018	2020
Pension benefits	643,153	630,538	609,814
Disability allowances	268,537	267,364	261,937
Sickness allowances	286,630	294,633	294,568
Parenthood allowances	149,092	144,027	137,836
Refunds for medical expenses	3,764,262	3,768,224	3,674,482
Rehabilitation services	120,165	131,174	150,091
Unemployment allowance / labor market subsidy	227,912	216,937	247,385
Child benefit (# of children)	1,003,635	996,358	977,024
Child care allowances (# of families)	80,084	75,749	66,968
General housing allowance (# of households)	381,529	376,529	402,559
Housing allowance for pensioners	207,322	209,617	213,183
Financial aid for students	224,752	223,458	250,217
Basic social assistance (# of households)	277,316	281,448	143,902
School transport subsidy	32,874	31,989	26,980

1 Introduction

The Social Insurance Institution of Finland (SII) is Finland's primary social benefits agency.[1] The SII provides basic social security for all persons residing in Finland. While not the only agency providing social benefits in Finland, it is by far the largest, both in scope of benefits and money paid out. In addition to handling social benefits, the SII is also responsible for informing the public about social benefits and services. The SII also carries out research and creates statistics, estimations, and projections necessary for the planning and development of the Finnish social security system. Additionally, the SII proposes improvements to social security legislation and provides electronic services for the National Archive of Health Information (the digitalized Kanta database).

Altogether, the SII handles slightly over 100 different types of benefits. A vast majority of Finnish residents receives one or more SII-handled benefits each year, which puts that figure into the millions, considering the total population of Finland is currently 5.5 million. Table 1 shows the number of recipients within various groups of benefits handled by the SII.

The SII pays out approximately € 15 billion in social benefits per year, as shown in Fig. 1. Benefit expenditure can vary significantly between the different benefit groups. It is also worth noting that there was no drastic change in benefits paid out during 2020, which was the first year of the COVID-19 pandemic.

The SII makes between 18 to 19 million benefit decisions per year, as shown in Table 2. There are large variations in the number of decisions made per benefit

[1] The SII is an independent agency under the trusteeship of the Parliament of Finland, organized as a legal person separate from the legal personality of the State.

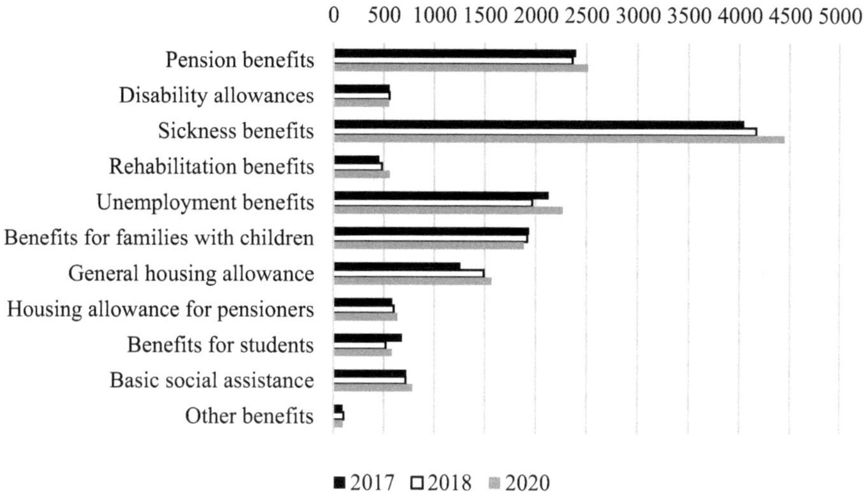

Fig. 1 SII benefit expenditure 2017, 2018, and 2020, million € (SII 2018, 2019a, 2021)

Table 2 Number of decisions per benefit group 2017–2018 and 2020. (SII internal statistics)

	2017	2018	2020
Pension benefits	160,306	157,427	157,881
Disability allowances	124,551	129,616	115,815
Sickness benefits	12,242,186	12,541,419	11,349,461
Rehabilitation benefits	229,724	254,315	296,678
Unemployment benefits	1,388,146	1,882,283	1,442,935
Benefits for families with children	599,084	549,714	491,041
General housing allowance	808,094	826,177	933,441
Housing allowance for pensioners	195,584	190,543	205,593
Benefits for students	349,657	355,349	367,708
Basic social assistance	1,707,828	1,911,415	1,851,407
Other benefits	250,907	261,544	356,454

group, but it is clear that many of the decision-making situations can be described as "mass decisions." However, the correlation between the quantity of decisions made and the benefit expenditure amount is not straightforward, because the expenditure per decision varies. Some benefits are also used regularly by a limited number of applicants. For example, in 2018, there were 216,937 applicants of unemployment benefits, and 1,882,283 decisions concerning them, which adds up to roughly nine decisions per applicant per year. The large number of sickness benefit decisions is handled mostly automatically. Often, intermediaries such as pharmacies and medical centers deduct the SII's subvention from the customer's bill and charge the SII for the subvention in cases where no individual-level consideration is needed.

As can be seen, the SII benefits vary in many ways. This is also true from an automation point of view. For example, although sickness-related benefits have the largest numbers of applications, such benefits are handled almost fully automatically at the SII. The reimbursement amount for medical expenses has been fixed using pre-determined rates (flat rate for medical expenses, flat percentage of prescription drug prices), which means that decision-making at an individual level is not necessary. At the other end of the spectrum, however, basic social assistance applications are handled separately, case by case, often based on a large number of documents such as invoices, bank account statements, and descriptions of various expenses, leading to the need for individual, manual decision-making. However, even in these more individualized cases, some parts of the benefit-granting process have been automated. These are usually semi-technical matters, such as creating a manual task in the work queue and linking the application and its appendices to the task, or notifying the handler about the complex interconnections between various benefits (for example, some benefits are mutually exclusive).

This chapter focuses on full and partial automation in decision-making related to social benefit applications handled by the SII. This chapter will also attempt to shed light on the following questions from the perspective of a government agency making millions of administrative decisions per year:

- How has the SII implemented automated decision-making in its benefit application process (both full and partial automation)?
- Who is accountable at the SII when decisions are made automatically?
- What is the role of artificial intelligence (AI) in the SII's automated decision-making?
- What are the main legal issues surrounding automated decision-making in benefit applications, and what is the SII's point of view on these issues?

This chapter does not discuss legislation on various SII benefits. Instead, the focus will be upon general legislation. This might be considered a limitation of this chapter, since in actual decision-making, the benefit decisions need to be grounded in different statutes in Finnish legislation, and the social benefit legislation is of course central in this process. For this chapter, actual social benefit legislation is essentially taken as a "given," although social benefit legislation may also need to be changed, after the new general legislation on automated administrative decision-making in Finland has been agreed upon and passed by the Parliament.

The starting point of this chapter has been the materials and discussions between the SII and the Finnish supervisors of legality, the Chancellor of Justice and the Parliamentary Ombudsman. These materials contain many references to various statements and considerations of the Finnish Parliament's Constitutional Law Committee, which is the authoritative interpreter of the Constitution of Finland.[2]

[2] See the chapters of Tuomas Pöysti and Markku Suksi in this volume.

2 The Process of Decision-Making Concerning Social Benefits at the SII

The general benefit-handling process is the same for all types of benefits. The steps are as follows:

- *Impulse detection*: An application arrives via mail or e-service but also verbally via the service phone or the service desk. Additionally, the SII receives information from other parties requiring action. For example, a customer receiving general housing allowance moves to another address, after which the SII receives the information about a new address automatically from Finland's Digital and Population Data Services Agency. The impulse can also come from within the SII, when, for example, a new benefit has been granted and that benefit has an effect on the other benefits of the recipient.
- *Preparation*: This is the most time-consuming task in manual handling. Information for decision(s) is gathered from various sources, most notably the benefit application and its appendices, as well as from other back-end systems and other sources, such as the Finnish Taxation Authority. The information is fed (partly manually, partly automatically) into a "benefit-handling system" designed for this purpose. A manual handler needs to become familiarized with the customer's life situation, benefit history, and other benefits. Quite often, the handler needs to ask the customer for clarification or further information. The final phase in this step is benefit calculation, which produces the draft decision and the phrases of the draft decision (which will constitute the main part of the decision document later on) based on the information available.
- *Checking*: The result of the calculation is checked and possibly corrected. Special circumstances are handled manually during this step, if needed.
- *Document formulation*: The decision document is formulated in the customer's language (either Finnish or Swedish; the decision can be translated to Sami languages upon request but decisions are not, at the moment, issued in English), based on the decision phrases produced by the calculation during the step "Preparation" and corrected during the step "Checking." The handler can modify some phrases, add phrases, and change the order of some phrases. The decision document presents the decision in accordance with the Finnish Administrative Procedure Act (434/2003). The decision is signed electronically by the handler or by using "the SII" as the collective denominator, if the decision has been made automatically.[3]
- *Decision*: The decision is officially registered in the various information systems, such as the system responsible for paying out the benefit, in case the benefit is

[3]The Finnish Chancellor of Justice has challenged this interpretation, stating that the SII needs to state a person for further information even in automated decisions. See decision by the Acting Assistant Chancellor of Justice Petri Martikainen of 4 September 2019, OKV/868/1/2018, Työmarkkinatukipäätöksessä ilmoitettavat tiedot lisätietojen antajasta, at: https://oikeuskansleri.fi/-/tyomarkkinatukipaatoksessa-ilmoitettavat-tiedot-lisatietojen-antajasta.

monetary. The decision document is then archived electronically. At this stage, the decision has been "officially made," and the benefit will be paid out in due time (in the case of monetary benefits).[4]

- *Delivery and further action*: The decision is delivered to the customer according to the method chosen by the customer.[5] In all cases, decisions are always available in the SII's e-service channel. Additionally, further action can be taken as needed. For example, some benefits are mutually exclusive: if you get one, you will lose the other. This is the case, inter alia, with the housing allowance for pensioners, since receiving that will result in losing the general housing allowance. The receipt of some benefits may change the level of other benefits. Cases of this kind cause new impulses to be sent in the decision-making process, which causes the whole process to start over again.

For this chapter, it is important to understand that all steps of the benefit-handling process can be completed manually or automatically, at least in theory. In practice, the Finnish social benefit legislation makes automated decision-making for some benefits practically impossible and/or non-feasible. However, concerning all benefits, there are possibilities for at least partial automation. Some of these partial automation possibilities are general, with the same solution applicable on all or a vast majority of benefits, while some of the partial automation possibilities are benefit-specific.

This section has presented the general process of benefit handling. The process for actual benefit handling is much more detailed and specific to each benefit. For example, an important aspect of the general housing allowance involves determining the household size, i.e., deciding how many persons are living in the household. The detailed instructions for deciding whether a person is a member of a household runs over eight pages.[6] The SII needs to be able to handle all the special situations, too, and therefore, full automation of all cases is not always feasible.

[4] Currently different benefits are paid out on set days. This means that a benefit that has been approved is not necessarily immediately paid out.

[5] At the time of writing, only a limited set of documents can be delivered electronically. Starting from late 2022, this situation will change, and most of the documents sent from the SII to customers can be delivered electronically (although Section 20a of the Act on the Social Insurance Institution (731/2001) explicitly states that decisions need to be "sent by post in a letter"). Electronic delivery of decisions and letters will proceed in stages.

[6] SII (2019b), Chap. 1.3.2.1.

3 Current State of Automation in Administrative Decision-Making at the SII

From the perspective of the General Data Protection Regulation (GDPR) of the European Union,[7] it is essential to separate between full automation and partial automation. Full automation is at hand when a decision is based "solely on automated processing," that is, when the decision has been made without human consideration or intervention. The difference between the two methods is essential since Article 22 of the GDPR explicitly grants the data subject the possibility to opt out of this kind of processing if such processing does not have proper support in national legislation.

When reference is made to "manual processing" in the SII, the processing is still partially automated. The electronic systems used in manual processing practically always carry out the preliminary calculation of the benefit level using procedural logic. In the phase "Preparation," the handler collects various pieces of information needed for the calculation. This can involve quite a lot of information, since an individual can, for instance, receive income in many different forms (most of which the SII can read automatically from the Finnish Incomes Register). Once this information is available, in most of the benefit processing systems, the system calculates the preliminary benefit and identifies the relevant phrases (which contain links to sections of legislation applied). In manual handling, the SII official has a possibility to override the results of this calculation and modify the phrases. In automated processing, the same logic is used, but without the possibility for manual editing. This approach strives to ensure that all users get the same treatment, no matter how their application is processed. The very same rule-based calculation logic is applied in all cases, be they manual or automatic.

The SII processes very few benefit applications fully automatically. The only major fully automated type of application is financial aid for students. As of June 2018, 50% of first-time applications for financial aid of university students has been handled automatically. Of all applications for financial aid for students, about 10% are handled automatically. Various features of the application may, however, direct the application to manual processing. The method used for this kind of processing is called "process automation." The method processes the benefit in roughly ten seconds, each individual application at a time. The processing uses exactly the same business logic and rules as the manual processing system. The cases handled automatically need to be selected very carefully.

The vast majority of automated processing in the SII takes place by using so-called "batch processes." This is the traditional, combat-proven, reliable automation method from the early history of automated information processing, and it

[7] Regulation (EU) 2016/679 of the European Parliament and of the Council of 27 April 2016 on the protection of natural persons with regard to the processing of personal data and on the free movement of such data, and repealing Directive 95/46/EC (General Data Protection Regulation), OJ L 119, 4.5.2016.

remains a valid automation method. In the SII, batch processing and manual processing utilize the same rule-based logic as process automation. The major difference between batch processing and process automation is that batch processing handles multiple cases at the same time, sometimes millions of cases. The cases are not handled exactly at the same time but as "bundles" of, say, a thousand at a time. Batch processing is extremely fast when compared to process automation. Batch processes are sometimes "chained," which means that another batch process starts upon completion of the previous one. Examples of batch processes include sending users a reminder message if the required appendices for a benefit have not been received in due time, or processing cost index changes for benefits. The latter is an example of a high-volume batch process, dealing with up to 800,000 new decision documents at the time the change of the index enters into force.[8]

The most recent addition to the SII's automation methods is RPA, or robotic process automation. This method is slightly different from the previous ones, since it happens mainly using existing user interfaces, and not using APIs (application programming interfaces), as previous automation methods had. Nevertheless, the same rule-based logic is again used. The SII has only recently started applying RPA, and the first robotic processes went live in late 2019. One example is "payment plan for benefit debt," in which a robot process picks a manual work item from the work queue where "payment plan proposals" from users have arrived. The robot then moves on to handle the proposal in the benefit debt processing system and sends a letter or a message to the customer, confirming the approved debt payment plan. Typically, RPA is used to automate "boring manual tasks," such as moving data from system A to system B when no programmatic interface is available.

All the mentioned automation methods have some things in common:

- They are always applied only in very clear-cut cases, based on objective facts. In fact, any other application method would be foolish indeed; creating bad or unclear decisions automatically would be counter-productive, since an appeals process is always manual and often very time-consuming for the SII;
- Manual handling and automated handing use the same logic. All applications need to be handled in a uniform way to ensure fair treatment of all applications, no matter how the applications are handled;
- Automation in the SII is always procedural, or "rule-based automation." This procedure is specified, documented, and implemented by employees of the SII. A responsible employee can always be identified, even if the handling is automated (for responsibilities and accountability, see below).

It is worth noting that all automation, including RPA, requires that logic can be described as rules that can be interpreted by a computer. However, describing these rules is not always easy. A Swedish study has articulated the challenges one faces

[8] Whether this kind of cost index change-related change in benefit level can be called a decision arrived "solely on automated processing" is an interesting question, and we will return to this later.

when trying to "codify" processes that actually involve a great deal of tacit knowledge and individual consideration.[9]

4 Designing and Implementing Full and Partial Automation in the SII

The SII designs and implements the above-mentioned automated information systems in-house. This is actually quite rare in the current IT landscape. The reason the SII designs and implements such systems in-house is that the Finnish social benefit legislation is unique and ever-changing, and when legislation is amended, there is often urgency to update the systems, which is a task handled more easily in-house. While taxation, for example, is to some extent universal, social benefit legislation, practices, and organization differ greatly from country to country. The SII is the only agency in the world responsible for implementing Finnish social security legislation. There are some software packages that target social security, but these do not consider the complex interconnections between different benefits in Finland. It has thus far proven to be easier in the long run to design and implement necessary systems in-house. This does not mean that all software the SII uses is custom developed; many times, benefit systems utilize commercial "middleware," and various open-source libraries, to complete tasks.

Designing an automated benefit handling system is effectively "translating law into code," as described by Dag Wiese Schartum in the Norwegian context.[10] The process involves gathering relevant legal sources, translating these sources into "rules" in more formal language, and the rules are then implemented in formal computer language.

From an information system point of view, the process of creating automated benefit handling systems at the SII follows a traditional "waterfall" method of information system design, with the following phases:

- *Requirement specification*: The business owner of the system (with the help of a large group of persons, including legal experts) describe, in business terms, what the system should do. In process automation, the business owner says which cases should be automated and which should not. This usually takes the form of a list of rules about when or when not to include a case. This is done in such a way that risks are minimized. To put it short: if there is some, however small, need for interpretation (for example, an unanswered message in another benefit relevant to the benefit being handled), the case is not handled automatically but manually. This is necessary since there is nobody to do the interpretation or write the

[9] Andersson et al. (2022).

[10] Wiese Schartum (2020).

decision document in a suitable way. It has to be clear-cut so that interpretation is not needed and so that a decision document can be effectively formulated.
- *Design*: IT personnel, with the help of the business owner and the business users, design a system (in this case, an automated handling process) that corresponds to the specification. In practice, a design document is written, which contains detailed design information for every rule on inclusion or non-inclusion in the automation process, such as where to fetch data needed for the rule, a description on the rule in a form suitable for implementation, how to do the calculation, and where to store the interim results. As described by Christoffer Andersson, Anette Hallin, and Chris Ivory, spelling out these rules explicitly is actually more difficult than it sounds; such articulation involves many practical, legal, and ethical questions.[11]
- *Implementation*: IT personnel implements the designed system according to the design made. This phase is usually quite technical and becomes more difficult in cases where technologies are used for the first time.
- *Quality assurance*: The implemented system is tested against the requirement specification and design documents. Quality assurance takes many forms, but typically testers design "test cases" that test various business rules of the system, such as the rules that sort which cases should or should not be included in automation. After that, the system is tested and checked to see if the outcome is as expected. If problems are found (and it is very rare indeed that no problems would be found), these are corrected by IT personnel, and tests are conducted again. Additionally, the system's performance and security aspects are tested. This stage ends when the quality assurance team agrees that the system works well enough according to specification—a formal approval document is created and signed. It is worth noting that usually this does not mean that the system is error-free; usually, there are "known bugs," but their risk level is low enough to allow the process to proceed to production.
- *Deployment*: IT personnel deploys the system into the production environment. This can be a lengthy phase, in case users need to be educated to use the new system, or data needs to be migrated from the old system. In an automation project, this phase is typically quite easy, since there are no users to train. In the process, a "production approval" document is created and signed by the business owner, the IT representative, and the quality assurance representative. This is done after a "production test" has been successfully carried out.
- *Maintenance*: when the system is in production, possible problems are corrected and tested, and the system can be further developed, for example to handle more cases automatically.

Although the process described above is presented as a top-down process (as a "waterfall"), in practice, things happen iteratively in the design, implementation, and quality assurance phases. Design can have an effect on requirements, and

[11] Andersson et al. (2022).

implementation on design, for example. Requirements may need to be revised, too. Usually, not all rules are implemented in the first iteration, only the most important ones so that quality assurance can commence. Sometimes a system is rolled into production in stages, for example so that some cases are automated first, and when it has been assessed that things work as planned, a new version handling more cases automatically is implemented, tested, and moved to production.

5 Accountability and Automated Administrative Decisions in the SII

With increasing automation, the question of accountability in automated processing at the SII becomes topical. As can be seen in the process described above, many persons in different roles are involved in implementing automated decision-making systems in the SII. Typically, all the persons described above are employees of the SII. (Occasionally, there can be consultants as part of an IT or quality assurance team, but practically all business owners and business users are SII employees). This means that the SII is the owner of the automated decision-making systems.

The policy of the SII is that responsibility in case of errors in automated processing depends on the source of error. If a document is improperly specified, the party responsible for approving the document would be accountable. If a case is handled erroneously because the business rules of inclusion, or non-inclusion of cases, have been specified improperly, the party approving the requirement specification would be accountable. If the requirements have been written properly, but the design is flawed and the system implemented according to design, the party that accepted the design document would be accountable. If the design is correct and the implementation is incorrect, IT persons (or quality assurance persons, depending on the case) are accountable. Finnish legislation hands the SII the responsibility of implementing certain statutes, and the SII delegates responsibilities to various persons to fulfill this task, according to needs. All responsibilities in the SII are handled in a similar manner with written responsibilities for each party; implementation of automated decision-making systems is no exception to this rule.

Thus, automated decision-making systems are implemented by identifiable persons with known responsibilities. The responsibilities of various parties and roles have been documented, and the design of information systems is based on written documents with defined persons responsible for each document. All lines of code implementing the systems are managed in such a way that it is always known who has written which lines of code. In short, the locus of accountability is always known, even if the decisions have been made automatically.

Accountability is an extremely important aspect in automated administrative decision-making. For example, the Finnish Taxation Authority has been subjected to a reprimanding decision by the Parliamentary Ombudsman for its implementation of automated decisions in taxation in Finland.[12] In this decision, it was interesting to see that the "process owner" could not be considered solely accountable for decisions taken by automated processes, although his/her responsibilities have been defined to contain the responsibility of decisions made automatically in the process "owned" by the person in question. The SII considers accountability to be shared among parties responsible for implementing automated decision-making systems, each according to the tasks delegated to them.

6 The Role of AI in Handling Social Benefits at the SII

AI and machine learning algorithms are, from a theoretical point of view, quite attractive for the SII. The SII has lots of good-quality data that could be used for teaching algorithms. In the SII, there is a legacy of automation spanning decades, and the SII even has relevant skills in-house: the implementation of AI systems requires skills in statistical analysis, which the SII already has, because some of the SII's tasks require such skills. Some benefits, such as the general housing allowance and unemployment benefits, are in principle quite simple calculations, not requiring that much human consideration. From this point of view, AI is a possible new tool in the SII's automation toolset.

It is easy to identify some relevant questions that could be answered with the help of machine learning algorithms:

- Is the person eligible for the applied benefit, given the data from the individual's application and other data available to the SII? This is a binary classification problem that can be addressed with a myriad of algorithms, such as logistic regression, support vector machines, nearest neighbor type algorithms, decision trees, and neural networks.
- What is the level or type of benefit granted, given the data from the application and other data available to the SII? This question could be answered, depending on the nature of the benefit, with, for example, linear regression or classification algorithms mentioned above. (Not all benefits are monetary, but they can also state, for example, the level of reimbursement of medication, which is a classification problem—selecting either reimbursement level of 0, 50, 75, or 100% of medication costs).

There are several problems, though, in applying machine learning algorithms in Finnish public administration——both legal and practical. The Finnish Administrative Procedure Act requires in Section 45 that decisions be reasoned, and reasons need to include facts and statements that have been considered. The sections of the

[12] Deputy Parliamentary Ombudsman Decision EOAK/3379/2018, 20 November 2019: Verohallinnon automatisoitu päätöksentekomenettely ei täytä perustuslain vaatimuksia, https://www.oikeusasiamies.fi/r/fi/ratkaisut/-/eoar/3379/2018.

material Acts applied in making the decision need to be mentioned in the decision, too. The main problems in applying machine learning algorithms in Finnish public administration are as follows:

- While some of the machine learning algorithms (such as decision trees, nearest neighbor type algorithms, MAX-SAT optimization algorithms) do provide an explanation of sorts, the explanation is mathematical, not legal. Is it not trivial (some could say it is impossible) to "jump" from the mathematical explanation to legal reasoning.[13]
- Change over time is embedded in the Finnish social security legislation. Benefit levels change typically on a yearly basis with Government Decrees, and minor and major changes in various sections of the legislation take place regularly, too. This is a grave problem for machine learning algorithms because changes easily render the currently-used machine learning model unusable—and in such a situation there does not exist any proper production data to train a new model.

Because of these major issues, the SII does not currently use machine learning algorithms in the actual decision-making part of benefit handling. This does not mean that the SII does not use any machine learning algorithms in benefit processing; it just means that the SII currently sees the role of machine learning only as a "helping hand" in benefit processing. AI-related solutions currently have following roles in benefit handling:

- The type of scanned document (applications and appendices that arrive on paper) is automatically detected. This makes handling of benefits more effective because handlers no longer need to detect which of the documents is a rental agreement and which is a bank account statement and so on.
- Appendices that arrive via an e-service channel are automatically turned "the right side up." (This might be surprising, but the problem is not trivial for computers).
- Categorizing of documents as in scanned, paper-based applications and appendices as described above is done using machine learning algorithms for the most commonly-used document types. (A great mass of documents is needed for a model to be successful, so this can only be done for commonly-used popular documents).
- Some chatbots are currently in active production use, giving our users answers in various specialized fields, such as help in applying for family benefits. A number of other chatbots are under implementation.

As can be seen from these examples, AI is a "supporting actor" in benefit handling. If case documents have been wrongly typed, or not successfully turned the right way up, handlers correct these problems using existing functionality in the handler's user interface, when manual case handling starts. There are no legal consequences that follow from such technical uses of AI. This is very much in line

[13] Cao et al. (2020).

with the expected EU-level legislation on use of AI in social benefit handling,[14] which sets social benefit handling in the "high risk to fundamental rights" category, resulting in extensive documentation and certification to be done by separate authorities.

6.1 *Balancing the GDPR and Effective Public Administration*

Finnish social security legislation, general administrative legislation, and the Constitution were slightly more relaxed towards automated decision-making prior to the GDPR. Automation was allowed if explicitly stated so in legislation (as in the GDPR), or when a decision was made "in connection with a legal agreement."[15] (This is not found in the GDPR). One can also say that the Finnish constitutional requirements of handling cases without undue delay, and uniform treatment of all citizens, are very much in line with automation. Automation makes case handling faster and treats everybody with the same set of rules.

The SII has statistical evidence showing that automatically-created benefit decisions are of significantly "better quality" than decisions made manually. This result is to be expected; the most important part in designing an automated decision-making system is ensuring that only very clear-cut cases are automated. For example, the internal quality assurance operations (in which expert users analyze administrative decisions post facto) at the SII show that around 3% of decisions for financial aid for students are erroneous when handled manually. The most common types of errors involve incomplete reasoning (not all relevant facts stated in the application and appendices are listed in the decision document), and that simple input errors occur (a piece of information in the application or its appendix is not correctly copied to the system in which benefit decisions are made). Both these errors may or may not have an effect on benefit eligibility or level of benefit. It is important to note that a carefully designed automated decision-making system is not prone to either of these sources of error. Errors in automated processes are quite rare: of 37,026 decisions for financial aid for students made using automated procedures in 2018 and 2019, only 24 have been erroneous, for three separate reasons. On other benefits, automatically made decisions at the SII are rarely changed in appeals procedure. This shows that the SII has been quite successful in limiting the scope of automated decision-making procedures to clear-cut decisions where the margin of error is slim.

[14] Proposal for a Regulation of the European Parliament and of the Council laying down harmonized rules on artificial intelligence (Artificial Intelligence Act) and amending certain Union legislative acts, Brussels, 21.4.2021, COM(2021) 206 final, 2021/0106 (COD).

[15] Finnish Parliament, Personal Data Act (henkilötietolaki, 523/1999, in Finnish), para 31. This law has been superseded by a GDPR-compliant law.

At the core of the current problem on automation of social security decisions is the fact that the national social security legislation in Finland has yet to catch up with Article 22 of the GDPR. The article grants the data subject the right to opt out of automated processing in situations where national legislation does not support automation. Currently, Finland does not have any general legislation that directly states the conditions for automated decision-making, and explicit support for automated decision-making in social security legislation is severely lacking, practically non-existent. Consequently, the SII would need consent for all fully automated decision-making procedures, and the SII should give an option to the applicant to opt out of automated processing. From the SII's point of view, allowing opt-out is not an ideal solution, because a person's opting-out of automated processing could have a very far-reaching effect. For example, if one household member has opted out, it would be impossible to handle automatically general housing allowances for that household. Formulating consent (or opt-out) would also be difficult, since there are numerous potential automated handling procedures, and consent would probably need to cover all of them separately, that is, a separate consent should be requested for each procedure.

Additionally, in some cases, it is difficult to decide what actually constitutes a decision based "solely on automated processing," as intended in the GDPR. Does the SII make a "decision based solely on automated processing" when a Government Decree changes social security levels based on cost index changes, and the SII then calculates a new benefit level based on this, creates a new decision document that states the new level, and sends this document to the customer? Is this an independent decision, or a new version of the original decision (which has not, in most cases, been made solely automatically)? There is no new application for any benefit here. Personal data processing does, however, take place. Is consent needed for this operation, too, since there is no support for automated decision-making in the social security legislation in question? What should be done if the customer has opted out, i.e., has not given his or her consent for automated decision-making? Should the SII really involve a manual step to handle index change decisions in these cases? Answers to these questions could have significant consequences for the efficiency of SII operations.

From the SII's point of view, Finnish legislation is in dire need of revision to enable effective public administration. Possibilities for automation are improving because information exchange between various public agencies has become increasingly automated. However, without proper support from national legislation, these possibilities cannot be utilized. It seems that the recent hype on AI has caused some confusion in legislative bodies—AI is different from more traditional methods of automation, and it should not be confused with rule-based automation. This difference should perhaps be reflected in legislation, too. AI is based on statistical analysis, and depending on the data used in teaching the algorithm, there can be bias in the decisions. In rule-based automation, the rules are explicit and documented, and these rules are usually based on legislation. Bias is therefore less of an issue in rule-based automation. Rule-based automation also works in situations where no data is available, such as when new legislation is first implemented, while machine learning-based algorithms do not work in such situations.

The following kind of legislative structure could act as a starting point for legislative work:

- The Administrative Procedure Act should be revised to support rule-based automation. The general conditions under which a decision can be automatically issued should be listed in the Act. Issues on accountability and openness of rules used in automated decisions should also be tackled. A good starting point for conditions under which automated decisions could be made would likely involve the following:
  - all facts are known
  - all facts are objective and unconditional
  - the facts do not require any kind of interpretation
  - related specific legislation does not require individual consideration

  Further, one could consider explicitly allowing automation for "technical changes," such as cost index-related changes. The legislation should also describe under which conditions the rules of automated handling should be made public, and in what way.

- Later, separately, new general legislation should be created to cover the use of machine learning algorithms, possibly only in public administration. Ethical issues, openness of algorithms used, and documenting the selection of data used in teaching the algorithms should be tackled. Covering AI in the Administrative Procedure Act could make the Act overly complex and make the process of drafting and approval of the amendments quite long. Quite simply, there would not be enough time for this.
- Specific social security legislation should be updated to list the situations in which automation could be used in accordance with the conditions of the revised Administrative Procedure Act. These statutes should be written carefully, so that the agency responsible for the implementation should not be required to request changes in legislation for each possible instance of automation. One possibility could be to list the facts which can be considered "objective, unconditional, and not requiring any interpretation," possibly in a Government Decree, and subsequently allow automation based on these facts.

7 Conclusions and *De Lege Ferenda*

The SII, a Finnish government agency handling social benefits, utilizes many kinds of automation. In fact, partial automation is the norm and fully automated decisions are rare. An exception to this rule would be the medical cost benefits, the processing of which is almost completely automated. All automation follows the same set of principles in the SII——only very clear-cut cases needing no individual consideration have been automated. All automation related to benefit decisions follows rule-based logic.

From the point of view of the SII, accountability in automated administrative decisions should follow from the tasks delegated to any particular employee, exactly as with manually-made administrative decisions. Process owners, IT personnel, and quality assurance all have their respective, documented responsibilities when automating benefit decisions, and these officials are thus accountable based on their respective responsibilities.

AI plays a supporting role in benefit handling, but no role at all in decision-making. It is unlikely that this would change in the near future. Rule-based automation is much better suited to administrative decision-making, both from a legal and practical point of view.

Lack of support for automated administrative decision-making in Finnish general and social security legislation is a major problem for the SII. The Finnish legislation has yet to "catch up with the GDPR." With the SII's decision volumes, requiring consent from data subjects is just not feasible. Urgent action is needed to update both general and social security legislation in Finland.

A good way forward would be to update the Administrative Procedure Act to cover the principles under which rule-based automation could be used, and cover accountability issues in automated decision-making, and to update social security legislation in accordance with the amended Administrative Procedure Act. Furthermore, at the legislative level, it would also be wise to separate rule-based automation from applications of AI in public administration. Rule-based automation is much more widely applied and much better suited to administrative decision-making. The controversies and potential problems flowing from the application of AI in administrative decision-making should not delay the urgent changes needed in existing general and social security legislation.

In fact, legislators in Finland have indeed started work on the areas presented in this chapter. The result has come in the form of draft legislation, prepared jointly by two ministries, the Ministry of Justice and the Ministry of Finance, in 2022. The proposal reached the Finnish Parliament in September 2022 and is still being processed. The final contents of this legislative proposals are not yet known, because the Finnish Parliament can and usually does revise proposals during the legislative process.

The proposed changes to legislation are as follows (Ministry of Justice and Ministry of Finance 2022):

- Small amendments to the Administrative Procedure Act (434/2003)
- Major amendments to the Act on Information Management in Public Administration (906/2019)
- Small amendments to the Act on the Provision of Digital Services (306/2019)

Most parties have greeted the proposed amendments to the Administrative Procedure Act and the Act on the Provision of Digital Services favorably in their official comments. The proposed amendments to the Act on Information Management in Public Administration, on the other hand, have been met with very strong opposition from many parties, especially from insurance and pensions insurance sectors. The SII has also voiced concerns on the proposed changes. This may mean that the proposals will change. The reasons for opposing the changes are mainly based on the detailed requirements for automated decision-making mechanisms and the somewhat "retroactive" nature of the proposal, meaning that even the existing automated decision-making mechanisms may need to be documented in a detailed way during a relatively short transition period.[16]

Given the pending legislative changes detailed above, the following rough comparisons could be made:

- The draft concerning the Administrative Procedure Act contains language allowing rule-based automation in cases where individual consideration is not needed. Data-based or AI-based administrative decisions would not be allowed, wording being "public administration can make an administrative decision automatically using pre-defined rules ... pre-defined rules need to be based on the pieces of legislation applied in the case."
- Administrative due process in automated decisions is implemented much in the way proposed in this chapter, based on careful documentation throughout the process. The legislative proposal on Act of Information Management in Public Administration, for example, states that the actual decision document needs to include a link to the document describing the go-live decision and its makers (and which further contains links to other design documents). The problem lies in the retroactive nature of the proposal, because these documents may not exist for automated decision mechanisms that were implemented, say, 25 years ago as a batch process in mainframe.

Overall, the proposed changes to the legislation are surprisingly well in line with the views presented in this chapter.

References

Andersson C, Hallin A, Ivory C (2022) Unpacking the digitalisation of public services: configuring work during automation in local government. Gov Inf Q 39:Article 101662

Cao H, Sarlin R, Jung A (2020) Learning explainable decision rules via maximum satisfiability. IEEE Access 8. https://doi.org/10.1109/ACCESS.2020.3041040

Finnish Parliament (2023) Eduskunnan vastaus EV 303/2022 vp HE 145/2022 vp (in Finnish). https://www.eduskunta.fi/FI/vaski/EduskunnanVastaus/Documents/EV_303+2022.pdf

Ministry of Justice and Ministry of Finance (2022) Proposal for legislation on automated decision-making in the public administration (Luonnos hallituksen esitykseksi Eduskunnalle julkisen hallinnon automaattista päätöksentekoa koskevaksi lainsäädännöksi) https://www.lausuntopalvelu.fi/FI/Proposal/DownloadProposalAttachment?attachmentId=17455

[16]Finnish Parliament passed the legislation in question 23 March 2023 with some changes. In particular, changes to the Act on Information Management in Public Administration were very much simplified. The retroactive nature of the proposal was removed.

SII (2018) Statistical yearbook of the Social Insurance Institution 2017 (partly in English) http://urn.fi/URN:NBN:fi-fe2018120349699

SII (2019a) Statistical yearbook of the Social Insurance Institution 2018 (partly in English) http://urn.fi/URN:NBN:fi-fe2019121247924

SII (2019b) Yleinen asumistuki (in Finnish) https://www.theSII.fi/documents/10192/3239691/Yleinen%20asumistuki.pdf (in Finnish)

SII (2021) Statistical yearbook of the Social Insurance Institution 2020 (partly in English) http://urn.fi/URN:NBN:fi-fe2021111755756

Wiese Schartum D (2020) From legal sources to programming code: automatic individual decisions in public administration and computers under the rule of law. In: Barfield W (ed) The Cambridge handbook of the law of algorithms. Cambridge University Press, Cambridge, pp 301–336

Artificial Intelligence, Public Administration, and the Rule of Law

Towards the Uncertainties of a New "Rule of Algorithms"

Yannick Meneceur

Abstract The impact of the development of artificial intelligence (AI) is often studied by contrasting benefits and risks to deduce a framework for action that will maximize the positive effects of this technology. However, a much more profound transformation escapes this type of analysis and affects the very foundations of the rule of law. This transformation of decision-making methods, substituting calculation and statistics for the provisions of law, is particularly evident in the use of AI in the public sector. This chapter therefore aims to document the emergence of what could be described as the "rule of algorithms," through concrete examples of the use of AI to combat fraud, establish compensation trends based on the analysis of court decisions or carry out border controls. This chapter presents a series of requirements to be applied by public administrations to properly regulate the use of algorithms, in a context where the ethics of AI and economically oriented public policies do not currently safeguard against potential misuses.

Keywords AI · Artificial intelligence · Rule of law · Rule of algorithms · Public sector

---

The content of this article is the sole responsibility of the author and does not reflect any official position of the Council of Europe.

Y. Meneceur (✉)
Faculty of Law, University of Strasbourg, Strasbourg, France
e-mail: contact.ym@pm.me

M. Suksi (ed.), *The Rule of Law and Automated Decision-Making*,
https://doi.org/10.1007/978-3-031-30142-1_6

1 Introduction

The profound impact of the application of artificial intelligence (AI)[1] on human rights, democracy, and the rule of law is no longer questionable. While many proactive discourses on the immediate (or future) benefits of AI continue to occupy the public space, mainly under the impetus of the digital industry,[2] an abundant literature also demonstrates that algorithms are not as neutral as some would like to imagine.[3] The principle of adopting binding legal regulations specific to AI is no longer taboo, at least under a double impulse: (1) the profusion of ethical rules that appeared at the end of the 2010s, which failed to convince of their ability to be operational instruments, and (2) the use of regulatory tools by the European Commission, particularly with the aim of aligning American and Asian competitors with market rules favorable to European digital industry.

But the regulators' motivation also stems from the need to respond to public distrust of some facets of AI: the debates remain very lively on, for example, the use of facial recognition technology in public surveillance, and the "prediction" of crime, or the use of AI in public administrations for decision-making purposes. The Snowden revelations of 2013 on the NSA's bulk data collection of online activity, the 2016 ProPublica investigation on discrimination resulting from algorithmic assessments of recidivism,[4] the Cambridge Analytica scandal in 2018 revealed by *The Guardian*, demonstrating the exploitation of data diverted from Facebook for electoral propaganda,[5] the success of television documentaries such as *The Social Dilemma* (2020) or *iHuman* (2020), the reach of books such as *Weapons of Maths Destruction* (C. O'Neil, Crown Books, 2016), *The Age of Surveillance Capitalism* (S. Zuboff, PublicAffairs, 2019), and *Atlas of AI* (K. Crawford, Yale University Press, 2021) are all examples that converge to compose a real and broad counter-discourse questioning the benefits of the digital,[6] often reinforced by Big Tech whistle-blowers. Additionally, AI technicians have offered convincing testimonies about the overvaluation of algorithmic capabilities for mercantile purposes.[7]

Fueled by this awareness, human rights defenders should find fertile ground to propose concrete and binding measures to prevent harm. However, highlighting the

---

[1]For editorial consistency, the acronym "AI" will be used instead of the more appropriate terms "AI systems," "AI tools," or "AI applications." All the technologies covered by this term naturally do not constitute an autonomous personality and the author would like to recall that we should avoid any anthropomorphism or confusion with the discipline by using only the acronym.

[2]See Scott Brennen (2018).

[3]On the critique of algorithm neutrality, see, for example, P. Walsh, Do Algorithms Have Politics? reproduced on the SoloTablet blog: https://www.solotablet.it/lifestyle/do-algorithms-have-politics.

[4]Angwin et al. (2016).

[5]See the website of *The Guardian*, on The Cambridge Analytica Files: https://www.theguardian.com/news/series/cambridge-analytica-files.

[6]See also Sadin (2018), Basdevant and Mignard (2018), Meneceur (2020a) or, for a wider global analysis of the critique in the media representation of AI controversies Crépel and Cardon (2022).

[7]See for instance David and Sauviat (2019), Ganascia (2022).

threats posed by the wide use of AI is a thankless task at a time when the development of digital tools remains primarily synonymous with progress among a large majority of public decision-makers, and where the harshest criticisms are classified (sometimes unfairly) as militant political discourse. It must be underlined that AI is promoted by the digital industry as a "universal solution" to an ever-increasing number of problems in our society, with the support of well-established communication and lobbying.[8] This is why AI and algorithms, even experimental ones, are entrusted with increasingly critical tasks, whether it is to rank or filter various content on social media, to warn of exposure to COVID-19, or to pre-select candidates in recruitment processes. Discourses expressing doubts about the relevance and sustainability of the digital transition, or recommending a certain form of caution, even if solidly substantiated, struggle to influence public policies and are either minimized, watered down, or "whitewashed" by actors mainly concerned with using the digital economy as a lever for growth, with the least possible obstacles. As the philosopher Günther Anders predicted, "[n]othing discredits a man today more easily than being suspected of criticizing machines."[9]

Therefore, the development of AI in public administration appears to be particularly sensitive, in large part due to the asymmetry of relations between an administration and its users. Applications are tested or implemented, sometimes without a clear legal framework, and they are presented unequivocally as necessary progress. I will present in this chapter, among a wide range of initiatives, a number of issues surrounding the fight against fraud, the quantified evaluation of compensation before the courts, and the use of facial recognition to facilitate screening operations at airports. These applications are not, however, only the expression of an effort to modernize administration. The use of AI to assist public decision-making with legal, economic, and social effects on individuals leads to a profound reconfiguration of the control and balance mechanisms of public services, which is not necessarily easy to assess. However, even if it cannot be disputed that many administrations objectively seek to better accomplish their missions, the time for objectively evaluating the impact of the use of AI is not always taken. After decades of *new public management* imposing new modes of governance by indicators and numbers,[10] AI has found in administration a fertile ground for expanded and increasing use.

The ambition to modernize public administrations through digital technology cannot, however, regard human rights, democracy, and the rule of law as interferences or mere external constraints.[11] These principles not only protect us in our daily lives, but they are also the essential keystone for any sustainable development of a

[8] One good example is given by Roberge et al. (2022), with the rise and fall of Element AI.

[9] Quote translated by the author from Anders (2002 [1956]), p. 17.

[10] See Supiot (2015).

[11] The weakening of human rights in many Western democracies and their assimilation by some policymakers to mere externalities or even activist rhetoric will not be discussed here. It should just be recalled that the United Kingdom government is currently proposing to reset how human rights law can be relied on by those with access to its courts.

society that claims to be truly modern. Innovation is only virtuous if it develops within this founding framework of modern Europe, and such innovation must be able to rely on clear and appropriate regulations to create both solid trust and good legal certainty. Finally, let us recall, the fragility of these achievements in an increasingly uncertain world, facing a series of crises (health, security, economic) shaking even the strongest democracies.

The application of AI in public administrations is already a reality in Europe, with promises to optimize internal work processes or deliver a more efficient and better public service. These ambitions, however, come up against a test of reality, with applications far from being mature and a treatment of situations subject to algorithms sometimes much more complex than the designers of these systems imagined. I will begin by examining three concrete examples of the application of AI to support public sector decision-making, and I will then discuss the difficulties encountered in the implementation of such systems (Sect. 2) to draw up a list of the main requirements that should be in place for automated decision-making systems in administration (Sect. 3). I will furthermore outline the reasons why AI ethics and current national public policies appear insufficient to meet these requirements and to prevent risks (Sect. 4), before concluding, in a more systemic way, on the current evolution from the rule of law to what could be described as a "rule of algorithms" (Sect. 5).

2 Algorithmic Decision-Making in Public Administrations

2.1 Examples and Assessment of Uses

In the Netherlands, the Fight Against Social Benefit Fraud: The SyRI Algorithm Stopped by the District Court of The Hague in 2020

Developed in the 2010s by the Ministry of Social Affairs and Employment of the Netherlands, the SyRI (*System Risk Indication*) system was designed to assess the likelihood of fraud in social assistance, taxes, and labor law. The term system will be used, as the acronym SyRI does not refer to a single application, but to a set of applications and projects that are essentially based on the centralization of data between different state stakeholders for the purpose of combating fraud. In 2012, a report by this ministry had set objectives to the precursor of the SyRI system as being able to contribute to "[reducing] administrative costs," to improving the "smart and effective detection of possible welfare fraud," and to have a "preventative effect if it is known that the government is monitoring behind the scenes."[12]

Deployed in low-income neighborhoods in the cities of Rotterdam and Amsterdam since 2014, the system has centralized considerable amounts of data on

[12]Report quoted and translated in English by van Veen (2020), original report accessible (in Dutch) on: https://anzdoc.com/download/bestandskoppelingen-bij-fraudebestrijding-nota-van-bevinding.html.

employment, debt, education, and housing, having subsequently processed the data by an algorithm indicating the individuals most at risk of committing fraud. Concretely, legislation, passed in 2014, provided a legal basis for previous experiments in authorizing public authorities, central and local, to cooperate to combat fraud in the field of social benefits, taxation, and labor law.[13] The legislation allows the authorities to share up to 17 broad, previously diffuse categories of data to assess the risks of fraud, in order to implement specific projects to identify individuals at risk. Each project was approved by the Minister for Social Affairs and Employment, who delegated the collection, anonymization, and analysis of data, using an algorithmic risk model. These data processes were carried out by a private agency known as the "intelligence agency" (*Stichting Inlichtingenbureau*). After obvious errors have been eliminated, the Minister's office refers the "high-risk individuals" to the cooperating authorities and includes their names in a "risk declaration register."

These elements are the only ones documented by the legislation implementing SyRI. Internal mechanisms (risk model, risk indicators, and accurate data) have never been made public and "high-risk" individuals have never been informed of their categorization or inclusion in the reporting register.

Following political pressure by a coalition of several NGOs, and the main Dutch trade union, the District Court of The Hague stopped, on 5 February 2020, the use of this algorithm by checking the conventionality of the 2014 legislation in relation to the European Convention on Human Rights. The Dutch court found a violation of Article 8 of the Convention because SyRI could lead to unjustified exclusion, discrimination, and stigmatization of the individuals concerned (paras. 6.91–6.92 of the decision).[14] The lack of transparency of the application, as well as the lack of balance between the main objective (the fight against fraud in social benefits), and the breach of individual privacy all seem to have played a role in the court's decision. Although the court found that the SyRI legislation in itself seeks to fulfil a sufficiently compelling purpose and a pressing social need which justifies interference in the private lives of individuals (para. 6.76), the court also noted the potentially discriminatory effects of SyRI (para. 6.91) as SyRI was used only in neighborhoods that have been unfairly profiled as potentially problematic (paras 6.93–6.94). This court decision also reveals the shortcomings of democratic processes, which sound robust in our Western countries, where the rule of law prevents the deployment and application of particularly discriminatory algorithms. Strong criticism from the

[13]The SyRI legislation in 2014 is the result of amendments to the SUWI (Work and Income Structure Implementation) Act and the SUWI Decree. This legislation about SyRI is compounded by Article 65 of the SUWI Act, viewed in conjunction with Article 64 of the SUWI Act and Chapter 5a of the SUWI Decree. The SUWI Act, enacted in 2002, implemented a new distribution of responsibilities of institutional actors with regard to the implementation of social security, social assistance and active labor market policies. It set also the combination of data by different public bodies in one register.

[14]NJCM et al. v. (2020) The Dutch State, The Hague District Court, ECLI:NL:RBDHA:2020:1878. Available at: https://uitspraken.rechtspraak.nl/inziendocument?id=ECLI:NL:RBDHA:2020:1878.

Dutch data protection authority,[15] the Council of State[16] and civil society failed to influence the legislation giving SyRI a legal basis. The quality of the debates before Parliament have also proved to be still in existence since several Members of Parliament, questioned by a newspaper on their degree of involvement, have had difficulty remembering the content of the discussions and the issues involved in this application. Although it would have been difficult for Parliamentarians to remember anything, as the SyRI legislation was adopted without debate.[17]

The decision of the District Court of The Hague therefore does not say much about automated fraud detection systems and does not exclude algorithms in principle in combatting fraud. Even if this decision is sometimes imprecise (notably on the distinction between privacy and data protection), it reveals the weaknesses of our current democratic-control mechanisms for guaranteeing the fundamental rights of individuals in a context of widespread use of algorithms for public decision-making.[18] On the one hand, we see that the principles stemming from the "ethics of AI" have not been able to compel designers or public policymakers to include mechanisms that prevent discrimination or make operating principles more transparent. On the other hand, and this is perhaps the most critical point, the lack of real parliamentary control shows that even the highest level of the legal framework is not in itself a sufficient guarantee to prevent violations of fundamental rights. It is the mechanism of the control of conventionality, which is not generalized in all the judicial systems of the European States, that has enabled the Dutch judges here to give precedence to what should have been obvious for the entire democratic chain involved in the drafting of laws.

2.2 In France, "Prediction" of Court Decisions: The DataJust Experiment Supported by the Council of State but Stopped by the Ministry of Justice in 2022

France is certainly one of the European countries, along with the United Kingdom, experiencing the largest growth in startups specializing in the field of law (legaltechs). Among the many computer applications available on the market, the "prediction" of court decisions (also referred to with the old term of "jurimetrics"[19]), based on the treatment of case law by various methods of computer processing, has been one of the most controversial areas. A study by University College London (UCL), published in 2016, documents precisely one method of "predicting" the

---

[15] Dutch Data Protection Authority [College Bescherming Persoonsgegevens] (2014).

[16] Dutch Council of State [Raad van State] (2014).

[17] Van Bekkum and Borgesius (2021).

[18] For a comprehensive review of the court decision see van Bekkum and Borgesius (2021).

[19] Term coined in Loevinger (1949).

outcome of a court case, based on machine learning.[20] The UCL researchers built a "predictive" model from 584 judgments of the European Court of Human Rights (ECtHR) by classifying them in two categories: violating and non-violating decisions.[21] The researchers reported that they achieved a predictive accuracy of 79% based on the factual description section of the judgment, concluding that judgments of the ECtHR depend more on non-legal facts than purely legal arguments. However, a closer look at the method used by UCL reveals that the researchers did not model the judges' reasoning as such but identified, through a statistical approach, the frequencies of words that most often lead to a decision of violation or non-violation.

For example, the words "injury," "protection," or "Ukraine" are identified as strong predictors of violations under Article 3 (inhuman or degrading treatment) of the European Convention on Human Rights, whereas the words "sentence," "year," or "life" would lead to non-violation decisions. This finding is supported by an examination of the accuracy of the predictions based on the section on the legal arguments used by the parties and the legal reasoning of the Court: the accuracy in this case falls to 62 % (it being specified that a prediction of 50% corresponds to a random choice between violation and non-violation). This study has been extensively discussed, even in the general press, to awkwardly qualify this AI as a "judge"[22] or to objectify the results obtained by the UCL to contribute to building guidelines for the use of AI in judicial systems.[23] The resurgence of the ambition of jurimetrics with AI[24] seems to have revived the imagination, long dissipated by many authors,[25] for a rule of law that would be logical and transformable into a mathematical model.

This relatively old finding by the UCL did not hinder the enthusiasm of some French entrepreneurs to make justice more predictable within the framework of the term AI. (It should be underlined that some applications seem to be more about linear regression than advanced uses of machine learning). The innovative appearance of this rejuvenated jurimetrics with an AI veneer has quickly resonated with public decision-makers and the highest French judicial authorities, with the hope of being able to relieve the courts of procedure and to better "discipline" the first levels of jurisdiction. The Ministry of Justice has therefore embarked on an experiment in the field of compensation for bodily injury, not necessarily seeking to establish precise predictions but rather scales of compensation for a particular case.

---

[20] Reference will be made to this study, as private sector applications of jurimetrics are covered by intellectual property and business secrecy, making it difficult to objectify the functioning of capacities.

[21] See Aletras et al. (2016).

[22] See Johnston (2016).

[23] European Commission for the efficiency of justice (CEPEJ) (2018) European ethical Charter on the use of Artificial Intelligence in judicial systems and their environment, Council of Europe, pp. 37–38.

[24] Hildebrandt (2017).

[25] On the "open texture of law," see Hart (1976); on the quote "the life of the law has not been logic; it has been experience," see Holmes (1997), pp. 991–1009 and Glastra van Loon (1958), pp. 1–9.

A decree of 27 March 2020, published in the middle of the first lockdown of the COVID-19 pandemic, came to create the "DataJust" algorithm with the objective of experimenting with this system from a set of decisions from courts of appeal. It must be said that this litigation, which grants the judge a very wide margin of appreciation for the individualization of reparation, imposes a high risk on the debtors of compensation claims—whether they are natural persons or private or public paying agencies. Actual compensation scales (based on simple statistics) established by the Court of Cassation (*Cour de cassation*) continue to serve as an informal guide for those receiving compensation for bodily injury, to ensure better territorial harmonization of the judicial response—although satisfactory compensation may not be awarded each time.[26] These scales are indicative only and can neither replace the law nor reduce the margin of interpretation that the judge has as a result of the law.[27]

However, "DataJust" is not just a modernized version of a compensation repository. Its method of establishing a public and official frame of reference is fully part of jurimetrics and thus borrows its power and weaknesses.

First, the training data of the algorithm correspond only to a part of the litigation of compensation for bodily injury, on a limited scale of time, and are not necessarily representative of the diversity of situations. Then, the arbitrations of the designers to annotate the data lead to a modelling of the litigation involving a certain number of biases, likely to give more weight to certain criteria than the judges give. Finally, it is the very adaptation of machine learning, i.e., statistics, to treat the "open texture" of the law that remains to be scientifically proven today, while the spurious correlations are already quite well documented.[28] To put it another way, all the ingredients of *data dredging* are present: it seems that the selection of decisions to drive the machine was made by retaining the judgments corresponding to the framework set by the designers, at the risk of favoring certain jurisdictions to the detriment of others that were not chosen by the designers according to all the criteria expected by the machine.

Seized by a coalition of various applicants, including a French association for the defense of digital rights (*La Quadrature du Net*), the Council of State (*Conseil d'État*) nevertheless confirmed the legal basis of the experimentation of "DataJust" on 30 December 2021. While the applicants complained that the algorithm replaced the law in setting compensation, that it was contrary to the principles of individualization of decisions, and of the full compensation for damages, as well as the principles of minimization and accuracy of data, the administrative judges of the "Palais Royal" in Paris stated that the software would tend, on the contrary, "to ensure easier access to the case-law on compensation for bodily injury in order to

[26]On the situation in France, see in particular Bourreau-Dubois (2019).

[27]This is what the Court of Cassation recalled about the scales of maintenance payments (Cass. 1st civ., 23 Oct. 2013, n° 12-25.301: JurisData n° 2013-023208).

[28]Calude and Longo (2015).

guarantee the accessibility and predictability of the law" (para 12).[29] However, the experiment was stopped by the Ministry of Justice a few days later, faced with the cumbersome measures that would have been necessary to ensure a better representativeness of the data and the reduction of bias.

The "DataJust" case thus serves as an example of a project that did not pass the stages of a real commissioning with substantial issues raised. It should however be noted that the abandonment of experimentation does not represent a total abandonment of ambition, since the training dataset (pseudonymized) is intended to be made available to the community, via open data, in the hope that a legaltech can continue this work and demonstrate the feasibility of calculating compensation scales.[30] Moreover, the motivation of the Council of State is not to be read as a simple repudiation of experimentation, but an expression of the belief that the predictability of law can be improved with the use of modern algorithmic techniques.

The end of the experiment of "DataJust" would therefore be more the consequence of a strategical delay of the development of applications criticized by civil society, and some of the legal professions, than of a real awareness of public decision-makers of the inadequacy of algorithms for this purpose. This analysis is confirmed in a report on a cycle of multidisciplinary workshops on the ethics of reuse of court decisions, submitted to the Ministry of Justice in July 2022.[31] While the participants, including the French Council of State and Court of Cassation, illustrated a wide range of opportunities and risks, these works never mentioned the lack of a serious scientific basis for the reuse of open data on court decisions for "predictive" purposes. Moreover, no clear conclusions emerged, particularly in the regulation and governance of such data.[32]

In France, currently, the Court of Cassation is where we must look for concrete applications of AI, albeit less spectacular applications, but ultimately effective ones. Thus, the implementation of a new legal search engine "Judilibre," exploiting the *open data* of court decisions, owes much to judicious arbitrations and the flexibility of a small multidisciplinary team. The Court of Cassation also uses AI to automatically pseudonymize the court decisions of French judicial courts placed in open data, and the Court uses AI to guide requests within its chambers.

[29] Conseil d'État, 10th and 9th chambers, 30/12/2021, 440376, ECLI:FR:CECHR:2021:440376.20211230.

[30] See Marzolf (2022a).

[31] See French Ministry of Justice [Ministère de la justice] (2022).

[32] See Marzolf (2022b).

2.3 In Europe, Detection of Lies During Border Crossings at Airports: The iBorderCtrl Experiment in 2019

To conclude the selection of examples of the application of AI in the public sector, a system developed by the European Commission for border protection is studied here. More specifically, the iBorderCtrl project was initiated in 2016 in European Union (EU) countries to assess the "reliability" of a person when crossing borders. Based on facial emotions,[33] the system is intended to direct at-risk travelers and others from regular queues towards specific queues with more advanced controls.

Tested in 2019 in three countries of the borders of the Schengen area (Greece, Hungary, and Latvia), the system required travelers to upload photos of their passport and visa, in addition to other elements, before their arrival at the border. Arriving at the airport, the travelers were then questioned by an AI via a loudspeaker, which analyzed the answers with a webcam to assess a series of 38 micro-expressions of the travelers' faces. A token in the form of a QR code was issued to travelers based on their likelihood of identity falsification, leading suspected travelers to first have their biometric data (fingerprints, palm vein scanning, and face matching) rechecked using a handheld device. If the data from the handheld device again pointed to a high risk for identity falsification, the traveler was then referred to a border guard for further questioning.

Following the request of MEP Patrick Breyer to access documents related to the iBorderCtrl research project in November of 2018, sent to the European Research Executive Agency (REA), the Commission refused to provide MEP Breyer with documents relating to this project – such as the ethical impact assessment – on the grounds that such a disclosure would threaten the commercial interests, including intellectual property, of the REA. The Commission also maintained that such a disclosure would have caused harm to the partners of the iBorderCtrl consortium, and that there would be no overriding public interest justifying such damage. The project was also the subject of media criticism, as the American news website *The Intercept* reported on the 2019 case of a journalist who was wrongly profiled as at risk by the system, when entering Hungary from Serbia. Even if the more extensive iBorderCtrl project checks were not, in the end, carried out, and despite no serious consequences from the journalist's experience with the project, *The Intercept* article highlights the methodological difficulties posed by the use of this algorithm.[34] The European Commissioner for Home Affairs, Ylva Johansson, publicly responded to MEP Breyer's concerns by indicating that iBorderCtrl was only a research project not intended for widespread deployment and that the evaluation, which would be communicated later in the experimentation process, would also consider the social acceptability of the system.

---

[33] For a critique of the revelation of emotions by AI, see in particular Feldman Barrett (2022).

[34] See Gallagher and Jonah (2019).

Despite these justifications, and the program's discontinuation in August of 2019, the project has remained heavily criticized. A European Parliament resolution on 6 October 2021 called for the abandonment of this type of experimentation, in view of the violations of fundamental rights by using biometric data for this purpose.[35] The General Court of the EU, seized in May 2019 by MEP Breyer,[36] ruled on 15 December 2021 that the European Commission's REA had been negligent in assessing MEP Breyer's requests, but the Court did not call into question the principle of the system (the recognition of emotions) or affirm the interest to organize public debates prior to experiments of this type.[37]

This experiment, which cost € 4.5 million, reveals other structural difficulties related to the deployment of algorithms. The first and certainly the most important difficulty lies in the actual capabilities of these systems. Even before discussing their impact on fundamental rights, the uncertain scientific foundations on which they are based should have led public decision-makers to exclude them from the scope of any serious experimentation. Since the rise of various forms of terrorism, aggravated by the war in Ukraine, the political weight of discourses relating to security now seems to take precedence over other considerations around civil liberties.

Another key difficulty with the deployment of algorithms stems from the lack of transparency of these initiatives, as arguments in alignment with industrial interests or intellectual property have been employed to shield certain technological systems from adversarial scrutiny. While information technology (IT) systems deployed under the responsibility of public authorities, already under increased control of various data protection provisions, should be subject to particularly close scrutiny because of the asymmetry of powers between the administration and its citizens, the iBorderCtrl experiment, on the contrary, shows a mixture of interests, public and private, that lead to a weakening of the protections of individuals and society.

3 The Main Requirements for Artificial Intelligence and Algorithms for Decision-Making in Public Administrations

3.1 Background

It should be recalled that the first texts relating to data protection and privacy found their motives in the potential abuses of the use of IT by public authorities. In 1974,

[35] See especially 2020/2016(INI) European Parliament resolution of 6 October 2021 on artificial intelligence in criminal law and its use by the police and judicial authorities in criminal matters, para 31.

[36] See Stolton (2020).

[37] Judgment of 15 December 2021, *Breyer v European Research Executive Agency (REA)*, T-158/19, EU:T:2021:902.

the French newspaper *Le Monde* revealed an important scandal relating to the "SAFARI" project, initiated by the INSEE (National Institute of Statistics and Economic Studies [*Institut National des Statistiques et des Etudes Economiques*]). The objective of this project was to centralize civil status files at the national level, and to interconnect these files with the file of identity cards and pension insurance. The article in *Le Monde*, which considered the project too vast to allow a filing of all the French population, led to a strong condemnation from then-French President Valéry Giscard d'Estaing. President Giscard d'Estaing's reaction, echoed by other politicians, gave rise to France's 1978 law on data processing and liberties (*Informatique et Libertés*), which created the French control authority, the CNIL (*Commission Nationale Informatique et Libertés*). It is thus not surprising that recent developments in the latest generations of "learner" algorithms, as well as the examples mentioned above, are renewing concerns about so-called "predictive" technological capabilities.

Therefore, there already exists an important literature on the different applications of AI in public services. Among the most significant contributions, given their depth and quality of analysis, would be two publications by AI Watch (a European Commission service that monitors the development, adoption, and impact of AI in Europe), namely "Artificial intelligence in public services"[38] and "Road to the Adoption of Artificial Intelligence by the Public Sector"[39]; a model impact study on the use of AI in public services carried out by the European Law Institute (ELI)[40]; and the developments of the Ad Hoc Committee on Artificial Intelligence, which is a feasibility study for a Council of Europe legal instrument.[41] Finally, reference can be made to an article by Jennifer Cobbe of the University of Cambridge's Computer Science Institute in which Dr. Cobbe reviews the factors for the proper use of automated decision-making systems.[42]

Without writing here a meta-analysis of the above-mentioned documents, the next section of this chapter will highlight the main requirements that should be in place for the use of automated decision-making by public administrations to respond to the most sensitive concerns illustrated in the aforementioned instances of automated decision-making use. These requirements will be set by criteria derived from five legal mandates; such automated decision-making systems must be in accordance with existing positive law (Sect. 3.2), keep a human agent legally liable for the decision (Sect. 3.3), manage biases (Sect. 3.4), prevent solutionism (Sect. 3.5), and guarantee possibilities for appeal (Sect. 3.6).

---

[38] See Misuraca and Van Noordt (2020).

[39] See Manzoni et al. (2022).

[40] See Wierzbowski (2022).

[41] CAHAI(2021)09rev – Possible elements of a legal framework on artificial intelligence, based on the Council of Europe's standards on human rights, democracy and the Rule of law, para 32 et seq.

[42] Cobbe (2019), pp. 636–655.

3.2 Applying Existing Positive Law

Even if this first requirement seems to be somewhat obvious, the examples previously developed have shown the limits of the existing legal architecture, the District Court of The Hague having had, for example, to justify its decision by review of conventionality with reference to the European Convention on Human Rights.

It should be remembered, however, that the EU's General Data Protection Regulation (GDPR) seems to prohibit, as a principle, the use of certain types of AI or decision-making algorithms.[43] With limited exceptions listed in paragraph 2 of the GDPR's Article 22, an individual cannot be the subject of a decision based solely on automated processing (including profiling), as long as this decision produces legal effects concerning the individual or otherwise significantly affects them. But the exceptions in the provisions of Article 22 include situations where national or EU law create a legal basis for the use of such systems. In addition, individuals affected by such processing must be informed of automated decision-making, including profiling, and affected individuals must be provided with meaningful information about the logic involved in the process, as well as the significance and envisaged consequences of such processing for the data subject.

Also relying on the GDPR, these systems can be examined from the perspective of the "purpose limitation principle," to assess whether a public authority has used data solely for the purpose(s) for which the data was collected or for other compatible purposes.

However, the limitation of the GDPR to be able to adequately regulate the use of AI and algorithms in public administration lies in its very purpose: the protection of privacy and personal data. Certain algorithmic processing carried out by public authorities is likely to escape the control of the GDPR, since the training would be carried out, for example, from anonymized datasets. Furthermore, such systems are likely to be used in a broad way, on non-nominative groups of the population. It should also be mentioned that in minor cases at the individual level, appeals to data protection authorities, or courts, may not necessarily be granted, although the cumulative effect that these denials of appeal have on society may be significant.

As mentioned above, the use of AI or other algorithmic decision-making systems may also be permitted by law for reasons considered legitimate and compelling, such as the SyRI system in the Netherlands, and thus such systems may escape the rules of the GDPR. It is to respond to these problems, located in grey areas and gaps, that initiatives such as the European Commission's proposal for a regulation (AI Act), or the Council of Europe's draft legal instrument have been drawn up, without waiting for the case law of the various European courts to be consolidated on the subject.

[43] On the interpretation of Article 22, to know whether it establishes a prohibition in principle or an individual right to opt out, see Suksi (2021), p. 92.

3.3 *Keeping a Human Agent Legally Liable for the Decision: Legality of the Conditions for the Transfer of Decision-Making Power*

Another question would be to what extent the use of AI or other algorithmic systems could be equated, in a legal sense, with a delegation, total or partial, of powers.

First, for clarity, the effects of using an algorithmic system to produce a decision will be examined here without emphasizing the degree to which autonomy, or power, has been entrusted to such a system. Even when automated systems are used as a support in seemingly simple decisions, the influence of cognitive biases (such as automation biases and anchoring biases) can be much greater than their designers anticipate.[44] In addition, I will only consider systems that comply with the provisions of Article 22 of the GDPR, which makes automated individual decision-making possible in three precise cases: when a decision (a) is necessary for the conclusion or performance of a contract between the data subject and a controller; (b) is authorized by Union law or the law of the Member State to which the controller is subject and which also provides for appropriate measures to safeguard the rights and freedoms and legitimate interests of the data subject; or (c) is based on the explicit consent of the data subject.

Some authors have argued that the introduction of fully-automated decision-making systems could be problematic because the scope of effective control by the human manager is not always clear.[45] It is true that the types of procedures that may be delegated by public administrations are usually formalized by a legal act, and that the obligations and responsibilities of the delegating agent and the delegate are typically specified in the same act or in other more general regulations. Very often, the introduction of algorithms has the characteristics of a simple tool to be used in the mission of the public administration. The characteristics of such "tools" are examined from the point of view of data protection and privacy concerns, and with relative ignorance of other potential difficulties, such as the real (not theoretical) degree of delegation of powers to the machine, or the biases and discrimination embedded in the system.

Mention should be made here also of the performative effect, made exponentially more harmful when coupled with automation bias, leading a system to normalize the following situation as its lifecycle progresses. The human user, confident in the algorithm's ability to suggest a better decision than him or herself, follows the system's recommendations, which leads the algorithm to suggest always the same type of recommendation when fed with new human decisions influenced by the algorithm. This effect is known, for example, for the recommendation of contents for

---

[44] On automation bias, see Parasuraman and Riley (1997) and Hadavas (2020). On anchoring bias, see Tversky and Kahneman (1974).

[45] Garapon and Lassègue (2018).

the diffusion of films, series, or music on line: the algorithms lock us gradually in a "bubble" where they suggest only contents which we seem to appreciate.

Moreover, even when an administrative authority has a certain level of discretion in its decision-making, such systems may have to comply with other higher-level principles.[46] Thus, the discretionary nature left to the administration in certain areas does not necessarily preclude the obligation to state reasons for judicial review. Under Anglo-American law, there is also the "non-fettering" principle in the exercise, by a public authority, of decision-making power containing a certain level of discretion. The intervention of algorithmic systems could here be analyzed as intervening in a relatively inappropriate way because such systems preclude an individual assessment of each situation.

In summary, even if humans are often presented by policy makers as "in control" of these systems, the use of algorithms might not necessarily be the simplest or smartest decision-making tool for a given task. The legal liability for automated decision-making in the context of public administration therefore still rests with a human operator, whose usual duties are complemented by specific obligations to verify possible abuses of these algorithms and, more broadly, to monitor operation in accordance with the objectives of the system and the public service mission.

3.4 *Managing Bias: Non-Discrimination, Equality Before the Law, Fairness, and Impartiality of Treatment*

One of the most frequently cited risks for AI and other algorithmic decision-making systems is the risk of unjustified discrimination, or a breach of equality due to bias in data, models, or programs. As demonstrated by the three examples of algorithms studied above, such systems carry the risk of wrongful profiling (false positives in SyRI or iBorderCtrl) or misclassification (DataJust). The use of solutions based on machine learning, sometimes depending on the combination of thousands, millions, or even billions of parameters, can, using "proxy variables," lead to differentiation of assessments based on criteria prohibited by law (sex, ethnic origin, etc.). Other times, it is the use of very simple spreadsheets in Excel, or simplistic programs, that can lead to discriminatory treatment.[47]

Systems operating groupings, or categorizations of individuals, may also lead to disregarding the principles of individualization of decisions, by basing decisions upon membership in a statistical group rather than the intrinsic elements of the situation assessed by the administration.

[46] On due process, see Suksi (2021).

[47] In, for example, the work of a collective of Dutch journalists, Lighthouse Reports, which had access to very simple tools used by municipalities in the Netherlands to assess the risk of fraud, available on: https://fraudescorekaart.lighthousereports.nl/#/ - accessed on 26 June 2022 (Dutch only).

Finally, the non-deterministic nature of machine-learning algorithms evolving continuously with the addition of new data to adjust their models raises the question of the equal treatment of citizens before the law.[48]

The total elimination of bias from algorithmic systems remains a largely theoretical ideal. The creation of a training dataset that is perfectly balanced and representative of the modeled environment is certainly a desirable goal – but one that is most likely impossible to achieve. Similarly, whether it is computer programming based on explicit (symbolic) rules, or model training by (connectionist) machine learning, designers necessarily make trade-offs: the choice of parameters, interpretation of qualitative variables, and hierarchy of content are just some of the choices made, sometimes quite discretionary, by system designers.

Therefore, it is crucial that regulators and scholars analyze and identify these possible disbalances, and seek to contextualize the result produced by algorithms, rather than operating under a false pretense of neutrality. In other words, lawmakers and system designers should understand the possible biases of such systems, rather than pretending to have solved the problem with technology that may simply create new biases. A constructive consequence of such considerations would be a change in perspective on the purpose(s) of use of these algorithms, especially in cases where qualitative information may be manipulated. Rather than setting a prescriptive goal (decision-making), these systems should be limited to descriptive capabilities, serving only general research or study purposes (perhaps in addition to other informational tasks).

In this context, it would seem unwise to advocate for a future where decision-making is completely or even largely delegated to algorithmic systems, if the objective pursued by the administration is indeed non-discrimination, equality before the law, fairness, and impartiality of treatment.

Ultimately, automated decision-making leads to a de facto transfer of power between the administration – which has been established to handle a public service – and the designers of these algorithmic systems. On the one hand, the administrations do not necessarily have the necessary expertise to ensure adequate control of the designers, thus leaving the designer free to make choices that are sometimes extremely decisive for the functioning of the system. On the other hand, it is not always possible to explain the underlying logic of the decision-making process to ensure that biases are minimized. This unexplainability may be due to the nature of the algorithm itself, but also, in some cases, as with iBorderCtrl, unexplainability results from the desire of certain actors to protect intellectual property and industrial secrecy. Under these conditions, how can hierarchical and judicial control be exercised?

---

[48] The CJEU ruled out the possibility of using machine learning to process PNR data (Passenger Name Record, collected by air carriers to enable the reservation and check-in processes) since the criteria for ensuring non-discrimination are likely to change without human intervention. Judgment of 21 June 2022, *Ligue des droits humains v Conseil des Ministres*, C-817/19, EU:C:2022:491, paras 193–195.

Even in the case of decisions that leave the administration a wide margin of discretion, decisions that have a significant impact on individuals (particularly from a legal, social, or economic point of view) must be subject to an external, human control. The sole authority of mathematics or statistics to assess a situation, and deliver a decision, cannot constitute a sufficient basis for a permanent delegation of decision-making to machines. As for the mechanisms that appear to have less direct impact on individuals, the real advantage derived from their use is sometimes questionable. The algorithmic devices examined in our examples all left the most sensitive part of the processing to humans and were only used for situation filtering functions (SyRI, iBorderCtrl) or for evaluating final compensation in a court (DataJust). The deployment of automated algorithmic systems to support decision-making cannot be motivated only by the economic gain obtained from the reduction of human operators, with an approximate consideration of the consequences of its implementation. Consideration of the impact on fundamental rights must be demonstrated by an evidence-based approach, as the AI Act seems to encourage high-risk systems. The very choice to use an algorithmic system should not be a solution to a lack of adequate funding for public services. The improvement of the organization of a public service, based on well-trained humans, can also allow for simpler and equally robust solutions, such as frequent random checks at borders or among beneficiaries of social funding, or, on the predictability of the law, regular reviews of case law and adequate continuous training of judges.

3.5 *Preventing Solutionism: Proportionality in the Use of AI and Algorithmic Decision-Making Systems*

The above developments, that demonstrate the risks of a technological solutionism, show that the principle of data minimization, well known today in data protection legislation, especially in cross-referencing possibilities, could well be transferred to algorithms.[49] If the trend today is to extend the use of algorithmic systems to various forms of decision-making, the interest and risks would be systematically measured in terms of the advantages and disadvantages compared to a human intervention. In addition, the use of an algorithm would not always be the best economic choice when considering direct and indirect costs of development, maintenance in operational conditions, or the environmental impacts, with the sometimes sizable carbon footprint of training a model and storing data.

As we have seen during the COVID-19 pandemic, especially with contact tracing applications whose effectiveness has been widely debated, the risk of solutionism is worsening. Some public decision-makers seem to consider that the *new public management* policies of administrations must be systematically accompanied by

[49] Meneceur (2020a), p. 387.

an IT component and algorithmic processing, even if it means transforming the problems to be solved into problems that can be treated by an algorithm.

By an objective search for the right balance, sometimes the use of AI or an algorithm is a disproportionate investment in relation to the needs of the circumstance.[50] According to the specificities of a given situation, it could be more effective to have recourse directly to a human assessment (with adequate procedural safeguards) rather than to spend time (and money) to calibrate an algorithm properly to mitigate various risks (such as discrimination).

3.6 Guaranteeing the Possibility of Appeal: Making Decisions Explainable, Ensuring the Adversarial Principle, Allowing Assistance to Users, and Opening Up Judicial Channels for Challenge

Paragraph 3 of Article 22 of the GDPR creates a right of the data subject to "obtain human intervention from the controller, to express his or her point of view and to contest the decision" in two of the three conditions already mentioned: if this algorithmic processing is made necessary for the performance of a contract or if it is based on the consent of the data subject. The same text introduces in its Article 13.2.f a right to information when automated decision-making is implemented, requiring "meaningful information about the logic involved, as well as the significance and the envisaged consequences of such processing for the data subject," but only in certain cases under Article 22.

While these provisions already address several concerns to ensure administrative or judicial remedies and an explanation of the methodology used by an AI or algorithm, these provisions do not cover all risk situations today. An administration, whether it has a simple Excel spreadsheet or a complex algorithmic model, can potentially rely on applications that escape the information obligation of the GDPR or judicial control of its activity. (For example, an administration may skirt GDPR obligations if their processing activity is authorized by law and the legal system does not provide for a possibility for judges to exercise a review of conventionality).

In a context of increased use of algorithms by public administrations, particularly the forms of AI whose models are relatively opaque and unexplainable, it might seem appropriate to be able to extend users' right to information more widely, to inform them of the existence of the intervention of an algorithm in the decision-making chain, to explain decisions, to ensure the assistance of a third party, and to rebalance the asymmetry between an administration, a specialist in their field, and individuals with no particular experience of a proceeding. Non-contentious and contentious appeals should also be opened so that the concerned party may be able

[50] For different proportionality considerations, see also the chapter by Lena Enqvist and Markus Naarttijärvi in this volume.

to obtain a review of the assessment of a decision taken, in whole or in part, based on algorithmic processing.

Less than total transparency, relatively theoretical (even with the publication of computer code when possible), it therefore seems to be necessary to guarantee good explainability, and possibly to exclude the use of certain types of AI (such as unsupervised learning) in situations where a precise motivation is necessary.

The right to be heard is also a concrete procedural translation of the adversarial principle, which can intervene both in the algorithmic decision-making phase and *a posteriori*, so that a user of a public service is able to provide the necessary explanations and justifications to the administration before an unfavorable decision is definitively taken against the user. This right is of course not absolute. For example, during an investigation phase, this right might be waived to preserve the integrity of evidence. However, this right should be granted to the user at every appropriate instance.

4 The Inadequacy of Artificial Intelligence Ethics and Public Policies to Prevent Damage Resulting from the Use of Artificial Intelligence

4.1 Background

The development of the use of AI and various forms of algorithms in public administration therefore already finds a legal framework in the texts relating to data protection and privacy at European or national level. However, these texts did not appear to sufficiently caution against the possible abuses of AI, particularly in the absence of processed personal data. In the late 2010s, the scientific, technical, and legal community turned to ethics to empower the designers of these systems with a significant body of principles, charters, and declarations.[51] As an example, in the field of public services, the Charter of the CEPEJ (European Commission for the Efficiency of Justice, under the Council of Europe) became the first European Ethical Charter on the use of AI in the judicial field.[52] The Charter, adopted in 2018 by representatives of the Ministries of Justice of 47 Member States of the Council of Europe,[53] is composed of five cardinal principles, meant to guide system designers to prevent human rights violations.[54]

[51]See Meneceur (2020b) to access a list of more than 500 texts including a ranking of ethical principles.

[52]CEPEJ (2018).

[53]Since 16 March 2022, the Council of Europe has 46 Member States, after the expulsion of the Federation of Russia.

[54]Principle of respect for fundamental rights, principle of non-discrimination, principle of quality and security, principle of transparency, neutrality and fairness, principle of user control.

However, these legally non-binding texts are not sufficient to meaningfully compel both public administrations and private solution providers to limit the functionalities of AI and algorithms when too many risks emerge. The CEPEJ Charter, for example, does not contain any binding provisions and sanctions as such, and only serves to make its readers aware of the particular issues at stake in the use of AI. Unscrupulous developers could perfectly well use the Charter to obtain a label of compatibility with human rights, without necessarily incurring great legal risks (even from the point of view of unfair commercial practices). Generally, the multiplication of declarative texts, with ambiguous and not always operational principles, added to public policies focused on economic growth, have led to the construction of an establishment consensus around AI, as an inevitable and necessary development for our society.

We will therefore see how the ethics of AI are insufficient (Sect. 4.2) in a context of very proactive national policies for the development of this technology (Sect. 4.3).

4.2 The Construction of Artificial Intelligence Ethics and Their Inadequacies

Sensitive to public concern and mistrust in the face of new "learning" algorithms, digital companies, but also parts of academic, technical, and think tank communities, have been committed, since the mid-2010s, to the drafting of non-legally-binding declaratory texts, inspired by moral philosophy or bioethics. Biomedicine was confronted early on with a whole series of moral dilemmas in the face of the development of complex technologies, allowing, for example, the manipulation of the genome, for which bioethics has provided satisfactory answers to the whole society. A wide variety of documents will undoubtedly emerge from this wave of AI ethics discourse, with a common intention: to propose readable frameworks of action for developers of various AI-solutions, based on high-level principles such as transparency, fairness, accountability, and robustness.

While there are many reasons for this increase in texts and discussions about the ethics of AI, Rodrigo Ochigame, a former researcher at the MIT Media Lab, identified one of the key drivers of this dynamic: the need of big technology companies to give credibility to self-regulation to postpone binding regulation.[55] At the same time, Brent Mittelstadt, a researcher at the Oxford Internet Institute, listed the reasons why the ethical principles of AI could not constitute serious foundations for effective regulation, especially because the digital sector does not have the same vocation as the health sector.[56] More generally, meta-analyses such as that of the Swiss Federal Institute of Technology in Zurich have rigorously

[55] See Ochigame (2019).

[56] See Mittelstadt (2019).

documented the polysemy of most of the principles and the difficulties, accordingly, in making these principles operational.[57]

The ethics of AI, while remaining present in public debates, and in the titles of university chairs or institutes, nevertheless have appeared to be gradually losing ground, since 2019, as the core feature of good governance with the use of AI. Instead, other well-known methods of governance of services and the industrial sector, namely compliance and certification, have emerged as the most prominent ideals in AI discourse.

4.3 Proactive National Public Policies for the Development of Artificial Intelligence

It is also from the mid-2010s that many governments (and the EU) have come to support the acceleration of AI development policies, with extremely proactive discourses aimed at the market and a rather small use of critical analyses. In France, both the law for a digital Republic (*Loi pour une République numérique*[58]), and the report prepared by MP Cédric Villani,[59] "promote innovation and the development of the digital economy" and "position France at the forefront of AI" with "agile and diffusing research." Most European states, and even beyond,[60] have adopted (or will likely adopt) strategies for the development of AI with substantial public financial support to remain in the race of global competition in this area. The French Minister of the Economy, Bruno Lemaire, announced in 2018 and 2019 funding of nearly € 1.5 billion with four objectives: to develop the ecosystem of startups specializing in AI solutions; to infuse AI in all sectors, including SMEs with the support of large groups; to attract foreign investment in France; and to build an ethical and transparent "French AI."[61]

Only reports from independent administrative authorities, such as those of the CNIL in 2017[62] or the Defender of Rights[63] (with the CNIL) in 2020, have instructed the development of AI with a less unequivocal narrative, centered on the protection of the rights of individuals. The opinion of the National Consultative Commission on Human Rights (CNCDH, *Commission Nationale Consultative des Droits de*

57 See Jobin et al. (2019), pp. 389–399.

58 On the context of the writing and adoption of this law, see Bellon (2021), pp. 27–53.

59 See Villani (2018).

60 See OECD AI Policy Observatory: https://www.oecd.ai/dashboards and the OECD State of Implementation of AI Principles (2021): https://www.oecd.org/fr/numerique/state-of-implementation-of-the-oecd-ai-principles-1cd40c44-en.htm or the Council of Europe website: https://www.coe.int/fr/web/artificial-intelligence/national-initiatives.

61 See Rolland (2019).

62 See CNIL (2017).

63 See Défenseur des droits and CNIL (2020).

l'Homme) of April 2022 should also be added, which considers the current legal framework for the development of AI to be deficient.[64] In Germany, the opinion of the Data Ethics Commission also stands out with a proposal for a risk-based framework, which inspires the European legislator since 2021 in the proposal for an AI Act.[65]

A clear tension therefore appears between different sets of imperatives for public decision-makers in the application of AI, particularly for decision-making (or decision-making support) in the public sector. On the one hand, digital technologies are undoubtedly one of the most dynamic levers of support for economic growth, in a sluggish context that has been experiencing a succession of crises (health, security, economic, etc.). Competition between continents to master the most advanced forms of AI, and thus gain a decisive technological advantage in strategic sectors such as military, industrial, or commercial fields, also encourages states to move as quickly as possible to innovate. In this seemingly Hobbesian context of a "war of all against all," a struggle which does not use its true description, the various systems of protection of individuals are no longer perceived as bulwarks against tyranny, but as hindrances, relics of another geopolitical context.

On the other hand, the very concrete damages resulting from the hasty and poorly controlled use of algorithms of all kinds are becoming increasingly better documented, or even sanctioned. As the CNCDH highlights in France, national legislation does not always appear to be appropriate, because of poorly informed debates, or because priority is given to innovation. Whether the issue is, as we have seen, the fight against fraud (SyRI) or arbitration between insurers and policyholders (e-Courts) in the Netherlands,[66] the grading of pupils in Great Britain,[67] or the tenure eligibility in Italy that will depend on automated topic modeling of the candidate's publications,[68] it is clear that these are not one-off problems of poor design that raise questions, but questions of principles relating to the new primacy of opaque computational systems over the law.

[64] See CNCDH (2022).

[65] See Daten Ethik Kommission (2019).

[66] See Pavillon (2018), pp. 51–55.

[67] See Shead (2020).

[68] See ROARS (2022).

5 Using Artificial Intelligence for Decision-Making in Public Administrations: From Rule of Law to a "Rule of Algorithms"

5.1 Background

The initiatives of regulators to develop legally binding texts, such as those of the Council of Europe in conjunction with the CAI (Committee on Artificial Intelligence), or the European Commission with its proposal for AI regulation which it presented on 21 April 2021, are therefore to be welcomed to reconcile innovation and damage prevention, in addition to texts relating to data protection and privacy.

However, the movement to transform society by digital means is not just a sum of sectoral transitions. In extension of Michel Foucault's concept of governmentality, the new regime being put in place is already well-documented, suggesting a whole series of difficulties specific to the use of AI for decision-making (or decision-making assistance) in public administration.[69] To sum-up that shift, we could consider that the increasing pre-eminence of calculation over law (Sect. 5.2) leads us to a new regime: a "rule of algorithms" (Sect. 5.3).

5.2 The Pre-Eminence of Calculation Over Law: A Permanent "Coup Data"

The action of an individual in our new digital age is no longer judged only in a contextualization of a pre-existing external norm, like the law. The action is now confronted, directly or indirectly, with the fields of possibility organized by the new digital environment.

This "algorithmic governmentality" structures the choices and behaviors of citizens often without their awareness. Whereas the law produces subjects of law, each one equal before the law according to a previously accepted procedure, each one able to challenge the application of the law before appeal authorities, the "algorithmic government" conversely is never able to be legitimized, explained, or challenged. Moreover, it does not impose itself on us by an organized conquest of power using sudden and brutal force, like a *coup d'Etat*. For Adrien Basdevant and Jean-Pierre Mignard, "we are experiencing a 'coup data', this reversal of the power of data choosing in real time the best configuration to deploy its program."[70]

[69] See Rouvroy and Berns (2013), pp. 163–196 or Batko and Kreft (2017), pp. 190–209 or Crawford (2015), pp. 77–92.

[70] See Basdevant and Mignard (2018), p. 59. Translation by the author.

This "coup data" would even seek to become *permanent*,[71] because it reinvents in real time the conditions of its domination without submitting itself, at any time, to any democratic debate. Not only does this "coup data" slowly colonize, with its own normativity, the gaps left available by all other forms of regulation of human behaviors, but this order also imposes itself as a filter from most other forms of regulation that it has not yet overturned and influenced. This is evidenced by the so-called "predictive" applications of justice, or the online dispute resolution methods of *legaltech* which, far from playing only an intermediation role, sometimes manage to impose their interpretation of the dispute by proposing ranges of compensation, without it being possible to really understand the exact legal foundations of their proposals.

In short, the "coup data" would attack the political head on, slowly leading us towards a mode of government based on a statistical expression of reality, without being interested in causes, intentions, or individuals.

Such a movement reveals the emergence of a reason and knowledge that would no longer imply the expression of any prior hypothesis based on a mixture of philosophical, societal, economic, and environmental vision of human matters. The very question of building a social project, based on collective deliberation, resulting from discussion and contradiction, has the potential to be simply made obsolete in favor of the sole achievement of objectives that are displaced and distributed in practice to the rhythm of the logical metronomes of the processors of computers.

This finding, about a profound change in governmentality, is reinforced by the weakness of representative democracies, which are in crisis in almost all Western countries. Enhancing a new way of governance, based on means (such as algorithms) that are *a priori* more rational and neutral, less corruptible, and less sensitive to human passions could represent an ideal for some politicians.

But this idea of rationality and neutrality is quite fallacious since the technique profoundly modifies our relationship with the world and even (re)shapes it.[72] To think that the whole society can keep control of power stems from a great naivety and a deep misunderstanding of the place of technology in our civilization. The socio-technical environment influences the evolution of society, of the relationships between individuals and of possible forms of governance. To limit the analysis of AI to a simple balance of benefits and risks is therefore to leave the field open to a certain form of authoritarianism: questioning the legitimacy of authority in such an algorithmic regime that has managed to prevent risks will certainly become incongruous in the name of the realism imposed by the quantity and apparent robustness of various programming mechanisms.

---

[71] In French, the term "coup d'Etat permanent" comes from the title of an essay by the politician and former French President François Mitterrand, who at the time criticized General de Gaulle's mode of exercising power. He considered that the latter had betrayed the letter of the Constitution of the Fifth Republic by concentrating too much decision-making power in his practice of the functions of President of the Republic.

[72] On the affordance of technology, see Gaver (1991), pp. 79–84.

Such a shift in governance induces a complete redefinition of public space. There, AI is entitled to protect us from any uncertainty and to avoid any form of crisis, conflict, or failure.

5.3 *The Pervasiveness of Computation in Society: The Emergence of a "Rule of Algorithms"*

But if the evolution of society no longer proceeds from a democratic debate to establish norms, even after harsh contradictory debates and potential ruptures, we will be condemned to ignore what is hidden behind appearances and to repeat harms by transferring to the algorithms the task to find a balance between conflicting interests. In other words, to respond to the crisis that representative democracy is undergoing, we are now inclined to resign ourselves, to admit as real that which is presented in the indisputable form of algorithmic truth and to simply accept the disappearance of the agora.

And it is exactly in that sense that the "coup data" would eliminate any form of politics: while the defining characteristic of politics is precisely the antagonism of points of view, and decision-making in uncertainty, governmentality by algorithms pre-empts the environment in which such a regime operates. This mode of rule thus organizes behaviors by reducing the margins of uncertainty, even making transgression impossible, since this possibility would no longer be left to the user.

This is an essential distinction between the two governmental regimes under consideration: while the rule of law sets, according to democratic deliberative modalities, preliminary rules to regulate present behavior and sanction past illicit behavior through legitimate authorities, "algorithmic government" or what we will call "rule of algorithms" aims, through a statistic representation of past behavior, to limit the possibilities of future behavior within the interpretative framework desired by its designers.

This evolution would naturally tend to gradually render the law obsolete, since in this new environment the fact becomes the norm by its sole statistical and algorithmic interpretation. But Basdevant and Mignard recall that "the difference between fact and law is precisely that between being and ought-to-be."[73]

In other words, by applying the law and interpreting it in the light of the facts of the case, the jurist constantly seeks to reconcile interests that are most often contradictory in a legal framework that has resulted from a societal consensus as to the principles to be respected, the values to be protected, and the objectives to be achieved. By sticking to a purely algorithmic mechanism for regulating human matters, the representativeness of reality is delegated to the sole interpretation of what has been, while potentially losing sight of the reasons why the facts occurred (as well as their context). This "rule of algorithms" cares very little about causality

[73] Basdevant and Mignard (2018), p. 74.

because such a system claims to apprehend the facts and bring out constants and laws, laws of nature, immanent and permanent, as revealed by the massive processing of data. The originality of the law is that it allows the possibility to deviate from itself: a sanction is, of course, incurred, but the sanction is not certain. For reasons which the law itself permits, justifications may be invoked and, from the original point of view of new facts of the case, the judge may decide to consider or exclude such facts.[74]

The originality of the algorithmic environment is that there will potentially be no more deviant behaviors since they are no longer even available in the field of possibilities . . . but at what cost?

In its foundations, a "rule of algorithms" thus simply makes any form of disobedience impossible and, by a performative effect, will even make it *inconceivable*. There is indeed a clear difference between the forbidden and the unthinkable: whereas a barrier or a sanction seeks to dissuade us from a behavior (a fine for speeding in your car), the *inconceivable*, by its very nature, is no longer represented in our fields of possibility and our mindsets (the car is restricted and will only be able to reach the authorized speeds). Like the *Newspeak* of Oceania in George Orwell's *1984*, how does one conceive of what is no longer named? In other words, with this new form of governance, the best way to prevent deviant behavior is no longer with the fear of punishment, but by creating conditions that leave individuals only with the ability to slip between *probable* states that correspond to what the designers of AI consider desirable. A new form of totalitarianism with the smiling mask of libertarian free will.

References

Aletras N, Tsarapatsanis D, Preoţiuc-Pietro D, Lampos V (2016) Predicting judicial decisions of the European Court of Human Rights: a natural language processing perspective. PeerJ Comput Sci 2:e93. https://doi.org/10.7717/peerj-cs.93

Anders G (2002 [1956]) L'Obsolescence de l'homme: Sur l'âme à l'époque de la deuxième révolution industrielle, L'Encyclopédie des Nuisances, Paris

Angwin J, Larson J, Mattu S, Kirchner L (2016) Machine bias: there's software used across the country to predict future criminals. And it's biased against blacks. ProPublica

Basdevant A, Mignard JP (2018) L'empire des données: Essai sur la société, les algorithms et la loi. Don Quichotte, Paris

Batko R, Kreft J (2017) The sixth estate: the rule of algorithms. Problemy Zarzadzania, University of Warsaw, Faculty of Management 15(68):190–209

Bellon VA (2021) L'elaboration de la loi République numérique au gouvernement. Réseaux 2021/1, 225:23–53

[74] We can recall that, in French law and in other legal systems, there are cases where, although one has caused damage or violated the law, one can be exempted from liability as for example in case of *force majeure* or due to the action of a third party (or of the victim). This is a discretionary power of judges that cannot be easily translated in a mathematical model or function, as contextualization of the situation would require a good representation of the world (not just the law).

Bourreau-Dubois C (2019) La barémisation de la justice: une approche par l'analyse économique du droit. Mission de recherche Droit et justice
Calude CS, Longo G (2015) The deluge of spurious correlations in big data. HAL, Nantes. https://hal.archives-ouvertes.fr/hal-01380626/document
Cobbe J (2019) Administrative law and the machines of government: judicial review of automated public-sector decision-making. Legal Stud 39(4) https://papers.ssrn.com/sol3/papers.cfm?abstract_id=3226913
Commission Nationale Consultative des Droits de l'Homme (CNCDH) (2022) Opinion on the impact of artificial intelligence on fundamental rights. https://www.cncdh.fr/sites/default/files/2022-05/A%20-%202022%20-%206%20%20-%20EN%20%20Artificial%20intelligence%20and%20fundamental%20rights%2C%20april%202022.pdf
Commission Nationale Informatique et Libertés (CNIL) (2017) How can humans keep the upper hand? Report on the ethical matters raised by algorithms and artificial intelligence. https://www.cnil.fr/en/how-can-humans-keep-upper-hand-report-ethical-matters-raised-algorithms-and-artificial-intelligence
Council of Europe, CAHAI(2021)09rev – Possible elements of a legal framework on artificial intelligence, based on the Council of Europe's standards on human rights, democracy and the rule of law. https://rm.coe.int/cahai-2021-09rev-elements/1680a6d90d
Crawford K (2015) Can an algorithm be agonistic? Ten scenes from life in calculated publics. Sci Technol Human Values 41(1):77–92. https://doi.org/10.1177/0162243915589635
Crépel M, Cardon D (2022) Robots vs. algorithms. Réseaux 40(232–233):129–167
Daten Ethik Kommission (2019) Opinion of the Data Ethics Commission. https://www.bmjv.de/SharedDocs/Downloads/DE/Themen/Fokusthemen/Gutachten_DEK_EN.pdf?__blob=publicationFile&v=1
David M, Sauviat C (2019) Intelligence artificielle: la nouvelle barbarie. Ed. du Rocher, Monaco
Défenseur des droits and CNIL (2020) Algorithms: preventing automated discrimination. https://www.defenseurdesdroits.fr/sites/default/files/atoms/files/836200280_ddd_synthalgos_access.pdf
Dutch Council of State [Raad van State] (2014) Advies Raad van State inzake het ontwerpbesluit houdende regels voor fraudeaanpak door gegevensuitwisselingen en het effectief gebruik van binnen de overheid bekend zijnde gegevens (Besluit SyRI). Staatscourant 2014:26306. https://zoek.officielebekendmakingen.nl/stcrt-2014-26306.html
Dutch Data Protection Authority [College Bescherming Persoonsgegevens] (2014) Advies conceptbesluit SyRI. z2013-00969. https://autoriteitpersoonsgegevens.nl/sites/default/files/atoms/files/z2013-00969.pdf
European Commission for the Efficiency of Justice (CEPEJ) (2018) European ethical Charter on the use of Artificial Intelligence in judicial systems and their environment. Council of Europe
Feldman Barrett L (2022) Facial expressions do not reveal emotions. Scientific American. https://www.scientificamerican.com/article/darwin-was-wrong-your-facial-expressions-do-not-reveal-your-emotions/
French Ministry of Justice [Ministère de la justice] (2022) Rapport du cycle d'ateliers sur l'éthique de la réutilisation des décisions de justice. http://www.justice.gouv.fr/art_pix/Rapport_decisions_justice.pdf
Gallagher R, Jonah L (2019) We tested Europe's new lie detector for travelers – and immediately triggered a false positive. The Intercept, 26 July 2019
Ganascia JG (2022) Servitudes virtuelles. Seuil, Paris
Garapon A, Lassègue J (2018) Justice digitale. Presses Universitaires de France, Paris
Gaver WG (1991) Technology affordances. Proceedings of CHI'91, ACM, New York
Glastra van Loon JFG (1958) Rules and commands. Mind LXVII, no. 268
Hadavas C (2020) How automation bias encourages the use of flawed algorithms. Slate, 6 March 2020
Hart H (1976) Le concept de droit. Saint-Louis University Departments, Brussels

Hildebrandt M (2017) Law as computation in the era of artificial legal intelligence. Speaking law to the power of statistics. SSRN. https://doi.org/10.2139/ssrn.2983045

Holmes OW (1997) The path of the law. Harv Law Rev 110:1039

Jobin A, Ienca M, Vayena E (2019) The global landscape of AI ethics guidelines. Nat Mach Intell 1: 389–399

Johnston C (2016) Artificial intelligence 'judge' developed by UCL computer scientists. The Guardian, 24 October 2016

Loevinger L (1949) Jurimetrics — the next step forward. Minn Law Rev 33:455

Manzoni M, Medaglia E, Tangi L, van Noordt C, Vaccari L, Gattwinkel D (2022) AI Watch. Road to the adoption of Artificial Intelligence by the public sector. Publications Office of the European Union. https://doi.org/10.2760/288757, JRC129100

Marzolf E (2022a) Exclusif: le ministère de la Justice renonce à son algorithme DataJust, Acteurs Publics. https://acteurspublics.fr/articles/exclusif-le-ministere-de-la-justice-renonce-a-son-algorithme-datajust

Marzolf E (2022b) Après l'ouverture des décisions de justice, la régulation fait débat. Acteurs Publics. https://acteurspublics.fr/articles/apres-louverture-des-decisions-de-justice-la-regulation-fait-debat

Meneceur Y (2020a) L'intelligence artificielle en procès: plaidoyer pour une réglementation internationale et européenne. Bruylant, Bruxelles

Meneceur Y (2020b) Inventory of ai, algorithms, big data, data science ethical and political frameworks (online database). Blog Les Temps Electriques. https://lestempselectriques.net/index.php/2020/05/06/ia-algorithmes-big-data-data-science-inventaire-des-cadres-ethiques-et-politiques/

Misuraca G, van Noordt C (2020) AI watch: artificial intelligence in public services. Publications Office of the European Union. https://doi.org/10.2760/039619, JRC120399

Mittelstadt B (2019) Principles alone cannot guarantee ethical AI. Nat Mach Intell 1:501–507. https://doi.org/10.2139/ssrn.3391293

Ochigame R (2019) The invention of 'ethical AI'. The Intercept. https://theintercept.com/2019/12/20/mit-ethical-ai-artificial-intelligence/

Parasuraman R, Riley V (1997) Humans and automation: use, misuse, disuse, abuse. Human Factors 39(2):230–253. https://doi.org/10.1518/001872097778543886

Pavillon C (2018) Justice alternative et numérique: des expériences mitigées aux Pays-Bas. La Semaine Juridique édition générale, supplément au 51:51–55

ROARS (2022) Riforma ASN: basta commissari umani, a giudicare sarà l'Intelligenza Artificiale. https://www.roars.it/online/riforma-asn-basta-commissari-umani-a-giudicare-sara-lintelligenza-artificiale/

Roberge J, Dandurand G, Morin K, Senneville M (2022) Do narwhals and unicorns hide to die? Réseaux 40(232–233):169–196

Rolland S (2019) Intelligence artificielle: Bruno Le Maire précise la stratégie française. La Tribune, 4 July 2019

Rouvroy A, Berns T (2013) Gouvernementalité algorithmique et perspectives d'émancipation. Réseaux 2013/1 177:163–196

Sadin E (2018) L'intelligence artificielle ou l'enjeu du siècle: anatomie d'un antihumanisme radical. Éditions L'échappée, Paris

Scott Brennen J (2018) An industry-led debate: how UK media cover artificial intelligence. University of Oxford, Reuters Institute for Study of Journalism

Shead S (2020) How a computer algorithm caused a grading crisis in British schools. CNBC, 21 August 2020

Stolton S (2020) MEP: Public has a 'right to know' about Commission's lie detector tech. EURACTIV. https://www.euractiv.com/section/digital/news/mep-public-has-a-right-to-know-about-commissions-lie-detector-tech/

Suksi M (2021) Administrative due process when using automated decision-making in public administration: some notes from a Finnish perspective. Artif Intell Law 29:87–110

Supiot A (2015) La gouvernance par les nombres. Cours au Collège de France (2012–2014). Fayard, coll. Poids et mesures du monde, Paris

Tversky A, Kahneman D (1974) Judgement under uncertainty: heuristics and biases. Science 185: 1124–1131

van Bekkum M, Borgesius FZ (2021) Digital welfare fraud detection and the Dutch SyRI judgement. Eur J Soc Secur 23(4):323–340

van Veen C (2020) Landmark judgment from the Netherlands on digital welfare states and human rights. OpenGlobalRights. https://www.openglobalrights.org/landmark-judgment-from-netherlands-on-digital-welfare-states/

Villani C (2018) For a meaningful artificial intelligence: towards a French and European strategy, Report to the Prime Minister. https://www.aiforhumanity.fr/pdfs/MissionVillani_Report_ENG-VF.pdf

Wierzbowski M dir (2022) Model rules on impact assessment of algorithmic decision-making systems used by public administration. European Law Institute (ELI), Vienna. https://www.europeanlawinstitute.eu/fileadmin/user_upload/p_eli/Publications/ELI_Model_Rules_on_Impact_Assessment_of_ADMSs_Used_by_Public_Administration.pdf

Discretion, Automation, and Proportionality

Lena Enqvist and Markus Naarttijärvi

Abstract This contribution examines the relationship between automation, discretion, and proportionality. It argues that automation efforts in public administration need to be further discussed and analyzed in relation to requirements of proportionality flowing from both national and European law, as the principle carries important implications for both the implementation of automated systems and the responsibilities of decision-makers within those systems. The different facets of proportionality flowing from, inter alia, constitutional, and human rights law, administrative law, and data protection law are explored, with four distinct stages of proportionality analysis identified: legislative, system, decision, and ex post proportionality. These stages all carry different implications for discretion and the prospects of automation. Through the requirements in these different stages, the authors conclude that proportionality ought to act as another driver of keeping human oversight of automated systems. This human oversight will however, in relation to proportionality, require further contextual awareness and control of correct output proportionality, a role which may be significantly more demanding than a more limited oversight implied by current legal discussions on "humans in the loop".

Keywords Proportionality · Automation · Discretion · Decision-making

1 Introduction

Throughout the rise of the modern welfare state, into the present, information and communications technology (ICT) has played an increasingly important role in public administration.[1] This development formed the impetus for early data

[1] See Henman (2010), p. 44; Bovens and Zouridis (2002), pp. 180–181.

L. Enqvist (✉) · M. Naarttijärvi
Department of Law, Umeå University, Umeå, Sweden
e-mail: lena.enqvist@umu.se; markus.naarttijarvi@umu.se

M. Suksi (ed.), *The Rule of Law and Automated Decision-Making*,
https://doi.org/10.1007/978-3-031-30142-1_7

protection rules in Europe,[2] but also shaped theoretical developments relating to privacy and public administration.[3] While early legal discussions on the use of ICT in public administration grappled with the associated privacy issues, discussions in public administration research have tended to focus more on discretion. The significant contribution into the research of administrative discretion by Michael Lipsky, coining the term *street level bureaucrats*, highlighted the role that discretion has played for human agents working within administrative authorities—and how such human agents have used discretion to balance conflicting expectations.[4]

Later developments in this strain of research have emphasized how, within bureaucracies, ICT has contributed to a shift from the street level to screen level, and later to the system level.[5] In public administration research, human discretion has been tied to issues such as bias, difficulties in reaching policy goals, or inconsistencies in applying the law.[6] Automation efforts have thus led to reductions of human discretion, a result that has been brought about consciously at times, and incidentally at others. This, in turn, raises questions about the aspects of legal judgment that might necessitate more sensitive and contextual analyses, such as proportionality in the exercise of public powers.

Well-documented in public administration research, the downsides of human discretion are on some level inevitable. People are after all humans,[7] and human discretion does carry the risk of slowing down decision-making, or injecting bias or inconsistencies in the application of the law. At the same time however, this strand of research has also acknowledged that human discretion, as exercised by street level bureaucrats, may also serve as a form of safeguard, allowing an official the chance to correct unreasonableness, or to revise a decision for the sake of fairness in light of individual circumstances.[8] As such, human discretion can add a touch of humanity to the application of law. It thus makes sense that reducing human discretion through ICT and automation risks making the resulting administration "less human"—for better or worse.

---

[2] For example, the Swedish Data Act of 1973, which served to protect citizens' privacy in relation to the increased depth and scope of data in public registers, see Offentlighets- och sekretesslagstiftningskommittén, Data och Integritet, SOU 1972:47, 1972, pp. 42–43.

[3] Strömholm (1967).

[4] Lipsky (2010).

[5] Bovens and Zouridis (2002); Zouridis et al. (2020).

[6] Ranerup and Henriksen (2020); Busch and Henriksen (2018).

[7] As William Bruce Cameron once described it in relation to sociological research focusing on quantitative data: "It would be nice if all of the data which sociologists require could be enumerated because then we could run them through IBM machines and draw charts as the economists do. However, not everything that can be counted counts, and not everything that counts can be counted. [. . .] people are human and there is not much that can be done about it. If this disturbs you, perhaps you should quit sociology and take up white rats, viruses, or electrons." Cameron (1963), p. 29.

[8] See Goldstein (1959); Goldstein (1963).

While successful automation efforts may indeed be efficient, and render the ability to consistently apply legal rules to individual cases (even at scale), researchers—informed by perspectives both within and outside the field of law—have raised numerous questions and concerns about the implications of automation. Examples of such concerns include whether automated decision-making can reach fairness and trustworthiness,[9] whether it can conform to ethical norms,[10] whether it can achieve transparency,[11] not to mention the question of whether automated decision-making has the ability to avoid inherent risks of algorithmic bias.[12] Recent EU developments,[13] as well as existing data protection rules,[14] have attempted to manage such issues through emphasizing the need for human oversight in automated systems. However, the principle of *proportionality* in automated efforts, and the role of "humans in the loop" for such automated decision-making, has been somewhat under-researched. Therefore, drawing from the European legal landscape, our aim is to show that proportionality is a key concern inherently tied to automation and human discretion in public administration, which also raises the question of to what extent human discretion needs to exist in decision-making systems for such systems to maintain the principle of proportionality.

As a point of departure for our analysis, we argue that proportionality as a principle in human rights law, EU law, constitutional law, data protection law, and administrative law places certain limits on government ambitions to automate decision-making and/or reduce human discretion. Both proportionality and discretion carry important connections to the rule of law, in that the rule of law as a concept is intended to limit the extent of discretion to avoid arbitrariness in the exercise of public power. Proportionality fulfills a key function in this pursuit for non-arbitrariness, in relation to the limitations of rights. It does this by requiring that such limitations fulfil legitimate aims and are necessary and proportional to the aims pursued. From a rule of law perspective, the proportionality principle helps ensure both that individual rights are respected—an important part of current definitions of the rule of law in a more substantive sense—and that arbitrariness in the rights-limiting context of public law is avoided. In effect, proportionality can thus safeguard against the abuse of discretion in the rights-limiting context.

However, proportionality, as we will show, carries multidirectional implications for discretion. It may, for example, increase the discretionary space for decision-makers in relation to legal *rules* through the requirement to set aside disproportional rules in individual cases. Proportionality may also in effect *require* a certain measure

[9]Zarsky (2016).

[10]Koulu (2020b).

[11]Merrer and Tredan (2019); Bayamlioğlu et al. (2018).

[12]Barocas and Selbst (2016).

[13]European Commission (2021) Proposal for a Regulation of the European Parliament and of the Council laying down harmonised rules on artificial intelligence (Artificial Intelligence Act) and amending certain union legislative acts.

[14]Bygrave (2020).

of human discretion, while simultaneously placing limits on the possible *output* of this discretion. Proportionality, as a principle, does not allow discretion to result in disproportional decisions. In this sense, proportionality may serve "as a yardstick for ascertaining and controlling whether the result of discretion, be it actions or omissions, is lawful or not."[15] This chapter will highlight the intricate balance between the rule of law, discretion, and proportionality.

2 The Many Faces of Proportionality

To explore how proportionality can impact automated decision-making in public administration, we first need to acknowledge that proportionality is a deeper level principle of (European public) law, and that proportionality has slightly different surface-level applications depending on where this principle is applied.[16] Proportionality as an umbrella term therefore includes a set of different proportionality principles sharing a common core—where the more specific proportionality principles possess slightly different properties in, inter alia, human rights law, EU law, constitutional law, data protection law, and administrative law. As we will see, this multiplicity of related definitions arises not only due to differing and specific legal contexts, but also due to differences in what is supposed to be proportional, and differences in who is responsible for ensuring such proportionality.[17]

Adding nuance to our claims above, we should point out that the "Europeanization" of European Union (EU) Member States' national public law suggests that the individual components and interpretation of proportionality may be converging, and that the different steps of the proportionality test are now more standardized across human rights law, the EU law, constitutional law, and administrative law.[18] The increasingly standardized components of proportionality are by now well-known and well-trodden in legal research, so we need only summarize them briefly: Once a government action has a legal basis, the proportionality test (again, as an umbrella-concept) essentially implies a first question of whether this measure—an action, decision, law, or other interference—has a legitimate aim.[19] The next step is to check if the measure is suitable and necessary to reach this aim. And finally, in the last step, the question is whether the measure is proportional,

[15] Yutaka Arai-Takahashi (1999), p. 12, referencing Ress (1985).

[16] The attribution of proportionality to this level structure is inspired by Tuori (2002).

[17] Cf. Billis et al. (2021), p. 17.

[18] Wenander (2020a); Jans et al. (2015), p. 491, arguing that the convergence flowing from the influence of EU law goes beyond the scope of EU law potentially resulting in an administrative *ius commune*.

[19] A debate has emerged about this step in constitutional legal theory, with Barak arguing it is an essential step in the proportionality analysis, while Alexy argues purpose limitation can be unhelpful and potentially harmful. For our purposes we need only recognize that it is an established step in adjudication of proportionality.

following a *strictu sensu* balancing the measure to its aims, and the extent to which the measure reaches them, given the impact on opposing interests or rights.[20]

Still, the implications of a proportionality test will remain different due to variances in what particular circumstances the test is applied to, at what stage it is applied, and what the legal and practical consequences of varying degrees of disproportionality are. So, even while in jurisprudence, proportionality traditionally has gained most attention in relation to limitations of constitutional rights and the review of such limitations by courts, proportionality requirements will (also) carry legal implications for legislators and administrative authorities. Such implications will be present before, during, and after a decision has been made.

By way of illustration, traditional rights-based proportionality is typically applicable only in relation to interferences with fundamental (human or constitutional) rights.[21] In the case of fundamental rights established at the European level, the responsibility of ensuring proportionality will primarily fall on the shoulders of the state as a collective entity—either as a party to the European Convention on Human Rights,[22] or a Member State of the EU[23]—or on the EU itself.[24] Here, actions of individual state authorities (and in some cases, private actors with delegated powers or fulfilling typical state-functions[25]) may be attributable to the state as such.[26] The proportionality test may, in this context, target the entire normative and operative chain, from the constitution,[27] to legislation,[28] to lower-level regulations,[29] and specific measures and decisions.[30] In some cases, the proportionality test may even target the internal decision-making structure or process,[31] or training within public authorities.[32]

20 Barak (2012), pp. 243–379; Rivers (2006); Jans et al. (2015), pp. 183–201.

21 Cf. Alexy (2002); Barak (2012).

22 See Art. 1 ECHR.

23 Member States of the EU are required to respect the rights of the Charter of Fundamental Rights of the European Union when acting within the scope of EU law, see Article 51 of the Charter of Fundamental Rights of the European Union.

24 Art. 51, Charter of Fundamental Rights of the European Union.

25 See ECtHR, *Van Der Mussele v. Belgium*, 8919/80, Judgment of 23 November 1983; ECtHR, *Costello-Roberts v. the United Kingdom*, 13134/87, Judgment of 25 March 1993; ECtHR, *Woś v. Poland*, 22860/02, Judgment of 6 August 2006.

26 This is true even when state agents are acting contrary to instructions or *contra legem*, see ECtHR [GC], *Ilaşcu and Others v. Moldova and Russia*, 48787/99, Judgment of 7 August 2004.

27 See ECtHR [GC], *Baka v. Hungary*, 20261/12, Judgment of 23 June 2016.

28 See ECtHR [GC], *A, B and C v. Ireland*, 25579/05, Judgment of 16 December 2010.

29 See ECtHR [GC], *Hatton and Others v. the United Kingdom*, 36022/97, Judgment of 7 August 2003.

30 See ECtHR [GC], *K. and T. v. Finland*, 25702/94, Judgment of 7 December 2001; ECtHR, *Valdís Fjölnisdóttir and Others v. Iceland*, 71552/17, Judgment of 18 May 2021.

31 See ECtHR [GC], *Strand Lobben and Others v. Norway*, 37283/13, Judgment of 9 October 2019.

32 See ECtHR, *Simsek and Others v. Turkey*, 35072/97, 37194/97, Judgment of 26 July 2005, paras 109–113.

The responsibility to ensure proportionality as a constitutional principle instead rests on specific actors within the constitutional framework of the state, such as the legislator, the executive government, courts, or administrative authorities.[33] While constitutional proportionality may—at least in theory—influence the legitimacy of constitutional amendments,[34] the principle will primarily influence the discretion of the legislator and other regulatory bodies, as well as the individual decisions or actions by public authorities and courts. In the application of constitutional proportionality, one may expect a certain emphasis on the "prepared proportionality" of legislation and regulations. Here, proportionality requirements may primarily serve to limit regulatory or governmental overreach. However, constitutional proportionality may also serve as an important principle for apex courts or constitutional courts in their review of the application of law by lower courts.

As an administrative principle, the burden of ensuring proportional decisions mainly fall on administrative authorities and, by extension, on the individual public servants tasked with making decisions. The proportionality principle will thus primarily target the balancing of means and ends in specific decisions and actions. The principle will, importantly, also include the proportionality of how any discretionary space in the legislation can be utilized in relation to potentially negative consequences for those affected by the decision or action.[35] As a consequence, administrative proportionality will, to a greater extent, target the "output proportionality" of individual decisions. The goal is to achieve an exercise of power which is not, in light of the circumstances, disproportionate. Therefore, administrative proportionality requirements could be described as a "key tool of modern administrative law to ensure the purposive rationality of public action."[36]

As shown so far, proportionality is entrenched in multiple *levels* of the legal system. And as we will see, the need to consider proportionality also surfaces in an *increasing range* of government action and decision-making.

3 The Extended Range of Proportionality and Its Impact on Automation

While proportionality has had a significant impact in relation to human and fundamental rights, it is important to remember that the impact of proportionality stretches far beyond clear-cut rights-based cases. A growing range of situations may activate

[33] There may be differences in the formal recognition of the state as a single entity or distinct authorities, but within constitutional democracies the responsibility to adhere to the constitution will be shouldered by all public powers.

[34] Roznai (2013).

[35] See Thomas (2000), p. 16, arguing that in continental Europe, "[i]n particular, the principle of proportionality is used to ensure sensitivity in public administration."

[36] Thomas (2000), p. 77.

proportionality requirements existing on all or some of the levels described above. This is partly due to rights inflation, whereby a wider range of interests tend to be covered by the potential umbrella of fundamental rights.[37] However, proportionality as a principle of public law can also target the exercise of power more generally.[38] Proportionality is therefore potentially relevant in much more commonplace interactions between public authorities and citizens, which will impact automation efforts. Also, several more specific trends contribute to the relevance of proportionality in interactions between public authorities and citizens. For example, socio-economic aspects may impact the effective enjoyment of more traditional negative rights established in human or constitutional rights, which may by extension add rights-based dimensions to public benefits,[39] where the use of automation has increasingly been a priority.[40] This can result in rights-based proportionality requirements seeping into areas of law traditionally thought to be exempt from such considerations.

Similarly, the protection of privacy, and proportionality as a data processing principle, become intrinsic parts of automation efforts, since automation generally implies the processing of personal data.[41] Through the risk of algorithmic bias, non-discrimination rules and associated principles may also become relevant (and with even greater force when there are EU law dimensions involved). This increased relevance of non-discrimination rules and associated principles includes proportionality-like assessments of whether differences in treatment can be objectively justified.[42] Balancing requirements, which contain implicit proportionality-assessments, may also follow as a result of associated principles, such as

[37]Möller (2014).

[38]This is apparent through the principle's historic roots in Prussian administrative law where it was used to limit administrative overreach in policing, see Yutaka Arai-Takahashi (1999).

[39]See ECtHR [GC], *Béláné Nagy v. Hungary*, 53080/13, Judgment of 13 December 2016, where the Court examined (through proportionality) the withdrawal of disability pensions under the protection of property in Article 1 of Protocol 1 to the ECHR. See also ECtHR, *McDonald v. the United Kingdom*, 4241/12, Judgment of 20 May 2014, where the Court found an interference with Article 8 and applied a proportionality analysis to the decision by a local authority to reduce the funds for the weekly care of a lady with severely limited mobility, forcing her night-time toileting needs that used to be assisted by a night-time carer to be replaced with the use of incontinence pads and absorbent sheets. See also ECtHR, *Airey v. Ireland*, 6289/73, Judgment of 10 September 1979 on the lack of legal aid in divorce proceedings undermining the right to access to a court under Article 6.

[40]Report of the Special Rapporteur on Extreme Poverty and Human Rights, Philip Alston on the digital welfare state, A/74/48037, 11 October 2019; European Union Agency for Fundamental Rights (2020), Getting the future right: artificial intelligence and fundamental rights: summary, p. 25 ff; Dencik and Kaun (2020).

[41]See Pazdej (2021). The possible implications of data used for risk analysis is well illustrated by the Dutch *SyRi* case (see below, Sect. 5.2), in which the District Court of The Hague struck down an automated risk assessment system used to detect welfare fraud as it was disproportional under Article 8 ECHR. See Bekker (2021).

[42]On the similarities and differences (and the benefits of using a proportionality test in this context) see Nilsson (2020).

"reasonableness" in relation to social and economic rights,[43] or "duty of care" as a principle of EU administrative law.[44] Finally, substantive requirements in specific rules may also call for proportionality-like balancing in specific situations, such as when the rules establish rights or obligations that are relative to the circumstances (e.g., to abstract standards such as "appropriate" or "reasonable").[45]

As illustrated above, proportionality quickly can move from an abstract constitutional principle representing one of the "defining features of global constitutionalism,"[46] to specific, substantive requirements burrowing into daily interactions between public authorities and citizens within the legal system. In this regard, proportionality can be seen as a requirement with a wide area of application, including virtually the entire exercise of public power. However, this does not imply that proportionality will need to be actively enforced in every application of law. Instead, certain thresholds in the different stages of making, applying, and reviewing law, will influence to what extent proportionality surfaces as an "operative" principle. In relation to automation efforts, it is therefore first necessary to consider the extent to which legislators and administrative authorities will be required to proactively uphold proportionality in a specific context. In contexts where proportionality requirements surface, failing to adhere to the principle will imply that the measure in question (a law, a regulation, a decision, etc.) violates higher order norms at the point in time when the measure is taken.[47]

One could argue that a disproportional administrative decision—under the specific circumstances affecting the proportionality of the measure—is also ultra vires, although it may have a formal basis in law. In any case, while legality and proportionality require separate compliance tests, a decision which meets the requirement of legality (*stricto sensu*), but fails to reach proportionality, has still not been made in accordance with the law—just like a law that disproportionately restricts a constitutional right is unconstitutional. Disproportionate administrative decisions can thus be said to exceed the powers delegated to the decision-maker, while disproportionate legislation exceeds the powers delegated under the constitution to the legislature.[48] This further highlights the connection between proportionality and the rule of law.[49]

While proportionality thus contains important implicit implications for the rule of law, and the legality of government action, it should be kept in mind that the role of courts and administrative authorities in reviewing the legality and proportionality

[43] Young (2017).

[44] Hofmann (2020).

[45] The implicit connection between reasonableness and proportionality is visible through the German term "*Zumutbarkeit*" ("reasonableness") used for the last step of the proportionality test, see Jans et al. (2015), p. 184.

[46] Sweet and Mathews (2008), p. 74.

[47] Except in situations where circumstances occurring later render the measure disproportional.

[48] Cf. Thornhill (2012).

[49] Cf. Allan (2014), pp. 201–211.

of legal rules and administrative acts and actions may vary. This is particularly true for administrative authorities. While there are examples of countries, such as Sweden—where administrative authorities, formally provided with a certain independence against the government in the application of law, are tasked with and given powers of "administrative review" similar to the judicial review of courts—this is far from the norm. We argue, however, that requirements established by the Court of Justice of the European Union (CJEU) on national administrative authorities acting within the scope of EU law increasingly provides national administrative authorities with a certain implicit independence towards their respective national governments, and a role of acting as part of a loyal European administration to safeguard EU law, when making decisions within its nebulous scope.[50] This further implies that administrative authorities are not only likely to be faced with proportionality requirements flowing from a number of different normative sources and levels, they are also given a more proactive role, with obligations to preemptively guard proportionality in areas, such as within the scope of EU law, where national law on its own might otherwise appear to be open for further automation.

4 The Human Nature of Proportionality and Discretion

4.1 Proportionality as an Expression of Human Judgment

So far, our short overview indicates that proportionality carries an inherent potential to be relevant for automation efforts in a wide range of circumstances and contexts. Looking at Robert Alexy's balancing formulas,[51] one may get the impression that balancing and proportionality are exercises of mathematical precision, well-suited for translation into code. In fact, some efforts have been made to operationalize proportionality as a legal principle to assist in future efforts to translate it into a set of tasks for automated systems.[52] Challenges to such codable operationalizations include relative factors, such as the complexity of the regulation (where possible, proportionality conflicts might be easier to identify and settle in advance), and the configuration of the systems used. As put by Karen Yeung, algorithmic decision-making refers to the use of algorithmically-generated knowledge systems to execute or inform decisions, which can vary widely in simplicity and sophistication.[53] As we will elaborate, the efforts or aspirations to translate proportionality into code are, however, also faced with inherent challenges due to the way in which proportionality—and the balancing it may entail through its very nature—remains a social and

[50] Enqvist and Naarttijärvi (2021); Wenander (2020b).

[51] Alexy (2005), pp. 575–576.

[52] Sartor (2010).

[53] Yeung (2018), p. 507.

contextual operation. The ensuring of proportional decision-making therefore requires a decision-maker to engage in reflection, imagination, and communication.

Machine-learning models generally use statistical methods to establish correlations in data that, with training based on certain features either selected by designers of a system, or the model itself, appear to lead to accurate predictions. From a legal point of view, this reliance on correlations has been criticized.[54] In what now seems a rather prescient article from 1977, Ronald Dworkin argued against basing legal judgments on statistical correlations. Among his arguments, Dworkin points to the fragility of the correlations in social phenomena, in the way such correlations can change quickly—even sometimes as a result of the fact that a correlation has been made. He also underlines the arbitrariness that can exist in choices about whose correlations are taken to be significant. This critique is mirrored in more recent studies of data-driven decision-making, where Emre Bayamlıoğlu and Ronald Leenes have pointed to the possible "demise of law as a causative enterprise," which might occur as a result of an "epistemology establishing causation between a multitude of data points through aggregation and recursive data analysis—insights of which may not be understood through direct human cognition."[55]

Correlative data-driven decisions thus differ from interpretive judgments of the kind that judges make. According to Dworkin, interpretive judgements avoid the same arbitrariness as they need to be "framed in the critical vocabulary of the community in question," which anchors the judgment. Dworkin further argues that interpretive judgments are more enduring, as such decisions are based on conventions and shared understanding that neither changes quickly, nor requires "a kind of technology that is for [the judge] arcane."[56]

While Dworkin focuses on interpretive judgments in general, others, like David M. Beatty, have made similar remarks in relation to proportionality—underscoring how legal reasoning and proportionality differ from the type of analysis carried out by other disciplines:

> Whether someone's rights have been violated in law is not computed by some utilitarian, mathematical calculation. It is not about adding and subtracting people's preferences. Nor is it a process in which factors are catalogued and quantified and balanced against each other.[57]

Beatty therefore diverges somewhat from Dworkin's general theory by claiming that the assessing of proportionality is different from regular acts of interpretation or applications of moral judgments. Instead, Beatty draws from Habermas,

---

[54] See Bayamlıoğlu and Leenes (2018), pp. 307–308. The Article 29 Working Party has even highlighted the need to develop safeguarding measures to address over-reliance on correlations in automated systems, Article 29 Data Protection Working Party (2017) Guidelines on Automated individual decision-making and Profiling for the purposes of Regulation 2016/679, p. 28.

[55] Bayamlıoğlu and Leenes (2018), p. 209. The authors also highlight how "[t]he collapse of the causative link may also be seen as a big leap towards dehumanisation of the social, economic, and political texture of our lives."

[56] Dworkin (1977), p. 274.

[57] Beatty (2004), p. 171.

emphasizing the "application discourse" of legal deliberation.[58] Beatty's argument holds that proportionality "avoids the subjectivity and indeterminacy that plagues interpretation and cost/benefit calculations alike," by turning "conflicts about people's most important interests and ideas into matters of fact."[59] In this regard, Beatty has been criticized for being naïve in overestimating the extent to which proportionality analysis can reduce subjectivity.[60] However, his emphasis on the relationship between discourse and proportionality still has merit, as this highlights important social and contextual aspects of proportionality as a legal concept.

These social and contextual aspects of proportionality become further visible through the critiques leveled *against* proportionality as a method of judicial review, due to the inability to find a common scale for measuring the impact on legal values (the argument of incommensurability).[61] This critique essentially holds that the values (rights, interests) that are to be balanced within proportionality *stricto sensu* are not just different, but so different they do not fit within the same paradigm of measurement—like balancing an elephant and the color blue; or the music of *Madrugada* against a thunderstorm. Defenders of proportionality rightly dispute the incommensurability critique, holding that incommensurability does not necessarily imply incomparability.[62] The debate still highlights something which joins together both the critics and defenders of proportionality. For while the language of proportionality connotes objectivity and measurement,[63] and while certain steps—like necessity—safeguard rationality in a logical sense, the balancing process involved in proportionality *strictu sensu* is more elucidative and deliberative than anything else. The balancing process tempers discretion by structuring the analysis.[64] This, in turn, forces decision-makers to furnish analyses anchored in the relevant legal context, which thus provides some clarity to the application of higher-order abstractions of human reason to social and moral values in legal deliberation.[65] The proportionality balancing does not, however, remove

[58] Habermas (1996), pp. 265–266.

[59] Beatty (2004), p. 171.

[60] da Silva (2011), p. 288. Empirical studies on the influence of personal preferences on proportionality analysis indicate this criticism is warranted. See Sulitzeanu-Kenan et al. (2016).

[61] Tsakyrakis (2009), p. 471.

[62] Da Silva rightly points out that "[j]ust as it is possible to compare apples and oranges relative to a given covering value (vitamin content, for instance), it is also possible to compare and balance constitutional rights relative to a given covering value: their degrees of satisfaction and non-satisfaction. The fact that these rights may be incommensurable in the abstract does not alter their comparability in concrete situations." da Silva (2011), p. 301; see also Poscher (2021), p. 59.

[63] See da Silva (2011), p. 276, "The very metaphors of weight and balance denote the necessity of measuring and comparing."

[64] Cf. Khosla (2010), p. 300; Rivers (2006), p. 195.

[65] Kumm (2010); see also Mylonopoulos (2021) arguing that balancing is not a "conceptual-logic relationship. On the contrary, it is a normative gradual relationship, i.e., a comparison between values. The values compared are assessed according to the degree to which they promote the central ideal behind all fundamental constitutional values, i.e., human dignity."

disagreement or provide a single right answer.[66] Instead, proportionality serves as both a tool for analyzing reasonableness and fairness within a limited legal understanding of those standards in relation to the exercise of power—and as a principle which limits those expressions of discretion which produce legislative, administrative, or human overreach. In relation to automated decision-making, proportionality (properly applied) may, in the same vein, serve as an important tool to ensure that the exercise of power is not suffering from *algorithmic overreach.*

4.2 Discretion and Proportionality: Connected But Different

Given the role that both automation and proportionality play in limiting discretion in the application of law, the relationship between proportionality and discretion should be further elaborated. As Julian Rivers has pointed out, "[c]onfusion about the role of discretion is caused in no small part by confusion about the nature of proportionality itself."[67]

Marlies van Eck, Rik Peeters, and Arjan Widlak argue that discretion (regulated by principles of good administration) and the design of administrative procedures used to be the two most important mechanisms for balancing "between the need for universal and predictable rules that allow us to build systems, either organizational or algorithmic, and the need to deviate from those rules guided by principles—such as fairness, proportionality and accountability—that allow us to do justice when the rules fall short."[68] Continuing their argument, van Eck et al. also note that both these mechanisms are changing because of the automation of "street-level" discretion.

In a similar respect, we argue that questions of how to ensure compliance with proportionality requirements parallel these "discretion dilemmas." As the influx of new technologies has accelerated, these technologies have been used as tools for further rationalization and standardization in public decision-making.[69] And in relation to proportionality, such standardization challenges the occurrence of any *ex officio* legal proportionality analysis. The much-discussed obstacle is that automated decision-making systems will (probably) not be able to infer when an exception to a rule should be made, or sensitively navigate different contextual factors to conclude the most optimal (and lawful) choice.[70] As the capacity to make such inferences is at the core of proportionality, we would argue that questions about how "output proportionality" is to be ensured in automated decision-making processes are called for. And as automated processes are, de facto, aimed at reducing

---

[66] da Silva (2011), pp. 291–292.

[67] Rivers (2006), p. 176.

[68] van Eck et al. (2020), p. 2.

[69] van Eck et al. (2020), p. 2. See also Pasquale (2015); Peeters and Schuilenburg (2018).

[70] See, for example, Bovens and Zouridis (2002); de Boer and Raaphorst (2021); Koulu (2020a); Petersen et al. (2020).

human oversight, questions on if, where, and when human judgment can or cannot be replaced is of theoretical as well as practical concern.

Above, we have questioned the possibility of translating proportionality into code. Another question is, however, whether the human judgment proportionality seems to entail could be emulated by machine reasoning. Reuben Binns raises the conceptual question of whether there could be such a thing as "machine discretion," which would challenge the basic assumption that human decision-makers are truly exceptional in their ability to infer the relevant features and reasoning for a given case.[71] Drawing on this reasoning, one could similarly ask if there could be something like "machine proportionality," on the basis of which automated systems could be capable of making inferences in parity with what could be expected from human decision-makers. If so, proportionality requirements would not ineradicably challenge automation efforts, even in more complex cases.

The kinship between discretion and proportionality that manifests in the consideration of context is important to understand when attempting to grasp the challenges inherent to achieving machine proportionality. This kinship leads to many of the pertinent questions and problems around automation in public decision-making being of a similar nature. As implied by our reference to Binns, one of these shared concerns relates to the (ir)replaceability of human judgment. However, the differences between proportionality and discretion also require circumstanced legal analysis—where proportionality is much less explored in the automation context.

Proportionality carries different traits than discretion, although there is an interconnectivity between the two. While both discretion and proportionality are "modifiers," discretion *enables* contextual considerations while proportionality *prescribes* them. And while discretion does not define what the law "is," and rather begins where the law "ends," proportionality is part of the law. So, while lawfully recognized discretion entails a restriction of judicial review, proportionality may be at the center of such review. Proportionality thus permeates the possible exercise of discretion but also limits it. If, for example, a social services public servant tasked with conditioning the issuance of benefits that place certain obligations on the receiver would be able to choose from, say, three alternatives within his or her discretion; one, two, or all these alternatives (even if aligned with the letter of the law) may still be disproportionate to the goals they are meant to achieve. And if all three choices are equally efficient, proportionality requirements hold that the least restrictive option should be chosen.[72] While discretion thus creates a legal space in

[71] Binns (2020), p. 4.

[72] In the EU (internal market) context, see ECJ, *Konsumentombudsmannen (KO) v De Agostini (Svenska) Förlag AB (C-34/95) and TV-Shop i Sverige AB (C-35/95 and C-36/95)*, Joined cases C-34/95, C-35/95, C-36/95, Judgment of 9 July 1997, paras 45–47. In the EU (common foreign and security policy) context, see GC, *Bouchra Al Assad v Council of the European Union*, Case T-202/12, Judgment of 12 March 2014. In the EU (fundamental rights) context, see ECJ, *Sky Österreich GmbH v Österreichischer Rundfunk*, Case C-283/11, Judgment of 22 January 2013, paras 54–55. In the context of the European Convention on Human Rights, see ECtHR [GC], *Nada v. Switzerland*, 10593/08, Judgment of 9 December 2012, para 183. See also Brems and Lavrysen (2015).

which automation can be implemented, proportionality serves as a limiter of that space.

The prospect of achieving "machine proportionality" is tempered by the fact that proportionality, even if it serves to limit discretion, cannot completely remove it. As such, proportionality contains a discretionary space of its own—in the sense that uncertainties may exist on what proportionality requires in a specific situation. Matthias Klatt and Moritz Meister have, in this context, distinguished between *structural* and *epistemic* discretion. *Structural discretion* exists when proportionality neither commands nor prohibits a specific action, such as when the necessity test allows for several different, equally intrusive, measures to be taken, and where the choice between these alternative measures remains political. *Epistemic discretion* exists because of epistemic uncertainties as to what proportionality requires. These uncertainties can be categorized as empirical when they relate to the underlying empirical premises of state actions, or the consequences of a specific policy. Epistemic uncertainties can also result in normative epistemic discretion, when the best way to balance two principles or rights is not clear. In this situation, discretion only exists between the different lawful alternatives contained by proportionality.[73]

In relation to automation efforts, the question of whether such efforts can be implemented with decisions being taken through the discretion existing *within* proportionality cannot be answered in the abstract and ex ante. Rather, we need to look at where and when proportionality is applied to properly examine the extent to which, and how, proportionality will limit discretion. This brings us to the question of the nature of proportionality assessments performed in the different stages of making, applying, and reviewing law—as well as by whom they must be performed. It also begs the further question to what extent these assessments can be shifted between different stages to accommodate further automation and to ensure proportional outputs of automated systems.

5 Safeguarding Proportionality Throughout the Stages of Making, Applying, and Reviewing Law in the Context of Automated Decision-Making

5.1 The Chronology of Proportionality

As we have seen in the previous section, legal requirements to ensure proportional decision-making may stem from different hierarchical levels, may surface in different areas of law, and may also carry different specific properties, including scope and relative "weight." Our choice to use the indefinite form "proportionality," rather than the definite (and singular) form "the proportionality principle," also reflects that it might be more correct to talk about multiple proportionality principles. Still, and

[73] Klatt and Meister (2012), pp. 79–84.

irrespective of the closer delineations at European and national levels, the different, specific proportionality principles share the common core of *contextualization* aimed at limiting the unfettered exercise of power—by ensuring that public means are proportional to their ends. Another commonality these principles share is that compliance to proportionality requirements may be safeguarded at different *chronological* stages. We will make a rough, fourfold categorization, and claim that proportionality may be assessed and safeguarded at a legislative, system, decisional, and ex post stage—all of which will impact the prospects of a legal implementation of automated decision-making. We will expand on the characteristics of each of these stages in the following section.

5.2 Proportionality at the Legislative Stage

Starting out at the legislative stage, this is where proportionality assessments are first made by different legislative bodies, and are embedded in the rules themselves. This implies that legislators have attempted to actively foresee and weigh different public and individual interests against each other, and that the legislators, via the design of the rules, have expressed a stance on the balancing in regulated cases. Efforts to enable automation are likely to increase the need for explicit and clear legislative guidance on proportionality. Any such weighting of public and individual interests against each other will, however, have been made *in abstracto*, as well as proactively: *in abstracto*, as the assessments are not based on the merits of an individual case, but rather on general considerations and precautions about what types of proportionality tensions that may occur, and proactively since the intent is to prevent the taking of disproportionate decisions at scale (ex ante).

Legislators will thus have made a type of "blanket" proportionality assessment which will, through its operationalization in binding provisions, provide guidance on the proportionality balancing in all cases covered by that specific regulation. There is an argument to be made that almost any type of regulation, at least indirectly, conveys the legislators' stance on proportionality, as any clear directives given through binding rules imply a priority of some values over others. Without express guidance on the proportionality balancing, such rules will most probably not, however, provide effective directives in so-called hard cases—where rare or unforeseen circumstances may render a specific decision disproportionate.

In discussions on drafting and adopting digital-ready or automation-friendly legislation, proportionality concerns seem to have been largely absent.[74] Added regulatory detail based on explicit proportionality assessments would, however, mesh with such legislative efforts. As basic concepts, the dynamics, or contingencies, of successful translation of rules into code are well known. The more that rules

[74] See, for example, Mohun and Roberts (2020); Moses (2020); Casanovas et al. (2008). See, however, for example Sartor (2010).

are designed around effectively "objective" or "fixed" facts, rather than vague or open-texture natural language, the more "automatable" these rules are.[75] Attempts to automate a decision-making process (fully, as well as partially) through legislative adaptation will thus require that legislators, as much as possible, try to fill in such "interpretive gaps" of the regulation. And although proportionality requirements often contain complex "interpretive gaps," one could say that, as far as proportionality considerations are made explicit, such considerations may not only be formalized, but they could also add "codable" detail to the rules.

As opposed to "discretion," which in essence relates to the exercise of one's own authority and judgment, proportionality assessments are legal assessments rather than based on "free" judgement. Therefore, compliance with proportionality requirements is achievable without direct human involvement in the implementation of rules. In this sense, it is primarily the legal complexity of proportionality requirements, where the requirements at all legal hierarchical levels need to be considered and related to a specific case, that stands in the way of making such requirements just as codable as any other legal substantive requirements. It necessitates that the whole spectrum of actors involved in the automation effort, from legislators to system designers, not only correctly predicts, but also identifies, and balances the legal values involved in a specific decision-making context. Meanwhile, the specific requirements on how to properly identify and balance those values may arise not only from relatively static constitutional or statutory norms and regulations, but from a complex, dynamic, and ever-evolving case law emanating from courts on the national as well as European level. This enterprise is further complicated by the sheer difficulty of foreseeing the possibly relevant individual circumstances that may come into play in a specific setting, with the potential to shift the equation in a way that needs to be considered.

Ideally, legislators will be able to navigate the complex task of foreseeing and addressing proportionality concerns, and thus also be able to provide express proportionality guidance that complies with proportionality requirements at other legal hierarchical levels which would facilitate automation of those levels. There are, however, several contributing factors challenging the achievement of output proportionality via *purely* preventive means at the legislative stage. These factors include the way hierarchical and multi-leveled origins of proportionality requirements may establish limits to legislative powers as such—especially when national legislators embed their own proportionality assessments into rules that are subject to conditions of proportionality flowing from the European level. Because even if the legislator has correctly considered those conditions, legal developments, such as changing case law in European courts, may alter their interpretation and application, and may thus come to undermine the proportionality of the national legislative product over time.[76] And although, within the discretionary space of a national

[75] Schartum (2020); Plesner and Justesen (2022).

[76] There are numerous examples of this, especially where developments of social norms or practices has shifted the foundations in judgments from the ECtHR. See ECtHR, *Dudgeon v. the United*

legislator, proportionality requirements established in higher order national norms may surface in relation to the application of such lower order norms that appear to give clear directions on the proportionality balancing. This is because national constitutional or administrative level proportionality requirements may require that even the clear provisions should be set aside when they generate disproportionate outcomes. Again, proportionality requirements in higher order norms may also develop and change out of sync with clear and specific lower-level legislation.

Lastly, the variety of values and circumstances that the realm of reality displays is also of general importance—it is rarely possible for legislators to foresee all the conceivable interests and values at play by the time a prospective law reaches the legislative stage. Accordingly, and importantly, as the circumstances of a case might be new, proportionality assessments cannot rely entirely on "blanket assessments." Proportionality implies a need to recognize that new circumstances in a case might also render new merits for that case.

At the legislative stage, lawmakers will need to analyze the impact of legal rules allowing for automated decisions in advance, as part of the legislative process. But the outputs and implications of such automation on a collective level will also need to be analyzed ex post and weighed against overarching aims and opposing legal interests. Automation efforts anchored in specific legal frameworks established at the legislative stage can still be nebulous and opaque, with intangible effects distributed over large populations. Based on examples from the similarly opaque and nebulous context of surveillance, there are indications that constitutional review of legislative-stage proportionality could be able to cope with this vagueness in legislation through a form of "collective proportionality analysis." In the data retention case of *Digital Rights Ireland*, the CJEU considered the types of communications data subject to retention and the implications for "practically the entire European population" and established that the legislation created disproportional interferences with the right to privacy and data protection.[77] In this judgment, the CJEU explicitly acknowledged subtle population-level effects, beyond the implications for individual citizens in the specific case.[78] In its opinion on the EU passenger name record agreement with Canada, the CJEU similarly considered both collective effects for all passengers

Kingdom, 7525/76, Judgment of 22 October 1981, para 60 on the criminalization of homosexual acts between consenting adults; ECtHR, *Rees v. the United Kingdom*, 9532/81, Judgment of 17 October 1986; compared to ECtHR [GC], *Christine Goodwin v. the United Kingdom*, 28957/95, Judgment of 7 November 2002 with regard to the legal recognition of changes in gender; ECtHR [GC], *Big Brother Watch and Others v. the United Kingdom*, 58170/13, 62322/14, 24960/15, Judgment of 25 May 2021, with regard to the need to develop surveillance case law in light of important differences between targeted interception and bulk interception.

[77] ECJ, *Digital Rights Ireland Ltd (C-293/12) v Minister for Communications, Marine and Natural Resources, Minister for Justice, Equality and Law Reform, The Commissioner of the Garda Síochána, Ireland and the Attorney General, and Kärntner Landesregierung, Michael Seitlinger, Christof Tschohl and Others (C-594/12)*, Judgment of 8 April 2014, para 56.

[78] Ibid., para 37.

subject to profiling, and the specific consequences that automated decision-making could have for those individuals for which the system generated adverse effects.[79]

The European Court of Human Rights (ECtHR) has applied a similar form of collective-oriented analysis in relation to "stop and search"-measures in the UK. Although this analysis was expressed in relation to the legality requirement of Article 8 of the European Convention on Human Rights (ECHR) ("in accordance with the law"), rather than proportionality. The ECtHR's analysis does, however, illustrate how the Court may be inclined to reference statistical evidence on the possible discriminatory application of measures at scale—even as the specific cases on trial related to two distinct instances where individuals were searched for a very brief time, and where no such discriminatory claims were raised.[80] Furthermore, both the ECtHR and the CJEU have engaged in the provision of prescriptive conditions in their respective analyses of legislation-stage proportionality, providing requirements which typically serve to make a system of covert surveillance conformant with fundamental rights.[81]

As shown in the Dutch *SyRi* case, where, on transparency and verifiability grounds, the District Court of The Hague disallowed the use of an automated risk assessment system in relation to social welfare benefits, proportionality can set limits on the lack of transparency in automated systems and the rules surrounding them as well.[82] Should the legislator fail to sufficiently limit the discretion of administrative authorities on the limitation of rights, this failure is often managed by the assessment of legality in a qualitative sense (focusing on, for example, its clarity, predictability, and level of arbitrariness).[83] A lack of sufficient legal safeguards limiting discretion and ensuring protection against abuse will, however, affect the proportionality of the legislation as well. This has been underlined specifically by the CJEU in relation to the processing of personal data,[84] holding that such legislation "must, in particular, indicate in what circumstances and under which conditions a measure providing for

[79] ECJ, *Opinion 1/15: Opinion of the Court (Grand Chamber) of 26 July 2017*, paras 186–232.

[80] ECtHR, *Gillan and Quinton v. the United Kingdom*, 4158/05, Judgment of 1 December 2010, paras 84–85.

[81] ECJ, *La Quadrature du Net and Others v Premier ministre and Others*, Joined Cases C-511/18, C-512/18, C-520/18, Judgment of 6 October 2020, para 168; ECtHR [GC], *Big Brother Watch and Others v. the United Kingdom*, 58170/13, 62322/14, 24960/15, Judgment of 25 May 2021, para 361.

[82] Bekker (2021).

[83] ECtHR, *Liberty and others v. the United Kingdom*, 58243/00, Judgment of 1 July 2008.

[84] ECJ, *Tietosuojavaltuutettu v Satakunnan Markkinapörssi Oy and Satamedia Oy*, Case C-73/07, Judgment of 16 December 2008, para 56; ECJ, *Digital Rights Ireland Ltd (C-293/12) v Minister for Communications, Marine and Natural Resources, Minister for Justice, Equality and Law Reform, The Commissioner of the Garda Síochána, Ireland and the Attorney General, and Kärntner Landesregierung, Michael Seitlinger, Christof Tschohl and Others (C-594/12)*, Judgment of 8 April 2014, paras 51–52; ECJ, *Maximillian Schrems v Data Protection Commissioner*, Case C-362/14, Judgment of 6 October 2015, para 92; CJEU, *Tele2 Sverige AB v Post- och telestyrelsen and Secretary of State for the Home Department v. Tom Watson and Others, Joined Cases C-203/ 15 and C-698/15*, ECLI:EU:C:2016:970, Judgment of 21 December 2016, paras 96 and 103.

the processing of such data may be adopted, thereby ensuring that the interference is limited to what is strictly necessary."[85] In the *Ligue des droits humains* case on automated profiling on airline passengers under the EU Passenger Name Directive, the CJEU highlighted that the need for safeguards established in the legislation to limit the interference to what is strictly necessary is all the greater when personal data is subject to automated processing.[86]

In relation to proportionality, those actors preparing legislation subject to automation, or otherwise authorizing the use of it, have a twofold responsibility. First, they must ensure that the aims of the legislation are proportional to the negative effects this legislation may have on a collective level. Second, they must attempt to anticipate (to the furthest extent possible) such situations where more individualized proportionality concerns may surface in a legislation that is otherwise sound. They can attempt this by providing guidance—within their own discretion—on how different rights and interests should be weighed against each other. There is, however, a risk that such efforts will make the legislation inflexible in relation to unforeseen circumstances. Attempts to preemptively manage proportionality at the legislative level, therefore and consequently, cannot offer any panacea that removes the need for individualized assessment in contexts where proportionality concerns surface in individual cases.

5.3 *Proportionality at the System Implementation Stage*

In automated and semi-automated decision-making, the automated system as such is, of course, another key part in ensuring proportionality in the decision-making process. In this section, we will approach system implementation as a second stage of relevant proportionality analysis. While conditions for the design and use of certain systems may be prepared at the legislative stage, systems often tend to be implemented within (or between) existing legal mandates which were not necessarily designed with automation in mind. This means that the design and implementation of a system enabling full or partial automation of decision-making procedures

[85] See ECJ, *Opinion 1/15: Opinion of the Court (Grand Chamber) of 26 July 2017*, para. 154; ECJ, *Digital Rights Ireland Ltd (C-293/12) v Minister for Communications, Marine and Natural Resources, Minister for Justice, Equality and Law Reform, The Commissioner of the Garda Síochána, Ireland and the Attorney General, and Kärntner Landesregierung, Michael Seitlinger, Christof Tschohl and Others (C-594/12)*, Judgment of 8 April 2014, paras 54–55; CJEU, *Tele2 Sverige AB v Post- och telestyrelsen and Secretary of State for the Home Department v. Tom Watson and Others, Joined Cases C-203/15 and C-698/15*, ECLI:EU:C:2016:970, Judgment of 21 December 2016, paras 109 and 117; see also to the same effect, ECtHR, *S. and Marper v. the United Kingdom*, 30562/04, Judgment of 4 December 2008, para 103.

[86] ECJ, *Ligue des droits humains ASBL v Conseil des ministers*, Case C-817/19, Judgment of 21 June 2022, para 117.

might come with substantive (advertent or inadvertent) insets into how proportionality concerns can be resolved in the design phase.

A system's capacity to produce proportional decisions or recommendations will depend on several factors that may in themselves be subject to proportionality requirements from a range of sources—and which, consequently, will have to be addressed at the system implementation stage. Examples include what type and range of data the system will process, and what types of inferences, recommendations, and decisions the system will be instructed to make (including considerations of when and how the system's operations should be subject to human oversight). Since automated or semi-automated systems are dependent on data (and often personal data), one important concern to address at the system implementation stage is that the processing of this data will activate proportionality requirements flowing from privacy and data protection rights in the ECHR and the EU Charter of Fundamental Rights, as well as in secondary data protection law. In essence, the specific rules and principles of data protection elaborated in the GDPR, as well as in the Data Protection Law Enforcement Directive, are examples of situated proportionality requirements for the data protection context.[87] They are essentially detailed elaborations on how to achieve a more overarching legality and proportionality where the rights of the individual in terms of data protection as a fundamental right are balanced against the needs of the processor.

These situated proportionality requirements will take aim at a diverse set of system-level attributes; for example, respecting the data minimization principle; the existence of proportional technical, and organizational measures to protect data; restrictions on the sharing of data; and more.[88] In contexts where data protection rules do not provide "pre-baked" solutions for balancing the rights of the data subject with the interests of the processor, data protection rules will include their own proportionality requirements, baked into conditions such as "except where such interests are overridden by the interests or fundamental rights and freedoms of the data subject."[89] Such data protection aspects add a further layer of obligations that automation systems need to meet, and which relate specifically to the associated processing of data.

Beyond compliance with data protection norms and principles, system-level proportionality will be dependent on decision-makers ensuring that system design choices do not result in automated systems that make or recommend decisions departing from the requirements of the law. In relation to proportionality, measures should be taken by system designers to ensure that blanket proportionality guidance provided by the legislator is effectively translated into any automated systems in use.

[87] See recital 4 GDPR; see also on sensitive data ECJ, *Proceedings brought by B*, Case C-439/19, Judgment of 22 June 2021, para 74; ECJ, *GC and Others v Commission nationale de l'informatique et des libertés (CNIL)*, Case C-136/17, Judgment of 24 September 2019, para 44.

[88] See generally Bygrave (2019), pp. 248–262; Bygrave (2020); Mendoza and Bygrave (2017), pp. 77–98.

[89] Art. 6(1)(f) GDPR.

Furthermore, the identification of "hard cases" not addressed by blanket assessments is important, so that these cases can be transferred to human decision-makers. Where the legislation leaves room for human discretion, such discretionary spaces should not be claimed by systems designers who, through their programming, make decisions and fixate proxies through which the cases are to be handled. Rather, these discretionary spaces must allow for proportionality to be considered via legal reasoning, rather than be the inadvertent result of preferred system design choices, or the algorithmic whims of a machine-learning system.

5.4 *Proportionality at the Decision Stage*

In the decision stage, proportionality is to be assessed in each specific case, with due regard to the particular circumstances at hand. Proportionality is, as a legal requirement, to be executed by the case administrator or automated system tasked with making decisions, with the assessment integral to the act of implementing the law. However, assessing proportionality *in casu* at the decisional stage is obviously more challenging in relation to automated decision-making, or decision support systems, as opposed to when human case administrators are the decision-makers. As the instrumental aim of automation is to limit human involvement, the extent to which individualized proportionality assessments remain enabled will depend on the capabilities of the system as such, and/or the inclusion of some form of human oversight in the decision-making process. And although we cannot rule out that future decision-making, or decision support systems, may become able to make complex inferences, a general level of complex "machine discretion" or "machine proportionality" has not yet been realized and remains elusive. Even more autonomous and comparatively more sophisticated systems under current technological circumstances, such as those deploying different types of machine-learning models, will base their training on historic data—but apply their inferences to new cases. The recognition of emergent circumstances or new merits in a case thus remain a particular challenge for such systems.[90]

It is worth pointing out that statutory rules may contain requirements for administrative agencies, and by extension, decision-makers, to consider individual circumstances and apply a proportionality assessment *in casu*, even where the overall legislative framework or system supporting the decision-maker can be considered proportional. The existence of procedures allowing individual proportionality to be considered by decision-makers is often a key part of achieving legislative-level proportionality.[91] A failure to account for individual circumstances warranting

---

[90]Bayamlıoğlu and Leenes (2018), pp. 310–311; Hildebrandt (2020).

[91]See, for example, ECtHR, *A.-M.V. v. Finland*, 53251/13, Judgment of 23 March 2017, para 84, where the Court held: "The procedural safeguards available to the individual will be especially material in determining whether the respondent State has, when fixing the regulatory framework,

exceptions, or the disapplication of norms in a specific case, may result in decision-stage disproportionality, even if legislative and system-stage proportionality has been achieved.[92]

Considering current limits to technology, human oversight is an important safeguard for proportionality at the decision stage. As indicated, involving "humans in the loop" is one measure that can temper algorithmic decision-making with human judgment. In relation to proportionality, one idealized function of "humans in the loop" is to ascertain that risks and clear imbalances between measures and their results can be identified, ensuring that proportionality between means and ends can be assessed. In practice, it might be somewhat optimistic to expect human decision-makers to make extensive proportionality assessments in full compliance with every requirement established throughout the full hierarchy of norms—at least in their everyday handling of cases *en masse*. It is also primarily (although not exclusively) in those cases where the means to achieve an end are of a certain restrictive nature that proportionality requirements will surface and become part of the (active) legal assessment.

Furthermore, although output proportionality is a substantive requirement that administrative authorities must consider when using their powers, the limits to administrative discretion that proportionality (at all hierarchical levels) introduces, are often vaguely framed in case law or other legal sources. These caveats considered, "humans in the loop" are still better prepared and more easily tasked with identifying those cases where the proportionality between means and ends needs to be assessed. The human overseer's ability to do so in a way that is meaningful and efficient will, however, depend on the conditions under which they are operating.[93] Their ability to identify cases where the means and ends may be disproportional, and thus warrant more careful scrutiny, will depend on their access to information, their mandates, time, training, and resources among other factors. Accordingly, while highly context dependent, such factors will influence the extent to which "humans in the loop" are properly equipped to assess the proportionality of an automated decision, or make suggestions in the same way as traditional decision-makers perhaps would be.

In sum, decision-makers acting at the decision stage will need to fulfil functions beyond those often associated with "humans in the loop" in a more limited capacity—functioning as a mechanism for system oversight. If human decision-making is

---

remained within its margin of appreciation. In particular, the Court must examine whether the decision-making process leading to measures of interference was fair and such as to afford due respect to the interests safeguarded to the individual by Article 8."

[92] See, for example, GC, *Donau Chemie AG v European Commission*, Case T-406/09, Judgment of 14 May 2014, para 308; ECtHR [GC], *Abdi Ibrahim v. Norway*, 15379/16, Judgment of 12 October 2021; ECtHR [GC], *Strand Lobben and Others v. Norway*, 37283/13, Judgment of 9 October 2019; ECtHR [GC], *Slivenko v. Latvia*, 48321/99, Judgment of 10 September 2003, para 117; ECtHR, *Silver and others v. the United Kingdom*, 5947/72, Judgment of 25 March 1983, para 105; ECtHR, *Segerstedt-Wiberg and Others v. Sweden*, 62332/00, Judgment of 6 June 2006, para 90.

[93] Koulu (2020a), p. 725 ff.; Santoni de Sio and van den Hoven (2018).

ceded to automated systems, it is important that functions exist to identify both contexts and cases where proportionality requirements established at different legal levels surface. In those contexts and cases, administrative officials will need to be positioned to make proper proportionality assessments. This, in turn, requires resources and decisional structures that are scaled for the task. In this sense, proportionality requirements highlight how systems of automated decision-making will need to exist in parallel and work in conjunction with human decision-makers, rather than replacing them, in contexts where proportionality requirements may surface.

5.5 *Proportionality at the Ex Post Stage*

Any legal system that pledges to respect the rule of law will include corrective functions, so that (inevitably occurring) errors can be corrected. Broadly defined, we refer to such corrective functions as ex post remedies or oversight mechanisms, and they comprise the range from the decisions of supervisory authorities to administrative review or court appeals. As such remedies are carried out after an initial decision has been made, but also relate to the proportionality of a specific decision, corrective remedies in the shape of courts or supervisory authorities will review compliance with proportionality requirements ex post. Such remedies may help correct errors in individual cases, in addition to preventing the introduction of new ones. And especially when done by courts, such remedies may include scrutiny of the proportionality assessments done both at the legislative, system implementation, and decision-making stages. This means that the proportionality of a certain decision can be reviewed both *in abstracto* (focusing on whether the mandates given to decision-makers based on the law are proportional), and *in casu* (focusing on whether a specific decision is proportional). Proportionality could, in this sense, be described as a standard of review to determine the lawfulness of a public authority's justification for infringing upon thc rights of individuals.[94]

One important shortcoming of ex post remedies is, naturally, that they imply a reliance on (predominantly) citizens to take action—or else there will be no correction of disproportionate decisions. An interrelated circumstance is also that there may be knowledge and resource dependencies which might affect citizens' tendency to contest decisions.[95] So, while proportionality assessments made at the ex post stage are highly important for safeguarding proportionality requirements established at all levels of the legal hierarchy, and thus for limiting unfettered use of powers by public authorities (or the legislator), proportionality assessments alone cannot guarantee output proportionality, especially *en masse*. Increased reliance on ex post

[94]Barak (2012), p. 439; Dyzenhaus (2014). That proportionality has a justification function is, however, debated. See Cohen-Eliya and Porat (2014).

[95]Lyons et al. (2021), p. 16.

contestation of decisions, while reducing ex ante human control of the proportionality of decisions, is problematic.[96] To some extent expanding the avenues of independent oversight may partially remedy more systemic issues. But for individuals subject to disproportional decisions, who may not be in a position to take advantage of the right to contest automated decisions, this solution may be inadequate.

When activated in courts or supervision, ex post proportionality review may, however, serve an important function. This review has the potential to address issues of proportionality at all hierarchical levels and all stages of decision-making. The fact that an appeal has been lodged will provide the review authority with a wider set of facts to base a review on, and will require a justification of the decision from the decision-making authority. While judicial review can correct for errors in the legislative balancing, ex post review will still be limited to ensuring *output* proportionality only in cases subject to review. This further highlights the limits of ex post review, in comparison with managing proportionality concerns at earlier stages of decision-making.

5.6 Where Proportionality Is Assessed Matters

Having introduced these four stages where the proportionality of decision-making may be assessed, these are clearly already present in all European legal systems and in no way preclude each other. And these stages can be combined with varying intensity and strength. There is, therefore, a certain space to maneuver in how to ensure output proportionality, which legislators at all hierarchical levels may dispose of in different ways. But since the targets of the proportionality requirements are somewhat different (and aimed at either limiting the legislator's or case administrator's discretion), the safeguarding of output proportionality is best ensured if actively safeguarded at all stages. Blanket proportionality assessments made by legislators may reduce the risk of disproportional decisional outcomes. Certain aspects of proportionality are inherently collective. For example, the balancing of what types and sources of data that may underpin a decision-making system must be considered at the legislative or system implementation stage and cannot in entirety be shifted to the decisional stage. An emphasis on (and trust in) blanket proportionality requirements to ensure output proportionality may, however, excessively shift the balancing to a priority of collective interests before individual ones. Likewise, an emphasis on, and trust in, ex post remedies to ensure output proportionality is also not enough, because this solution risks placing greater responsibility on citizens to take action, and therefore tilts the power relations between state and citizen even further to the advantage of the state. To ensure that the proportionality of public decisions can be

[96] See Lyons et al. (2021), p. 16, holding that contestability should be seen as a last line of defense against faulty decisions.

assessed at the decision stage is therefore a necessary safeguarding measure. And, as will be argued in next section, this is best assured if public automated decision-making processes are combined with a sufficient degree of human oversight at the decision stage.

6 The Human in the (Proportionality) Loop

While both are central elements to the rule of law, proportionality has a certain juxtaposing element in relation to legality. This is because proportionality requirements may call for the letter of the law to be set aside in cases where the consequences of a formalistic application of the law are too disadvantageous for the affected. From this perspective, proportionality could be regarded as a value-based principle of law, rather than a formal one. But while proportionality prevents legislators from abusing their formal legislative powers (by exercising unfettered powers), it also serves to offer legal guidance on how to resolve complex cases in which "the law" prescribes the consideration of different values, which cannot all be fully realized (and thus cannot all be present to safeguard the rule of law).[97] Proportionality therefore supports making the legal system as a whole resilient against the inner tensions between the different and sometimes counterbalancing aims it accomodates. As proportionality relates to the weighing of different values, it is inherently susceptible to change (and also risks having a negative effect on foreseeability). Proportionality requirements thus make the law and its application somewhat responsive to societal values, as well as to scientific developments. Therefore, borrowing a conceptualization associated with automation, one could claim that a function of proportionality is to keep the law (or rather its application) "in the loop" in relation to collective and individual aims. In this sense, proportionality is a process, rather than a fixed and attainable state.

Against this background summarized above, our contribution has highlighted why proportionality needs to be taken seriously in relation to automation efforts in decision-making. Not only has proportionality become a principle of significant importance in the European legal order, it has become so in many, if not most, national legal orders within Europe. The need to account for proportionality also surfaces in a widening range of circumstances, due to the increased scope and influence of fundamental rights and fundamental constitutional and administrative principles. Proportionality is also important due to the various legal functions the principle fulfils. As we have illustrated, proportionality can add a human dimension to the implementation of law when functioning as a barrier against government overreach, or irrational or unreasonable exercises of power.

Proportionality also serves as a catalyst for deliberation and communication through the way it promotes and requires reason-giving and articulation in relation

[97] Alexy (2002), pp. 50–57.

to policy goals, interests, and the balancing of values. Additionally, proportionality carries implications for the rule of law, by ensuring that the exercise of government power is carried out within the boundaries established through the constitution and the powers delegated to administrative authorities, as well as to individual decision-makers (which are inherently circumscribed by the principle). Consequently, proportionality needs to be safeguarded in all decision-making, including decision-making processes subject to varying degrees of automation. Such safeguarding is best achieved by considering proportionality in the full lifecycle of decision-making, from the legislative stage to ex post facto review of decisions.

Meanwhile, attempts to automate proportionality will be faced with considerable challenges. The nature of these challenges varies between the different stages of preparing legislation, implementing automation, and making and reviewing decisions. To some extent, aspects of necessity and balancing can be anticipated and prepared ex ante through the legislative process, either through interpretive guidance on how interests should be weighed, or through codified expressions of such balancing in rules. These anticipatory measures could offer a partial guide for automation efforts, but are unlikely to solve the issue of proportionality in later stages of decision-making. This is partly due to the differing dimensions of proportionality surfacing at the different stages. It may also be difficult (if not impossible) for the legislative process to properly anticipate and resolve all relevant factors in a proportionality assessment in advance, except for such decision-making taking aim at more mechanical subsumption with little room for discretion or contextual factors. Finally, developments in national or supra-national case law may evolve the interpretation of rules, principles, or rights involved in the decision-making, which would make the baked-in or blanket proportionality analysis provided by the legislator incomplete or obsolete.

As we have highlighted, proportionality also has *in casu* components, requiring individual circumstances and consequences to be considered. Even if the legislation can provide some guidance in this regard, the need for individual assessment is the key aspect separating *making law* from *making decisions* (i.e., applying law). This is especially true in relation to proportionality, where one of the primary functions is to manage situations where the legislation, applied *as is*, would result in unreasonable outcomes. Recognizing and pinpointing situations where there is a risk of disproportionate decisions or actions may require considering the entire legal hierarchy, as well as the explicit and implicit values represented in a variety of rules and principles. Finally, as we have already mentioned, the balancing exercise included in proportionality is a deliberative, communicative, and thereby a deeply *social* exercise, emphasizing the human dimension it involves. One could even argue that proportionality incorporates into the law a certain expression of *compassion*.[98]

[98] This is partly visible in the application of proportionality to the use of force. While individuals may have acted in ways which make it legal and necessary to use force against them, proportionality holds both that the force used should not exceed what is necessary to reach the aim, and when the use of force would result in effects that are disproportional to the expected outcomes, the use of force may need to be ruled out.

While our study thus points to the significant difficulty of automating proportionality, our conclusion is not that proportionality precludes automation as such. Rather, it points to the need to analyze *which* proportionality becomes applicable, *at what stage* this proportionality needs to be assessed, and *to what extent* proportionality at the decisional stage can be either proactively managed by previous stages or through ex post controls. Our study suggests, however, that when proportionality requirements surface in relation to the decision stage, for example, due to fundamental rights dimensions or substantive requirements incorporating proportionality-like assessments, these requirements are likely to necessitate substantial human participation (to account for the abstract and contextual assessment of values and consequences involved for proper *in casu* determinations of proportionality).

We also argue that the legal expectations flowing from proportionality differ from those usually associated with "humans in the loop". Ensuring proportionality at the decision stage requires a more holistic, contextual, and nuanced analysis of individual circumstances. Statistical decision-making models look to the many to decide on the implications for the few, and the one. They look to the past to decide about the future. Proportionality, however, requires that we also look to the few, and the one, to understand the implications for the many. It requires us to look beyond the past, towards future consequences, to decide about the present. It then asks us to explain those decisions through the provision of reasons anchored in the critical vocabulary of the community, rather than opinions. It tells us to look beyond numbers, to actual consequences, where we can find the foundations for common sense and humanity in the application of law. This will be a challenge to meet if human actors in automated or semi-automated decision-making environments are not informed and engaged in the decision-making process enough to be able to properly check the outcome of automated systems against contextually sensitive circumstances and effects.

While human oversight of automated processes is sometimes a requirement in substantive law, these requirements do not directly address, or "solve," the concerns we have raised on how to safeguard proportionality in automated decision-making. Turning to the well-known human oversight requirement in Article 22 of the GDPR, this part of the Regulation grants a (limited) right to human intervention through a right for data subjects not to be subject to decisions based solely on automated processing, including profiling.[99] Also at the EU level, Article 14 of the proposed EU AI regulation will, if implemented, require that so-called "high-risk AI systems" be designed and developed so that they can be effectively overseen by natural persons during their use.[100] We also argue that human oversight might, in addition, be an obligation stemming implicitly from proportionality requirements established

[99] A particularly relevant limitation in the context of public decision-making is that this right does not apply where the automated decision is authorized by Union or Member State law, Article 22(2) (b) GDPR. See, also, Tosoni (2021).

[100] Article 14(1) European Commission (2021) Proposal for a Regulation of the European Parliament and of the Council laying down harmonised rules on artificial intelligence (Artificial Intelligence Act) and amending certain union legislative acts.

in human rights, EU, constitutional, and administrative law. Because, in cases where the law does not give clear enough directions on proportionality, and where the automated decision-making systems are not advanced enough to ensure "machine proportionality," there will be interpretive gaps in need of human oversight. The role and responsibilities of humans overseeing automated decision-making processes are, however, not fixed.

If we, for example, return to Article 22 of the GDPR, the Article focuses on a procedural right to have a "human in the loop," while the suggested human oversight requirement in Article 14 of the proposed EU AI regulation is primarily a part of system-level control (as the obligation is placed on providers of AI systems and is aimed at ensuring a system capacity to perform oversight rather than entailing an obligation to do so). Through their approaches, these regulatory frameworks, therefore, do not address the more particular legal responsibilities of "humans in the loop," of which ensuring compliance with proportionality requirements may be one. Therefore, while one could claim that the emphasis that the EU particularly places on human involvement in automated decision-making matches quite well with these implicit oversight requirements, the EU regulations are certainly not the end point of the discussion on the need for human oversight and the responsibilities of "humans in the loop" in ensuring that contextual factors are considered and inform the proportionality assessment.

So, what to do? In approaching automated public decision-making, we argue that there is a need to balance alarmism and solutionism. As we have seen, proportionality is a core concern, but one that is often overlooked. At the same time, the importance of proportionality is growing due to the Europeanization of law. This brings the further implication that the answer to the question "what is proportional?" is increasingly found beyond the national legal order, with public authorities in Member States having to consider and mediate between values and principles existing on multiple levels, with different arbiters and possibly different outcomes. Proportionality thus seems to serve an important function in mediating between multi-level and multi-state regulations (addressing the chaos that pluralism brings).

The implications for automation efforts in public administration are multifold. Keeping humans in the loop cannot be *the* single solution to ensure proportionality in automated decision-making. This pursuit requires measures taken both before and after decision-making. It is, however, difficult to bypass the need for the sensitive judgement which automated systems lack, to ensure proportionality. This also brings to the forefront the conditions and practicalities facing humans in the loop. If they are tasked with guaranteeing proportionality in individual decisions, this considerably raises the bar in terms of ensuring proper agency, access to information, availability of legal expertise, and of course time. This is not to say the expectations exceed those of regular human decision-making in public authorities, but given that automation is generally implemented to bring efficiency through speed, scale, or the analysis of a wider set of data, simply the existence of *similar* requirements of "humans in the loop" within automated systems are enough to challenge the very gains that automation efforts are implemented to achieve. Given these dependencies, the decision to *implement* automated systems, and the conditions facing decision-making within those systems, needs to be proportional to the risk of not being able to ensure proportionality within the decisions such systems generate.

In the end, proportionality must be regarded as another key factor in assessing the legal prospects of implementing automation. Proportionality adds to an already crowded array of issues around automation, such as discrimination, bias, transparency, ethics, etc. However, given the normative foundation of proportionality, the way the principle operates on multiple hierarchical levels, in all stages preceding and succeeding decision-making—and considering its foundational importance to fundamental rights and the rationality and humanity of law—we believe that proportionality should be at the core of socio-legal and technical perspectives on law surrounding automated decision-making.

Funding Statement This research was funded by the Swedish Research Council, grant no. 2020-02278_VR.

References

Alexy R (2002) A theory of constitutional rights. Oxford University Press, Oxford

Alexy R (2005) Balancing, constitutional review, and representation. Int J Const Law 3:572–581. https://doi.org/10.1093/icon/moi040

Allan TRS (2014) Democracy, legality, and proportionality. In: Huscroft G, Miller BW, Webber GCN (eds) Proportionality and the rule of law: rights, justification, reasoning. Cambridge University Press, New York, NY

Barak A (2012) Proportionality: constitutional rights and their limitations. Cambridge University Press, Cambridge

Barocas S, Selbst A (2016) Big data's disparate impact. CalLRev 104:671. https://doi.org/10.15779/Z38BG31

Bayamlıoğlu E, Leenes R (2018) The 'rule of law' implications of data-driven decision-making: a techno-regulatory perspective. Law Innov Technol 10:295–313. https://doi.org/10.1080/17579961.2018.1527475

Bayamlioğlu E, Baraliuc I, Janssens L, Hildebrandt M (eds) (2018) Being profiled: cogitas ergo sum: 10 years of profiling the European citizen. Amsterdam University Press, Amsterdam

Beatty DM (2004) The ultimate rule of law. Oxford University Press, Oxford

Bekker S (2021) Fundamental fights in digital welfare states: the case of SyRI in the Netherlands. In: Spijkers O, Werner WG, Wessel RA (eds) Netherlands yearbook of international law 2019. T.M.C. Asser Press, The Hague, pp 289–307

Billis E, Knust N, Rui JP (2021) The typology of proportionality. In: Billis E, Knust N, Rui JP (eds) Proportionality in crime control and criminal justice. Hart Publishing

Binns R (2020) Human judgment in algorithmic loops: individual justice and automated decision-making. Regul Gov. https://doi.org/10.1111/rego.12358

Bovens M, Zouridis S (2002) From street-level to system-level bureaucracies: how information and communication technology is transforming administrative discretion and constitutional control. Public Adm Rev 62:174–184. https://doi.org/10.1111/0033-3352.00168

Brems E, Lavrysen L (2015) 'Don't use a sledgehammer to crack a nut': less restrictive means in the case law of the European Court of Human Rights. HRLRev 15:139–168. https://doi.org/10.1093/hrlr/ngu040

Busch PA, Henriksen HZ (2018) Digital discretion: a systematic literature review of ICT and street-level discretion. IP 23:3–28. https://doi.org/10.3233/IP-170050

Bygrave LA (2019) Minding the machine v2.0: The EU General Data Protection Regulation and automated decision-making. In: Yeung K (ed) Algorithmic regulation. Oxford University Press, Oxford, pp 248–262

Bygrave LA (2020) Article 22 Automated individual decision-making, including profiling. In: The EU General Data Protection Regulation (GDPR). Oxford University Press, Oxford

Cameron WB (1963) Informal sociology: a casual introduction to sociological thinking. Random House, New York

Casanovas P, Sartor G, Casellas N, Rubino R (eds) (2008) Computable models of the law: languages, dialogues, games, ontologies. Springer, Berlin, Heidelberg

Cohen-Eliya M, Porat I (2014) Proportionality and justification. Univ Toronto Law J 64:458–477. https://doi.org/10.3138/utlj.020614RA

da Silva VA (2011) Comparing the incommensurable: constitutional principles, balancing and rational decision. OJLS 31:273–301. https://doi.org/10.1093/ojls/gqr004

de Boer N, Raaphorst N (2021) Automation and discretion: explaining the effect of automation on how street-level bureaucrats enforce. Public Manag Rev 1–21. https://doi.org/10.1080/14719037.2021.1937684

Dencik L, Kaun A (2020) Datafication and the welfare state. Global Perspect 1. https://doi.org/10.1525/gp.2020.12912

Dworkin R (1977) Social sciences and constitutional rights. Educ Forum 41:271–280. https://doi.org/10.1080/00131727709336251

Dyzenhaus D (2014) Proportionality and deference in a culture of justification. In: Huscroft G, Miller BW, Webber G (eds) Proportionality and the rule of law: rights, justification, reasoning. Cambridge University Press, New York

Enqvist L, Naarttijärvi M (2021) Administrative independence under EU law: stuck between a rock and Costanzo? Eur Public Law 27:707–732. https://doi.org/10.54648/EURO2021035

European Union Agency for Fundamental Rights (2020) Getting the future right: artificial intelligence and fundamental rights. Publications Office of the European Union, Luxembourg

Goldstein H (1963) Police discretion: The ideal versus the real. Public Adm Rev 23:140–148

Goldstein J (1959) Police discretion not to invoke the criminal process: low-visibility decisions in the administration of justice. YaleLJ 69:543

Habermas J (1996) Between facts and norms: contributions to a discourse theory of law and democracy. Polity, London

Henman P (2010) Governing electronically: e-government and the reconfiguration of public administration, policy and power. Palgrave Macmillan UK, London

Hildebrandt M (2020) Code-driven law: freezing the future and scaling the past. In: Deakin SF, Markou C (eds) Is law computable? Critical perspectives on law and artificial intelligence. Hart Publishing, an imprint of Bloomsbury Publishing, Oxford, UK; New York, NY

Hofmann HCH (2020) The duty of care in EU public law: a principle between discretion and proportionality. Rev Eur Adm Law 13:87–112. https://doi.org/10.7590/187479820X15930701852265

Jans JH, Prechal S, Widdershoven R, van den Brink JE (eds) (2015) Europeanisation of public law, 2nd edn. Europa Law Publishing, Groningen

Khosla M (2010) Proportionality: an assault on human rights?: a reply. Int J Const Law 8:298–306. https://doi.org/10.1093/icon/moq002

Klatt M, Meister M (2012) The constitutional structure of proportionality, 1st edn. Oxford University Press, Oxford

Koulu R (2020a) Proceduralizing control and discretion: human oversight in artificial intelligence policy. Maastricht J Eur Comp Law 27:720–735. https://doi.org/10.1177/1023263X20978649

Koulu R (2020b) Human control over automation: EU policy and AI ethics. Eur J Legal Stud 12(1): 9–46. https://doi.org/10.2924/EJLS.2019.019

Kumm M (2010) The idea of Socratic contestation and the right to justification: the point of rights-based proportionality review. Law Ethics Human Rights 4:142–175. https://doi.org/10.2202/1938-2545.1047

Lipsky M (2010) Street-level bureaucracy: dilemmas of the individual in public services, 30th anniversary expanded edn. Russell Sage Foundation, New York
Lyons H, Velloso E, Miller T (2021) Conceptualising contestability: perspectives on contesting algorithmic decisions. Proc ACM Human-Comput Interact 5:1–25. https://doi.org/10.1145/3449180
Mendoza I, Bygrave LA (2017) The right not to be subject to automated decisions based on profiling. In: Synodinou TE, Jougleux P, Markou C, Prastitou T (eds) EU internet law: regulation and enforcement. Springer International Publishing, Cham, pp 77–98
Merrer EL, Tredan G (2019) The bouncer problem: challenges to remote explainability. arXiv:191001432 [cs, stat]
Mohun J, Roberts A (2020) Cracking the code: rulemaking for humans and machines. OECD Working Papers on Public Governance No. 42. https://doi.org/10.1787/3afe6ba5-en
Möller K (2014) Proportionality and rights inflation. In: Huscroft G, Miller BW, Webber G (eds) Proportionality and the rule of law: rights, justification, reasoning. Cambridge University Press, New York
Moses LB (2020) From rule of law to legal singularity. In: Deakin S, Markou C (eds) Is law computable? Hart, Critical perspectives on law and artificial intelligence
Mylonopoulos C (2021) The contribution of fuzzy logic and comparative concepts to the rational application of proportionality stricto sensu. In: Billis E, Knust N, Rui JP (eds) Proportionality in crime control and criminal justice. Hart
Nilsson A (2020) Same, same but different: proportionality assessments and equality norms. Oslo Law Rev 7:126–144. https://doi.org/10.18261/ISSN.2387-3299-2020-03-01
Pasquale F (2015) The black box society: the secret algorithms that control money and information. Harvard University Press, Cambridge
Pazdej AP (2021) The proportionality principle in privacy and data protection law. J Data Protect Priv 4:322–331
Peeters R, Schuilenburg M (2018) Machine justice: governing security through the bureaucracy of algorithms. Inf Polity 23:267–280. https://doi.org/10.3233/IP-180074
Petersen ACM, Christensen LR, Hildebrandt TT (2020) The role of discretion in the age of automation. Computer Supported Cooperative Work (CSCW) 29:303–333. https://doi.org/10.1007/s10606-020-09371-3
Plesner U, Justesen L (2022) The double darkness of digitalization: shaping digital-ready legislation to reshape the conditions for public-sector digitalization. Sci Technol Hum Values 47:146–173. https://doi.org/10.1177/0162243921999715
Poscher R (2021) Proportionality and the bindingness of fundamental rights. In: Billis E, Knust N, Rui JP (eds) Proportionality in crime control and criminal justice. Hart
Ranerup A, Henriksen HZ (2020) Digital discretion: unpacking human and technological agency in automated decision making in Sweden's social services. Soc Sci Comput Rev 40(2):1–17. https://doi.org/10.1177/0894439320980434
Ress G (1985) Der Grundsatz der Verhaltnismassigkeit im deutschen Recht. In: Kutscher H, International Commission of Jurists (1952-) (eds) Der Grundsatz der Verhältnismässigkeit in europäischen Rechtsordnungen. C.F. Müller, Heidelberg
Rivers J (2006) Proportionality and variable intensity of review. CLJ 65:174–207. https://doi.org/10.1017/S0008197306007082
Roznai Y (2013) Unconstitutional constitutional amendments: the migration and success of a constitutional idea. Am J Comp Law 61:657–719. https://doi.org/10.5131/AJCL.2012.0027
Santoni de Sio F, van den Hoven J (2018) Meaningful human control over autonomous systems: a philosophical account. Front Robot AI 5. https://doi.org/10.3389/frobt.2018.00015
Sartor G (2010) Doing justice to rights and values: teleological reasoning and proportionality. Artif Intell Law 18:175–215. https://doi.org/10.1007/s10506-010-9095-7
Schartum DW (2020) From legal sources to programming code: automatic individual decisions in public administration and computers under the rule of law. In: Barfield W (ed) The Cambridge

handbook of the law of algorithms, 1st edn. Cambridge University Press, Cambridge, pp 301–336

Strömholm S (1967) Right of privacy and rights of the personality: a comparative survey. Norstedt, Stockholm

Sulitzeanu-Kenan R, Kremnitzer M, Alon S (2016) Facts, preferences, and doctrine: an empirical analysis of proportionality judgment. Law Soc Rev 50:348–382

Sweet AS, Mathews J (2008) Proportionality balancing and global constitutionalism. ColumJTransnatlL 47:72–164

Thomas R (2000) Legitimate expectations and proportionality in administrative law. Hart, Oxford

Thornhill C (2012) Contemporary constitutionalism and the dialectic of constituent power. Global Const 1:369–404. https://doi.org/10.1017/S2045381712000159

Tosoni L (2021) The right to object to automated individual decisions: resolving the ambiguity of Article 22(1) of the General Data Protection Regulation. Int Data Priv Law 11:145–162. https://doi.org/10.1093/idpl/ipaa024

Tsakyrakis S (2009) Proportionality: an assault on human rights? Int J Const Law 7:468–493. https://doi.org/10.1093/icon/mop011

Tuori K (2002) Critical legal positivism. Ashgate, Aldershot, Hants, England; Burlington, VT

van Eck M, Peeters R, Widlak A (2020) Towards principles of good digital administration: fairness, accountability and proportionality in automated decision making. In: Schuilenburg M, Peeters R (eds) The algorithmic society: technology, power, and knowledge, 1st edn. Routledge, Abingdon

Wenander H (2020a) Europeanisation of the proportionality principle in Denmark, Finland and Sweden. Rev Eur Adm Law 13:133–153. https://doi.org/10.7590/187479820X15930701852283

Wenander H (2020b) Administrative constitutional review in Sweden: between subordination and independence. Eur Public Law 26:987–1010. https://doi.org/10.54648/EURO2020074

Yeung K (2018) Algorithmic regulation: a critical interrogation. Regul Gov 12:505–523. https://doi.org/10.1111/rego.12158

Young KG (2017) Proportionality, reasonableness, and economic and social rights. In: Jackson VC, Tushnet M (eds) Proportionality. Cambridge University Press, Cambridge, pp 248–272

Yutaka Arai-Takahashi (1999) Proportionality: a German approach. Amicus Curiae

Zarsky T (2016) The trouble with algorithmic decisions: an analytic road map to examine efficiency and fairness in automated and opaque decision making. Sci Technol Human Values 41:118–132. https://doi.org/10.1177/0162243915605575

Zouridis S, van Eck M, Bovens M (2020) Automated discretion. In: Evans T, Hupe P (eds) Discretion and the quest for controlled freedom. Springer, Cham, pp 313–329

Legislating AI: A Matter of High-Risk Administration?

Anna-Sara Lind

Abstract For 50 years, in national administrative law, automatization and handling new technological tools that function with the law have been important areas of interest for legal scholars and practitioners. In the Nordic Federation of Public Administration, this can be seen when we study the programs of the meetings that have been held from the 1970s onwards. And this rapid technological development shows no signs of slowing down. On the contrary, new technologies continuously emerge and challenge the flexibility of the legal rules. Artificial intelligence (AI) and the new forms of automated decision-making represent recent developments that have tested national administrations. In April 2021, the European Commission proposed a new Regulation, the AI Act, which classifies AI by risk level. Automated decision-making and the national administrations are not clearly visualized in the Commission's proposal although these are definitely intertwined with AI. Many of the measures taken in a national and European context could be fruitful to highlight in the suggested future reforms, especially for automated decision-making. In this chapter the concept of the rule of law will be the frame-work when investigating and linking the AI Act and its implications to the national and European constitutional structures.

Keywords Automatization · AI Act · Rule of law · Administrative law

1 Introduction

For the past half century, the use of artificial intelligence (AI), automation, and other new technological tools has been an important issue in national administrative law. For example, the Nordic Federation of Public Administration has discussed this

---

A.-S. Lind (✉)
WASP-HS, PI of the project Artificial intelligence, democracy and human dignity, Faculty of Law Uppsala University, Uppsala, Sweden
e-mail: Anna-Sara.Lind@jur.uu.se

M. Suksi (ed.), *The Rule of Law and Automated Decision-Making*,
https://doi.org/10.1007/978-3-031-30142-1_8

issue in their meetings since the 1970s,[1] and in Sweden, the first Data Act was enacted as early as 1973.[2]

This chapter will analyze some of the administrative issues that could potentially result from the European Commission's proposed European Union (EU) AI Act.[3] This recent proposal follows a highly important legislative development comprising the General Data Protection Regulation (GDPR) 2016/679,[4] Directive 2016/680,[5] and Regulation 2018/1725.[6] All of these legislative acts have led to extensive national adaptations and also to some administrative changes. The impact of the data protection package is enormous, and the legislative work in Member States, such as Sweden, cannot be overestimated. More than 40 public inquiries have been arranged in Sweden since the enactment of the GDPR. The legislative reforms have been comprehensive. New, broader surveillance systems are up and running, and information about the GDPR has been disseminated widely by banks, stores, social media companies, and others since early 2018; virtually all actors in each of these sectors have been asking for consent to process personal data to comply with the GDPR. Since then, the English acronym for the Regulation, "GDPR," has been mentioned more than the Swedish words referring to the Constitution, the transparency and secrecy acts, and other national laws safeguarding personal integrity while securing a functioning administration.

The EU AI Act aims to enhance economic growth—in addition to fostering EU innovation and global competitiveness—and bring societal benefits. The Commission suggests that the EU AI Act should be subsidiary to the GDPR when data protection is relevant. The EU AI Act is intended to be technology neutral when defining AI systems, and the Act is intended to ensure that safety, security, and fundamental rights issues are managed in a good manner.

[1] This is seen also in the written contributions to the journal of the Nordic Federation of Public Administration, https://www.nafnet.fi/se/julkaisut/nordisk-administrativt-tidsskrift/.

[2] Datalag (1973:289).

[3] For a brief summary of the legislative steps and the core of the AI Act, see European Parliament Legislative Train 04.2022.

[4] Regulation (EU) 2016/679 of the European Parliament and of the Council of 27 April 2016 on the protection of natural persons with regard to the processing of personal data and on the free movement of such data, and repealing Directive 95/46/EC (General Data Protection Regulation).

[5] Directive (EU) 2016/680 of the European Parliament and of the Council of 27 April 2016 on the protection of natural persons with regard to the processing of personal data by competent authorities for the purposes of the prevention, investigation, detection or prosecution of criminal offences or the execution of criminal penalties, and on the free movement of such data, and repealing Council Framework Decision 2008/977/JHA.

[6] Regulation (EU) 2018/1725 of the European Parliament and of the Council of 23 October 2018 on the protection of natural persons with regard to the processing of personal data by the Union institutions, bodies, offices and agencies and on the free movement of such data, and repealing Regulation (EC) No. 45/2001 and Decision No. 1247/2002/EC (Text with EEA relevance).

To achieve this, a risk-based approach is suggested in the Commission's proposal.[7] AI systems that could lead to harmful uses of AI, that are contrary to EU values, are considered as "unacceptable risk AI" in the EU AI Act and are forbidden. "High-risk AI" are those systems that were suggested to be listed in the Act's Annex I. In the Presidency's most recent proposal, it is suggested that the Annex should be taken away, and that the descriptions of machine learning and AI systems should be found directly in the EU AI Act.[8] High-risk AI are systems that are creating an adverse impact on people's safety or their fundamental rights. Such systems can be allowed if they meet a list of mandatory requirements (for example a conformity assessment). Limited-risk AI are the systems that would only be subject to a limited set of obligations (transparency). Finally, minimal-risk AI are all the other systems that can be developed and used in the EU without additional legal requirements beyond existing legislation.

This background is highly intriguing, especially when we raise constitutional reflections. When working with this proposed EU AI Act, one realizes that experience in a national, or historical, context could be fruitful to examine in order to anticipate future reforms, especially concerning automated decision-making. And by taking the concept of the rule of law as the framework, it is possible to study the ongoing legislative process and connect it to the national and European constitutional structures.

The current chapter is structured as follows. First, the concept of the rule of law will be briefly introduced, with attention to the different jurisdictions relevant to this chapter. Next, some salient features of algorithmic decisions and AI will be described, which will serve to ground the reader's understanding of such technologies within a legal context. This chapter then turns to the legislative process of the GDPR and discusses some insights that can be drawn from this process. The legislative process of the GDPR will furthermore be discussed, with the rule of law, for the ways these two elements inform ongoing legislative initiatives, both at the European as well as at the national Swedish level. As we will see, the complexity of developing good legal frameworks for the aforementioned emergent technologies is substantial in Swedish law, as in other jurisdictions. This chapter concludes with three main reflections that will hopefully be relevant for future scholarship at the intersection of law and technology.

[7] Here, one can gather that the ambition to be neutral risks to lead to less nuances. When discussing artificial intelligence and software programs, one easily forgets that there are different sorts of hardware (open and closed) that in turn can be relevant.

[8] Second Presidency compromise text of 15 July 2022 (11124/22; Interinstitutional File: 2021/0106 (COD), at https://artificialintelligenceact.eu/wp-content/uploads/2022/07/AIA-CZ-1st-Proposal-15-July.pdf (accessed on 25 August 2022).

2 Rule of Law: Common Denominators in All Jurisdictions Involved

The commitment in Europe to create legal frameworks for AI started with the data protection negotiations in 2012 in the European Union. An explicit request for legislative action came from the European Parliament and the European Council in 2017 and ultimately led to the 2021 proposal made by the European Commission. In the Council of Europe (CoE), there have also been efforts to create a legal framework, and in April of 2022, the CoE's Committee on Artificial Intelligence (CAI) held their inaugural meeting.[9] The Organisation for Economic Co-operation and Development has also developed principles intended to help AI use become more trustworthy and innovative.[10] A common feature of all these initiatives is their respective referencing of the rule of law. For example, the CAI has been instructed by the CoE's Committee of Ministers to establish an international negotiation process for the implementation of a legal framework on the development, design, and application of AI, based on the CoE's standards on human rights, democracy, and the rule of law.

The rule of law can be explained in different ways, while focusing upon different dimensions of this doctrine. Legality, legitimacy, equality, transparency, participation, access to court, and accountability are features that historically have been put forth as essential elements of the rule of law.[11] Today, fundamental and human rights can be counted among this list of dimensions of the rule of law. The national administrative and constitutional systems have furthermore merged these fundamental dimensions through the practice of law. This merging can also be seen in the European setting; the layers of the rule of law have progressively been woven into the EU legal system. Although the words pertaining to the rule of law might be the same in national, international, and European law, their meaning and content can differ depending on the legal context. This becomes clear with complicated issues such as AI and automated decision-making.

In the Swedish system, transparency has a special dimension through a major constitutional arrangement where transparency is protected in three fundamental laws. This constitutional arrangement has often posed a challenge when balancing national and EU law during the decades Sweden has been a member of the EU.[12] In the CoE, the Venice Commission has suggested that the rule of law could be explained through four parameters: legal certainty, prevention of abuse/misuse of

---

[9] For more information, see https://www.coe.int/en/web/artificial-intelligence/cai. In the Council of Europe, several groups are working on AI related issues and therefore an AI Co-ordination group has been formed. This will continue its work parallel to CAI.

[10] For more information, see https://www.oecd.org/digital/artificial-intelligence/.

[11] See Sajó (2011), Chap. 1 and also Bull (2013), p. 235.

[12] See Lind (2015).

powers, equality before the law, and non-discrimination and access to justice.[13] In public decision-making, the rule of law is comprised of three types of requirements: formal, procedural, and material. This means that decisions that are taken should be based upon the law, that procedural rules should be respected when decisions are taken, and the rules for the content of the decision are established in law.[14]

Other important requirements of the rule of law include participation, which is the right of every person to be heard before any measure which would affect them adversely is taken. Included in this context is also the right of the affected individual to receive information about the administrative process and the resulting decision. In this regard, digital and technological development carries risks that may undermine the rule of law. What information and processes are possible to understand if a highly-advanced system is making a decision? As has been asked in legal research: do we need to be technically specialized to be able to understand what lies behind a decision?[15] Accountability is also another matter that must be addressed for the rule of law to be maintained. For administrative systems to be legitimate, and for the administrative laws to function, the Swedish Government has established safeguards to ensure that there is always someone, a public servant, who is legally responsible for administrative decisions.

Based on its preamble, the proposed EU AI Act aims to increase trust through the achievement of four key goals. First, the AI Act aims to make sure that all AI systems on the market are trustworthy and in line with the EU's values and fundamental rights. This market aim is also an important reason why the European Commission has indicated that the Act would take the form of a regulation, rather than a directive.[16] Along with this initial market goal, increased innovation and investment in AI are also included as goals in the AI Act, as well as the intention to support the development of AI on the market. Lastly, the Act aims to secure efficient supervision of AI.[17] But all these goals are gathered under the overarching purpose of the Regulation: to serve as a tool to improve the functioning of the internal market. The meaning of what is considered as "trustworthy," however, is not clear, nor is it explained in the preamble. Noteworthy from a legal point of view is the existence of an individual responsibility in criminal law as well as one in tort, both of which would be highly difficult to capture for AI and not foreseen in the draft AI Act.

---

[13] Report on the rule of law - Adopted by the Venice Commission at its 86th plenary session (Venice, 25–26 March 2011). See also Rule of Law Checklist, adopted by the Venice Commission at its 106th Plenary Session (Venice, 11–12 March 2016).

[14] Suksi (2022), pp. 176–177.

[15] Suksi (2017).

[16] Subsidiarity and proportionality as fundamental principles of EU law are stated in Article 5 Treaty on European Union (TEU).

[17] AI Act, preamble paras 1–5.

3 Algorithmic Decisions and Artificial Intelligence

"AI system" is defined in Article 3.1 of the European Commission proposal for an EU AI Act as "software that is developed with one or more of the techniques and approaches listed in Annex I and can, for a given set of human-defined objectives, generate outputs such as content, predictions, recommendations, or decisions influencing the environments they interact with." This is a broad definition and at the same time a rather narrow one.[18] AI can be considered as having a wider impact and meaning than the one of a mere software. And it is with this definition rather difficult to understand what kind of software would be covered by the definition. In the Presidency compromise, written seven months after the Commission proposal, the definition of an AI system has been changed. At the same time, it can be seen as narrower and comprises mainly machine learning systems that transform input data to output data, according to a rule that stems from training data.[19] The transformation of this definition, when considering how it had been perceived by the AI Expert group in 2019, is remarkable. This group defined AI systems as being construed by humans, steered towards a certain goal, depending on data, and adjustable and reactive with some sorts of agency.

Algorithmic systems already have a significant influence over administrative decision-making processes in many European countries. AI has already been a substantial factor in the formation of public opinion and political consent, particularly in the domains of digital information and communication. Such influence is a factor in shaping flows of information in any digital contexts where algorithms influence the perceptions of the recipient.

As a general remark, one can distinguish between three levels of AI-systems. First, there are simple algorithms used in data-filtering processes and other rudimentary situations. Then, there are more advanced systems, based in evolving algorithms or self-learning applications that are capable of processing large amounts of data and identifying factors relevant for future decisions. These systems can be characterized by an inherent unpredictability, even from the programmer's perspective. Third, there is the hypothetical category of "strong AI," exhibiting behavior indistinguishable from that of human agents, in principle able to perform any type of decision-making task.

Different definitions of the rule of law are used in different organizations and jurisdictions. Likewise, different definitions of AI are also used in different (and to some extent parallel) legislative processes. And, at the same time, the European Commission proposal is dependent on the definition of a certain technique (the definition of AI) while aiming to be neutral. Automated decision-making is not a

[18] See also de Vries (2022), pp. 11–12.

[19] See Presidency Compromise, November 2021, on Article 3.1. See also Second Presidency compromise text of 15 July 2022 (11124/22; Interinstitutional File: 2021/0106(COD), at https://artificialintelligenceact.eu/wp-content/uploads/2022/07/AIA-CZ-1st-Proposal-15-July.pdf (accessed on 25 August 2022), where this narrower definition is underlined.

concept, nor a term, that is included in the EU AI Act. But decision-making based upon algorithms, as part of the fulfillment of public services, do fall within the proposal's scope.

Interestingly enough, the EU AI Act is suggested to be based upon Article 114 in the Treaty on the Functioning of the European Union (TFEU). This Article relates to the realization of the free movement and the internal market, and it is extensive to stretch the Article so far that it becomes a legal basis for the handling of automated decision-making in the national administrations of the Member States. The EU AI Act proposal has a general scope and contains harmonizing rules. Public and private spheres would therefore be affected by the Act when it enters into force, and although public activities are not specially mentioned, the judicial systems and democratic processes are mentioned as AI systems of high risk.[20] It is thus relevant, in this situation, to question if the EU has competence to legislate in a way that restricts or reshapes the activities of national authorities, even if this activity would be automated.[21]

Algorithmic decisions in national administration become more important as societal demands on the welfare state increase. Such welfare state decisions can lead to better services and more efficiency, enhance the quality of decision-making (generally speaking), and improve working conditions. But we also need to map out the obstacles and problems such decision-making systems can raise. Lessons of the GDPR could be helpful in that regard.

4 Article 22 GDPR: Reflections in the Aftermath of Its Entering into Force

Under Article 2.1 of the GDPR, the GDPR is applicable on the processing of personal data. It is consequently relevant for all automated decision-making that involves personal data. In Article 4.1 of the GDPR, personal data is broadly defined and that leads to the conclusion that all public decision-making directed to physical persons is included in the concept. Article 2.2(a) of the GDPR states that the regulation is applicable to EU law. Sweden, however, has chosen to enlarge the scope of application of the GDPR: it applies generally in all areas of society.[22]

---

[20] See EU AI Act proposal, Annex III.

[21] Noteworthy is that information gathering linked to exercise of power might not be correct if solely grounded on the AI Act. In the Swedish setting a new Act (discussed below) restricts this option. The fundamental principles of subsidiarity and proportionality must be respected when a new legislative act is enacted in the European Union. Unfortunately, these principles are just touched upon, when the Commission briefly concludes that they are respected in the proposal (cf. Art. 5 TEU). The legislative path taken here resembles the one of the GDPR. Regulations are more common today than was earlier the case and during the negotiations of the GDPR few were the ones who strived for a directive solution. See also Enqvist and Naarttijärvi (2021).

[22] Lag (2018:218) med kompletterande bestämmelser till EU:s dataskyddsförordning 1:2.

Accordingly, the GDPR currently applies to, for example, automated administrative systems of municipalities, as soon as personal data is handled.

Under Article 22 of the GDPR, the data subject shall have the right not to be subject to a decision based solely on automated processing, including profiling, which produces legal effects concerning him or her or similarly significantly affects him or her. What this means is not totally clear; is the Article intended to be a prohibition, as automated decision-making as a general rule is prohibited,[23] or is it a right?[24] Article 22 could be considered a right because the main rule is that there is a right *not* to be subject to automated decision-making. Furthermore, is all automated decision-making included, or is automated decision-making included only when profiling also occurs?[25] No matter what: Article 22 does limit the possibilities to automate certain types of decisions.

If the decision is solely automated, and has legal implications, then there is a problem in relation to Article 22. But if the use of algorithms is allowed according to law and proper safeguards have been guaranteed, then it appears that such a decision would be permitted under EU law. These forms of decisions are also permitted if necessary to achieve a contract or if informed consent has been given by the data subject. Although the general rule is that decisions based solely upon automated processing under Article 22 are forbidden, there is an exception in Article 22.2(b), namely, when such decisions are authorized by EU or Member State law to which the controller is subject, and when that law also lays down suitable measures to safeguard the data subject's rights, freedoms, and legitimate interests. In contact with public authorities, consent is seldom the legal basis, which means that Member State legislation needs to regulate the issue thoroughly and not too broadly.

Transparency is an important aspect of the exercise of power in open societies for several reasons, and it is also a key feature of the rule of law. Transparency safeguards accountability for errors and abuses; furthermore, this accountability depends on a visible chain of decisions and a clearly established causation. Transparency is also crucial for functional democratic influence over government decision-making processes, without which there can be no proper open deliberation over governance and the distribution of power. In Swedish constitutional law, transparency is expressed in several ways. It is embraced and promoted in the Freedom of the Press Act, where the right to access official documents is stated. Transparency is also achieved through the constitutional demand that the work of courts and legislative bodies should be done publicly. In the Administrative Procedure Act, documentation and motivation of decisions are expressed as a rule and a

[23] The Working Party on the Protection of Individuals with Regard to the Processing of Data, Guidelines on Automated individual decision-making and Profiling for the purposes of Regulation 2016/679, Adopted on 3 October 2017, p. 9; Karlsson (2020), p. 65.

[24] Öman, GDPR, artikel 22 (JUNO).

[25] Prop. 2017/18:95 s 100; see also Karlsson (2020), pp. 55–60.

general demand for all public bodies and those who have been given the right to take administrative decisions.[26]

5 A Swedish Initiative for the Local Administration: Revealing National Constitutional Issues

An initiative to enable municipalities to use automated decision-making in their administration, in the way that has earlier been done according to the Administrative Procedure Act for national Agencies, was presented in 2020,[27] and a Government Bill was presented to the Parliament at the beginning of 2022.[28] This initiative was taken to allay concerns that automated decisions taken in the municipalities were not legally correct, because the legal basis was lacking.[29] Prior to the initiative, self-learning algorithms had been used in municipal administration, but they could not be used in a decision-making capacity. In such a context, however, it is important that a public servant assumes responsibility and acts as the final decision-maker, and is not ruled by the program.

On 1 July 2022, the legislative amendments in the Municipalities Act entered into force.[30] From this date, a municipal committee may delegate decision-making to the chairperson, a sub-committee, a substitute, or an automated decision-making function in a specific case, or concerning a certain group of cases.[31] There are, however, limits to this delegation, and they are explicitly listed in Chapter 6, Section 38 of the Municipalities Act. Generally, delegation to automated processes is not allowed in cases regarding (1) the aim, structure, scope or quality of the activities of the municipality nor (2) communications to the Municipal Council or communications issued due to an appeal of decisions taken by a board or the council, nor is it (3) permissible to delegate cases that involve the exercise of public power relating to individuals, if the cases concern issues of principle or are of greater importance. Thus, within the Municipalities Act, the rule of law for the individual is emphasized. The legality is further underlined by the statement that decision-making power cannot be delegated in cases where the law or other statutes forbid delegation.[32]

---

[26] Indeed, even in an authoritarian society, a minimal level of transparency with regard to the exercise of power is arguably necessary to enable regulatory oversight and to avoid abuse and the entrenchment of corruption, if for no other reason than to maintain basic safety, the efficiency of production, and social cohesion and stability.

[27] SOU 2021:16 En väl fungerande ordning för val och beslutsfattande i kommuner och regioner.

[28] Prop. 2021/22:125 Val och beslut i kommuner och regioner.

[29] Cf. Karlander (2021), pp. 223–232.

[30] See lag (2022:638) om ändring i kommunallagen (2017:725) [Act 2022:638 on amending the Municipalities Act].

[31] Chap. 6 Sect. 37 Municipalities Act.

[32] This is also a means to communicate the constitutional idea that some matters are so important that they should be kept for the Parliament to be decided, see Chapter 8 Instrument of Government.

Along with these rules for automated processes, in the same Section of the Municipalities Act, there is an additional explicit prohibition against delegating decision-making powers to an automated decision function in certain situations. The situations listed here are (1) cases that can be subject to appeal under Chapter 13 of the Municipalities Act (legality review), (2) cases where decisions are not allowed to be appealed due to law or other statute, (3) cases relating to public procurement and (4) cases relating to public services that can be chosen by the individual (some social services and health care).

The national inquiry presented in 2021 was highly criticized as it did not consider features relating to the rule of law. For instance, labor unions have maintained that public power should always be performed by public servants, as matters of accountability are regulated in a different way in public law than in private law. It was also pointed out by the labor unions that if the documentation is carried out by private partners, and the municipality only enters to take the final decision, then there is a problem relating to the rule of law.[33] It is even more troublesome if the documentation is handled solely by algorithms and the decision is not taken by a human being. To some extent, these fears have been addressed in the new legislation. The Government stressed that the legislation should be construed with a view to having the constitutional basis for decision-making in municipalities as its main goal, not focusing on technical options or possibilities.[34] And as we have seen, the decisions by the Municipal Council, which is the democratically-elected, highest decision-making body in a municipality, should under no circumstances be made in an automated way.[35]

The wording of the Municipalities Act stresses an important dimension of the rule of law: the principle of legality. But an addition to this dimension is that the exercise of public authority should be based on reasons accessible to citizens, derived from the principle that those who are its subjects are owed an explanation and justification. This principle is recognized in many legal contexts, including in the fundamental treaties of the EU, where Article 296 of the TFEU states that "[l]egal acts shall state the reasons on which they are based," but also in national provisions. The basic rationale for providing reasons in public decision-making is that citizens have a fundamental interest to be able to confirm that public power is exercised in a way that is consistent with the basic values of equality, the rule of law, and maybe to some extent also core values of the welfare state.

Public decision-making should be carried out in accordance with the principle of transparency. Related to transparency is the principle of public justifiability, which, developed in the liberal tradition, is the idea that public authority must be grounded in reason. According to the principle of public justifiability, authority must be based on reasons, and these reasons must be accessible and acceptable by the governed. Absent this principle, a non-legitimate sovereign may abuse their power by not

[33] See Akademikerförbundet, remissvar 2021.

[34] Prop. 2021/22:125 p. 27.

[35] Prop. 2021/22:125 pp. 27–28.

letting people see or understand legal texts, or the reasons behind their implementation. In the Swedish case, the Government has stressed that no exceptions nor changes to the constitutional Freedom of the Press Act or the Transparence and Secrecy Act will be allowed. The constitutional basis for transparency and possibilities to get information are accordingly to be left unchanged.[36]

AI technology has the potential to make public decisions more efficient, more effective, and, at the same time, less discriminating and less biased—if automated decision-making is rightly construed and implemented, that is. There have been situations where enhanced administrative abilities of doing justice have come at the expense of delivering justice. Another way to express this is that administration (and administrative law) always involves dimensions of form and content that need to be balanced and motivated.

But at the same time, risks to democracy are increasingly recognized by scholars worldwide. Machine learning can be a tool for authoritarian regimes and, also, for repression in democracies. Accordingly, machine learning can be perceived as a new threat to democracy. Many scholars, including contributors to this volume, have written about the risks of more efficient and targeted uses of this technology.[37] Algorithms in statistics can, for example, open up for statistical discrimination. Likewise, data collection methods may invade privacy, and political polarization can be enhanced through the use of AI. The introduction of machine learning in the decision-making processes of public authorities may be detrimental to transparency due to the opacity of the reasons for the conclusions of algorithmic recommendations or decisions. Public authority that is opaque undermines the capacity of citizens to examine, understand, and potentially contest the grounds for public decisions to which the citizenry are subjected.

At the same time, the use of AI in public authority is typically introduced to improve the quality and speed of public decisions. AI may make the bureaucracy more efficient, thus saving resources to the benefit of citizens. More importantly, AI could also make bureaucratic decision-making more effective, which in some cases is crucial for protecting human rights (e.g., property rights or asylum rights). In other words, the implications that AI may have for public authority are ambiguous: AI might promote the instrumental value of democratic authority while reducing the intrinsic value of democratic authority. The more basic issue in democracy theory, provoked by the introduction of AI in public decision-making, is how to balance instrumental and intrinsic values of democracy.

In the Swedish example, the criticism of automated decision-making is illustrated in the following situation. In 2019, a labor union (Akademikerförbundet SSR) requested information about the algorithm that was used in the Swedish municipality, Trelleborg. The labor union wanted information about how the algorithm was used in cases where the municipality decided if applicants should get financial social support. As the labor union did not receive any answers, it turned to the

---

[36] Prop. 2021/22:125 p. 32.

[37] See for example Beckman et al. (2022) and O'Neil (2016).

Parliamentary Ombudsman who analyzed the case and then criticized the municipality for not explaining how the algorithm worked.[38] The legality was thus questioned. This situation demonstrates the importance of outlining, in the law, how administrative models function.

Here, the decision taken by the Parliamentary Ombudsman is relevant.[39] The labor union asked for information about how the algorithm makes decisions. To the union's disappointment, their request to get "meaningful information" about the algorithm in question was only addressed briefly in the decision taken by the Parliamentary Ombudsman. Democracy cannot be dependent upon technology, which would be the case if democratic involvement was limited to just the mere technical information of an algorithm. To understand the content and the meaning would be a different thing. A bit surprising is that AI is not mentioned in the national inquiry of 2021, although it covers important legal matters relating to automated decision-making.[40] Would it then be enough to let the EU establish the legal framework for the use of AI? I would say EU regulations would not be adequate—it would be difficult for an initiative at the European level, based on the free movement article", to consider all the dimensions relating to national spheres, especially the constitutional ones.[41]

Automated decision-making has thus recently been legislated for municipalities and counties in Sweden. It remains to be seen if there are sufficient mechanisms to ensure the rule of law and transparency in local and regional contexts. For the individual, it is crucial to have such mechanisms in place. And the legitimacy of the government can be questioned if these requirements are insufficient.

6 Conclusion

To conclude, there are three main points that need to be stressed, namely the challenges for how to legislate technological phenomena, how to handle the rule of law in a pluralistic legal context, and, finally, how to create a holistic approach embracing several facets of the rule of law.

---

[38] JO decision, dnr 6783-2019.

[39] See also Gothenburg Court of Appeal, Kammarratten i Göteborgs dom 2020-02-21 i mål nr 6973-19.

[40] SOU 2021:16 En väl fungerande ordning för val och beslutsfattande i kommuner och regioner.

[41] The legal basis is suggested to be Article 114 TFEU, although in some cases Article 16 TFEU should be the legal basis. Article 16 is thus considered to be *lex specialis* (see para 23 in the preamble of the AI Act).

6.1 Difficulty of Regulating Algorithms, AI, and Related Technological Phenomena

Focusing on the rule of law, and especially the issue of transparency, several problems can occur, as we have seen. If we add to the equation the self-learning aspect of advanced AI, we also have an inherent unpredictability in the situation which essentially precludes full transparency, even from the perspective of those providing the initial programming. In other words, a self-learning, decision-making algorithm may effect changes in relation to a fluid information environment—changes which, at the outset, are in principle unpredictable.

When AI is applied to large-scale opinion formation mechanisms, a great influence is exercised over popular opinion and ultimately parliamentary processes.[42] The European Commission has chosen to refer to "regulatory fitness" as a parameter for explaining why the proposed AI Act has been written as it is. Clear definitions of and explanations about how related rules and legislation should be handled are examples of how we can judge whether the legislation is thoroughly crafted and of high quality. These examples could constitute "regulatory fitness" at its core. But AI is nevertheless a constantly evolving tool which the EU is attempting to regulate in the proposal for an AI Act. This evolving nature of AI makes it difficult to uphold the legislation over time in a consistent manner. Here, a closer study of how a functionality approach to AI could be legislated might have been fruitful. This is underlined when one considers that it is AI systems with high risk that are mainly legislated in the proposal for an AI Act. For the rest, codes of conduct and a more voluntary approach is suggested in the AI Act.

6.2 The Pluralism of Contemporary Law: The Rule of Law at Stake?

The development of contemporary law shows that an increasing number of legislative systems and jurisdictions are dealing with similar questions. This leads to more fragmentation, as more rules regulate the same issue from different perspectives and in different jurisdictions. These disparately located rules sometimes overlap. As we have seen, an increasing number of legislators are involved, and they each represent different jurisdictions (for example, the CoE, the EU, and the Swedish national system). Communication between these actors is not always prioritized, as they all, to a great extent, have supreme constitutional positions in their respective systems. These participating jurisdictions need to reconcile the risk of a blurred divide between the national, international, and supranational spheres but also between what is considered private and public, respectively.

---

[42] Eddebo and Lind (2022), pp. 505–507.

The European Commission has stated that the safeguarding of fundamental rights is a main impetus for the proposed EU AI Act. In a European context, fundamental rights point to a variety of rights, some contested or not easily defined. The rights emanating from the EU treaties are in their constitutional capacity "fundamental," as are free movement rights and rights stated in the EU Charter of Fundamental Rights. Human rights are of course relevant as fundamental rights stated in the Charter, but such rights are also relevant as the European Convention on Human Rights is part of the principles of EU law. Human rights are furthermore codified in the Treaty on European Union.[43] But fundamental as well as human rights are only briefly mentioned in the wording of the AI Act. As these rights, together with the EU's basic values, are designated as a main goal of the AI Act, it is noteworthy that they are not integrated in a more comprehensive manner, nor explained in the wording of the proposal. Human rights for everyone, and especially for minorities and vulnerable groups, are not further explained or prioritized in the proposal, nor are there any special demands on measures for protecting human rights. For equality standards to be met (as part of both human rights and the rule of law), it would be relevant to include mechanisms that work against bias when creating different forms of automated decision-making. And following human rights case law, vulnerable groups and minorities need even more protection and special measures.

6.3 *Striving for a Holistic Approach?*

And what can we take with us to the process of continued work on AI? Law as it is communicated and construed in different jurisdictions, and at different levels of governance, has become more fragmented and pluralistic than in the past. This fragmentation has led to a stronger presence of the constitutional dimensions of law, which in turn integrate the dimensions of power and legitimacy relevant at all levels of legislation and administration and serve as a common denominator of all jurisdictions. This situation is also true for European law and the interplay between European, international, and national law.

To understand and explain these mechanisms and phenomena in relation to AI is however not the sole task of the legal domain. Law needs to interact and communicate with society in many ways; law is mirrored in the changes that occur in society. To explain, make visible, and test future challenges is however an endeavor that in and of itself must, by definition, be multidisciplinary. This deliberation must invite all parts of civil society as far as possible, in the interest of consolidating the foundations of liberal democracy in this transformative period characterized by complex and diverse challenges relating to new technologies.

[43] Also, as part of national identity (Art. 4(2) TEU), Member States' national identities, inherent in their fundamental structures, political and constitutional, should be respected.

One could then wonder if a holistic approach can be achieved by more and stronger administrative structures. As the EU has developed, the distinction between national and European administrations has been blurring or at least changing. The constitutional thought of having separate administrations performing their respective tasks is constantly put to the test. The national authorities acting as European authorities in a national context has been mirrored by European authorities acting as national authorities in the field of data protection. In the AI Act, a new administrative structure has been proposed. A European AI Board will have as its mission to surveil how the AI Act is implemented and additionally, national authorities will contribute to the process and, also, collaborate with each other. In terms of structure, the functioning of the AI Act would thus resemble the structure and functioning of the GDPR. It is stressed in the AI Act that the Act will be subsidiary to the GDPR in this sense, and that data protection rules prevail.

High risks are not only associated with the structures and phenomena of technologies. Technologies can potentially create new risks inherently intertwined in the interactive administrative structures of contemporary law.[44] When administrative rules and principles are combined with human rights, fundamental rights, and constitutional principles, then we might reasonably expect acceptable management of the high risk associated with the use of AI and automated decision-making in administration. The rule of law must oversee and guide the use of algorithms and automation.

References

Beckman L, Hultin Rosenberg J, Jebari K (2022) Artificial intelligence and democratic legitimacy. The problem of publicity in public authority. AI Soc. https://doi.org/10.1007/s00146-022-01493-0

Bull T (2013) Global governance: need for a new theory or the return of an old friend? In: Lind AS, Reichel J (eds) Administrative law beyond the state. Martinus Nijhoff Publishers & Liber, Stockholm, pp 230–239

de Vries K (2022), Introduction. In: de Vries K, Dahlberg M (eds) Law, AI and digitalisation. Iustus förlag, Uppsala

Eddebo J, Lind AS (2022) Artificial intelligence and imperceptible governance via opinion formation: reflections on power and transparency from a cross-disciplinary encounter. In: de Vries K, Dahlberg M (eds) Law, AI and digitalisation. Iustus förlag, Uppsala

Enqvist L, Naarttijärvi M (2021) Administrative independence under EU law: stuck between a rock and Costanzo? Eur Public Law 27:707–732. https://doi.org/10.54648/EURO2021035

Karlander L (2021) Artificiella beslutsfattare i den kommunala förvaltningen. In: Lind AS, Lundin O (eds) Mänskliga rättigheter i det lokala Sverige. Studentlitteratur, Lund, pp 223–232

Karlsson R (2020) Den digitala statsförvaltningen: rättsliga förutsättningar för automatisering, profilering och AI. Förvaltningsrättslig tidskrift:51–80

[44] This is explained by Markku Suksi in his contribution to this volume, when illustrating the procedural, material, and formal dimensions of the rule of law. See also Suksi (2022).

Lind AS (2015) Sweden: free press as a first fundamental right. In: Suksi M et al (eds) First fundamental rights documents in Europe. Intersentia, Antwerp, pp 151–162

O'Neil C (2016) Weapons of math destruction: how big data increases inequality and threatens democracy. Crown Publishers, New York

Sajó A (2011) Constitutional sentiments. Yale University Press, New Haven & London

SOU 2021:16 En väl fungerande ordning för val och beslutsfattande i kommuner och regioner. Statens Offentliga Utredningar, Stockholm

Suksi M (2017) On the openness of the digital society: from religion via language to algorithm as the basis for the exercise of public powers. In: Lind AS et al (eds) Transparency in the future: Swedish openness 250 years. Ragulka förlag, Visby, pp 285–317

Suksi M (2022) Lagbundenhetskravet vid automatiserat beslutsfattande i myndighetsverksamhet enligt finsk rätt. In: de Vries K, Dahlberg M (eds) Law, AI and digitalisation. Iustus förlag, Uppsala, pp 157–177

Algorithms in Public Administration

Legal Implications

Cecilia Magnusson Sjöberg

Abstract A central issue in the establishment of legal automation in public administration concerns the transformation of legal information into digital environments. In this context, regulation of automated decision-making (ADM), machine learning (ML), and artificial intelligence (AI) give rise to several key questions. Legal implications of algorithms of different kinds call for special attention. One distinction to be made has to do with general algorithms on the one hand and (case) specific ones on the other. Often, but not always, transformation of open texture in law (primarily vague and ambiguous concepts) results in legal steering mechanisms resembling what may be referred to as code in a normative way. Furthermore, the rule of law requires awareness of the kind of consequences that come with so-called dynamic (changeable) algorithms, as opposed to the static ones. To a considerable extent, societal development boils down to a quest for proactive law as a supplement to traditional preventive law. Legal infrastructures need to be considered at early stages of system design, development, implementation, and management.

Keywords Algorithms · Administrative law · Artificial intelligence

1 Introduction

Fully- or partly-automated measures are playing an increasingly significant role in today's digitalized society. This particularly applies to the public sector and its agencies where such developments have been in progress for more than three decades. Furthermore, automation has without a doubt also been on the rise in the legal domain.

C. M. Sjöberg (✉)
Faculty of Law, Stockholm University, Stockholm, Sweden
e-mail: cecilia.magnussonsjoberg@juridicum.su.se

M. Suksi (ed.), *The Rule of Law and Automated Decision-Making*,
https://doi.org/10.1007/978-3-031-30142-1_9

The legal framework surrounding this chapter is based within the interdisciplinary field of Law & Informatics,[1] supplemented primarily by national studies of a multidisciplinary character. This chapter will address some Information and Communications Technology (ICT) Law issues, although to a limited degree. A broader perspective would have addressed law not only in interaction with administrative procedure law, but also with intellectual property rights,[2] competition law, European law, and other areas of law. Here, however, public law will be the main focus of our attention.

Over the years, a highly valuable interplay has evolved between these academic and legal disciplines and the associated methods—including law in practice—for studies of different kinds, not least in the context of various learning activities.[3] At the same time, legal scholars have acted as a driving force in many fruitful, innovative projects, discussions, and other initiatives spurring collaboration between science in general and law in various digital research environments.

With a few exceptions, this chapter does not include in-depth overviews and analyses of current legislative actions or developments on the digital market and in other sectors of artificial intelligence (AI) activity. [4] Rather, it aims to illuminate the current state of affairs on legal automation, primarily in the public sector. The overall aim of this chapter is to open up a discussion for transfer of knowledge and experiences from legal informatics into related digital environments. The jurisdictions subsequently covered fall within the scope of the European Union (EU). In the EU, there is a growing interest to include legal scholars in a wide variety of EU projects, for instance, for positions in both internal and external legal advisory boards. A consequence of this has been the development of a kind of hybrid legislation, given the well-known impact that the EU has had upon national regulatory actions.

The title of this chapter, "Algorithms in public administration—legal implications," was chosen to indicate a technological approach beyond what are typically considered to be conventional personhoods. An algorithm can roughly be described as a mechanism for (structured, step-by step) problem solving. To simplify, a cooking recipe can also be conceived of as an algorithm. From the area of law, we find an example based on the principle of openness (and the required conditions for a document to qualify as a public official document), and this is the approach that we will investigate somewhat further in the context of algorithmic decision-making. In this part of the book the focus will be upon digital citizenship as it currently exists in the format of digital environments,[5] where access to justice is contingent upon some

---

[1] Magnusson Sjöberg (2021a, b).

[2] See, e.g., Westman (2021).

[3] See, e.g., Carlsson et al. (2017).

[4] See, for instance, the (recent) political agreement on the Digital Markets Act, 2020/0374(COD).

[5] For instance, developments in Estonia concerning e-residency for entrepreneurial purposes are interesting. See https://www.e-resident.gov.ee/ (accessed on 9 September 2022).

kind of membership or other legal status,[6] i.e., proven qualifications to gain official recognition. More precisely, we could distinguish between natural persons and legal persons, and imagine that there are digital persons.[7]

Furthermore, technology is often referred to as neutral, i.e., neither good nor bad from a humanitarian point of view. Still—if the rule of law is to be upheld[8]—attention must at least be paid to the following technological and societal developments. To begin, there is the emergence of legal automation, then there is the transformation of legal information into digital environments, and the regulation of core automation and AI.

With the reasoning above in mind, a few more items can be put on a legal wish list. Advantages from the above-mentioned developments can be related to more proactive and preventive law (instead of merely traditional reactive law). ICT-adjusted legislation (revised legislative techniques) is also interesting, as would be a right to file a complaint over administrative applications (applications including algorithms) in terms of a modern view of administrative law. Finally, there lies a potential to digitalize the welfare state more rapidly (a sector-wise approach has potential). In this context, critical success factors are, particularly, AI and machine learning.

2 Emergence of Legal Automation

An important starting point is that there is no formal definition of "legal automation" as such. Instead, this term is commonly used in reference to legal issues that appear when ICT is used wholly or partly without human intervention. Adding to the picture is the widespread metaphor of the computer being merely a tool, like any other device. However, this view proves to be too narrow in practice. As it turns out, ICT often serves as a comprehensive steering mechanism—a fact that calls for attention, not least in the context of legal safety (legal compliance). This is particularly relevant when software in the form of computer programs (code) is used as a means for decision-making in the setting of mass administration and/or supervision. Mention could also be made of the digitalization of social insurance, social security, taxation, and study administration at universities. Legal automation also takes the form of embedded technical standards for production of legal information, e.g., preparatory

[6] For instance, Personal Identification Number and Coordination Numbers.

[7] See further Kurki (2019). See also Magnusson Sjöberg (2020).

[8] For an updated general discussion, see Suksi (2022). It can be noted that the legal situation varies somewhat between Finland and Sweden, the latter having formally accepted legal automation (Sect. 28 in the Swedish Administrative Procedure Act), while it is based on practice in the former, at least until 2023, when legislation concerning automated decision-making is expected to be in place. At the same time, digitalization is in Finland as in other Scandinavian countries a well-established characteristic of modern e-government.

works, legislation, and settled court cases. Another example of legal automation is legal document management and long-term storage in e-archives.[9] Lastly, but not least, legal compliance as regards information security also requires steering mechanisms.

Despite recent noteworthy developments, legal automation is not a new technological feature within the legal domain. On the contrary, we can find Nordic initiatives dating back several decades. As an example, the Swedish Working Party for Electronic Data Processing and Law was established in Stockholm in 1968. During the 1970s and 1980s, a number of academic dissertations and public reports were presented and defended, opening up discussions about, for instance, the legality of digital administrative decisions.

When technologies evolve, so do the risks for mistakes resulting in erroneous administrative decisions. The 1980s revealed particular challenges in attempts to acknowledge the rule of law in the digital legal domain. Responsible actors were eager to find both advantages and disadvantages of modern computing activities at the time.

Similar discussions developed throughout the 1990s, and the number of academic dissertations also increased, enlightened by earlier attempts at AI being applied in the form of "expert systems," as they are called, taking advantage of the tacit knowledge provided by "knowledge engineers," as they can be called. At the start of the new millennium, AI was adding value to old-fashioned automation. The current situation has been captured well in the work of the Royal Swedish Academy of Engineering Sciences,[10] where a major finding has been the importance of time and rapid actions as a critical success factor. What the future will bring, however, remains to be seen.[11]

In summary, legal automation can be described as a network of applications, almost like a decision tree,[12] in which the surrounding rules and regulations in force for each application are of particular interest. Here, a distinction should be made between public legal automation and private legal automation. To give an example, the legal conditions for personal data processing vary considerably between so-called data controllers in the private sector and those in the public sector.[13]

---

[9] On the topic of legal developments regarding backup copies in the public sector, see the Supreme Administrative Court Case number 4905-21, 1 April 2022.

[10] Kungliga Ingenjörsvetenskapsakademien (2022).

[11] There is no lack of political ambition. See, e.g., Department of Infrastructure (2021). See also Digitaliseringsrättsutredningen (2018).

[12] In fact, the Swedish Ombudsman (JO) has in a decision (Decision of 9 June 2021, dnr 6783-2019) pointed at the legal implications of a decision tree and its availability as a service on the part of a municipality. Unfortunately, JO did not make any assessments with regard to the principle of openness and right of access to official documents including digital recordings.

[13] Regulation (EU) 2016/679 of the European Parliament and of the Council of 27 April 2016 on the protection of natural persons with regard to the processing of personal data and on the free movement of such data, and repealing Directive 95/46/EC (General Data Protection Regulation). See also Proposal for a Regulation of the European Parliament and of the Council on harmonised rules on fair access to and use of data (Data Act) COM(2022) 68 final.

This need not be more complex than the common division of the legal field into the two major areas public and private law. When it comes to public legal automation, it is also important to separate administrative legal automation taking place in public agencies from judicial legal automation taking place in courts. Furthermore, federal legal automation[14] may differ from municipal legal automation. Unfortunately, this has been the situation of legal automation in Sweden. However, the legality of automation in Swedish municipalities has been quite unclear, which poses a challenge to the rule of law. Therefore, it is most rewarding to find that the Swedish lawmaker has amended applicable law as of 1 July 2022, thus formally laying the legal foundation for automated administration also in the municipal area.[15] As already indicated, legal automation has been a widely-used tool of public administration in other Nordic countries, too.

3 Transformation of Legal Information into Digital Environments

Legal automation requires the transformation of legally relevant information into code. Some sources can be more relevant for a particular application, while others can be less relevant. The selection process is comprised of both traditional legal sources and new ones, such as certain software components, commonly code (computer programs). The selection of sources is furthermore governed by the fact that legal rules are commonly expressed in natural (human) language, while computers run on artificial programming language (code). The rule transformation is based on an understanding of the open textures that characterize legal texts. More precisely, the rule transformation often concerns vague criteria that are being transformed into strict criteria. Sometimes, the transformation is trivial, but other times, it can be quite complex. Consider the difficulty of coding a concept such as "a reasonable standard of living" in the context of social services, and then compare that task with coding a fixed sum as applied by a taxation agency.

Ambiguities in law may complicate matters even further. To improve the quality of automated decision support, processes of categorization would likely be helpful. The underlying idea is that while some forms of transformation are trivial, others will

[14]This is a reference to what can be a national federal state and its regulatory framework that to some extent can be supplemented by means of municipal legislation. Being an EU Member State is of importance when Directives are to be implemented and rules should be followed.

[15]On municipal legal automation and a recently implemented new governing legal framework, see further Utredningen om en väl fungerande ordning för val och beslutsfattande i kommuner och regioner (2021). By government proposal Prop. 2021/22:125 a revision of the general Municipalities Act (2017:725) has clarified matters so that legal automation as a major rule is permitted as of 1 July 2022 (Act 2022:638) in Chapter 6, Section 37, according to which a municipal committee may delegate its decision-making power to the presidium, a sub-committee, a member or to an automated decision-making function.

be much more advanced and demanding. One example here could be a minor financial transaction connected to an assessment of the right to national citizenship. Considering the diversity of public sector administration, five more precise categories (variables) can be extracted. Copying of the data to be transformed is the trivial case. Translation comes next, and then adjustment. Expanding represents a fourth category. Lastly, there is the situation where the transformation results in new (normative) information.

4 Regulation of Core Automation and AI

Now let us turn our attention to legal algorithms introduced into public administration. This highlights certain aspects of digitalization that can be briefly explained as structures for problem solving of various kinds. There is a need for categorization of different types of algorithms, so as not to simplify the analysis to a scope that is too limited. Simply put, there is a fundamental difference between algorithms generally applied within, for instance, taxation, social insurance, and study administration at universities, and algorithms adjusted to individual cases. Another aspect of digitalization concerns the time factor expressed in terms of algorithms emanating from the past, the present, and (presumably) the future.

Incidentally, the author of this text has recently experienced personal consequences of algorithm-related, erroneous legal automation in the area of taxation.[16] The case in question reflects the importance of both efficiency and the rule of law in modern information society. More precisely, the issue concerned the legal conditions and procedures of (Swedish) income tax.[17]

In the tax declaration, an income amounting to SEK 909 090 was correctly reported. The Taxation Agency, however, made a digital mistake and a figure of SEK 9 091 090 was instead registered by the system. From a taxpayer's point of view, it was an unpleasant surprise (to say the least) to receive a formal taxation decision based on such a large amount. Why was there no check on whether the outcome of the system running was at all reasonable? Why were the incorrect figures not removed as soon as it became known to the agency that a technical misinterpretation had taken place in the digital environment? Was it really necessary to wait for a new taxation decision (Swe: *omprövningsbeslut*) instead of accomplishing an immediate response to the error?

Additionally, according to the Taxation Agency, it was not possible to receive an expeditious rectifying measure. When the approximately SEK 8 million fault was

[16] See further the now rather old notifications by the Swedish Ombudsman on erroneous tax charges, JO om felaktiga skattekrav—synpunkter på några viktiga rutiner i skatteuppbörd och indrivningsverksamhet, 1982:S 3.

[17] More on the Swedish Tax Authority, see https://www.skatteverket.se/servicelankar/otherlanguages/inenglish.4.12815e4f14a62bc048f4edc.html (accessed on 27 October 2022).

discovered, this error still could not be corrected right away. The rectifying measure was delayed until a new declaration was filed, although there was no doubt about the applicability of personal data processing legislation that could have been used for rectification. Adding to this unsatisfactory process is the fact that a public official document, one that includes personal data, has also been generated and disseminated. Presently there are still core national transaction systems that are unable to meet the very fundamental issues of safe legal automation.

The text that follows next continues a brief overview of algorithmic decision-making, including challenges and steps forward. The overall perspective is still the rule of law and how algorithms require the engagement of not only tech experts, but also legal scholars. Among the crucial factors are transparency,[18] equality, and predictability. From a legal analytical perspective, algorithms must be understood both narrowly (individually customized) and broadly (generally applicable). Expressed in another way, there is a distinction to be made between models and algorithmic code.

Furthermore, a critical issue concerns the foundations for traditional legal automation on the one hand, and the foundations of the design of AI applications on the other. These respective foundations consist of datasets of different kinds. A common starting point for conventional legal automation is traditional legal sources, such as legislative material, e.g., government bills, laws at various hierarchical levels, settled court cases, administrative decisions, and EU law. This grows more challenging when different stakeholders request the inclusion of other governance materials in system design, development, implementation, and management. In short: who has the right—or authority—to select legal information?

Recent developments include the European Commission's proposal for a regulation with harmonized rules on AI: the EU AI Act.[19] Particularly, the proposed definitions of so-called training data (Article 29), validation data (Article 30), and testing data (Article 31), with associated model(s), call for attention in a discourse of the kind found in this volume. The number of normative rules embedded in the proposal—and its explanatory memorandum, recitals, articles, and annexes—is very large. The reference to Annex I in the Commission proposal below serves as an illustration.

[18] See further, e.g., Dexe (2022).

[19] Proposal for a regulation of the European Parliament and of the Council laying down harmonized rules on artificial intelligence (Artificial Intelligence Act) and amending certain Union legislative acts, COM(2021) 206 final. The AI Act proposal is likely to have undergone modifications at the point when it is enacted into law. See Presidency compromise text of 29 November 2021, https://data.consilium.europa.eu/doc/document/ST-14278-2021-INIT/en/pdf (accessed on 22 August 2022) and Second Presidency compromise text of 15 July 2022 (11124/22; Interinstitutional File: 2021/0106(COD), at: https://artificialintelligenceact.eu/wp-content/uploads/2022/07/AIA-CZ-1st-Proposal-15-July.pdf (accessed on 25 August 2022). The modifications are likely to impact on the contents of what is written here about Article 3 and Annex I of the proposal.

One line of criticism during the evaluation of the proposal pertained to the vast number of legal definitions that it includes. Here is one definition as an illustration:

> Title 1, General provisions, Article 3
>
> Definitions (44), e.g.,
>
> AI-systems (Article 1)
>
> 'artificial intelligence system' (AI system) means software that is developed with one or more of the techniques and approaches listed in Annex I and can, for a given set of human-defined objectives, generate outputs such as content, predictions, recommendations, or decisions influencing the environments they interact with;

Without going into much detail, it can be said that the regulatory methodology boils down to a so-called risk-based approach. Humanity has not yet succeeded in regulating technologies, nor properly integrating them into society. Will we be better off this time, based on the following grading scale?

Unacceptable risk—Banned use of algorithms
High-risk—Strict obligations for the use of algorithms
Limited risk—Awareness in the use of algorithms
Minimal risk—Free use of algorithms

There are many challenges to be addressed when introducing algorithms into public administration, as this gives rise to both constraints and possibilities, as well as considerations about traditional automation versus AI, and legacy versus innovation. The conclusion must be that legal frameworks, including some limited case law, may supplement legal informatics by means of substantive ICT law, particularly in reference to data protection, openness and secrecy, administrative law, record management in digital archives, and information security. Additionally, there is the importance of adequate professional skills[20] in connection with the design, implementation, and management of legal algorithms in public administration. Both interdisciplinary and multidisciplinary expertise are valuable in such digitalization.

To illuminate this reasoning, a section of the proposed AI Act is included below:

> ANNEX I
>
> ARTIFICIAL INTELLIGENCE TECHNIQUES AND APPROACHES referred to in Article 3, point 1
>
> (a) Machine learning approaches, including supervised, unsupervised and reinforcement learning, using a wide variety of methods including deep learning;
> (b) Logic- and knowledge-based approaches, including knowledge representation, inductive (logic) programming, knowledge bases, inference and deductive engines, (symbolic) reasoning and expert systems;
> (c) Statistical approaches, Bayesian estimation, search and optimization methods.

[20] This footnote highlights the importance of not only working with already skilled people but also beginners. A common misunderstanding is that all legal automation nowadays is based on AI which is not true. Instead, most ICT support is applied by way of conventional data support. This distinction might matter during procurement of applications.

When adopting new business models, it is important to balance pros and cons in response to any obvious shortcomings. One approach that has been suggested by the EU is commonly called "Trustworthy AI."[21] This term refers to critical success factors for innovation, among other things. More precisely, it can be described in terms of value-based AI being built on well-founded or unfounded trust. Another approach to balance advantages and disadvantages of new technology can be linked to the rule of law, with components such as foreseeability, equality, and transparency. Legal aspects of information security must also be considered. Here, we are primarily concerned with confidentiality, integrity, and availability.

In future research, we can anticipate much more comprehensive and in-depth analyses of legal algorithms that have been introduced into the public sector. One major distinction that should be highlighted is, as already pointed out, the one between general algorithms on the one hand and individual algorithms on the other (see above).

Narrowing the scope somewhat, we can find examples of both types of algorithm emanating from Swedish national administrative law (SFS 2017:900), taking its starting point in Government Bill 2016/17:180, entitled *En modern och rättssäker förvaltning—ny förvaltningslag* [A modern administration based on the rule of law—a new Administrative Procedure Act]. Without making any further specifications, the legislation (formally) permits the use of automated decision-making (Section 28). In this context, it is important to keep in mind the EU's General Data Protection Regulation's (GDPR) provisions on automated decision-making (Article 22) and profiling (Article 4.4). In some cases, these Articles can have implications, especially in interaction with national supplementary legislation. In Sweden, there are approximately 200 rules and regulations of this kind that need to be considered to get the full regulatory picture.

Considering the regulatory complexity and complications, it is worthwhile to briefly reflect upon how algorithms were initially introduced into public administration in Sweden. This implementation began with a question by many stakeholders decades ago of whether machines could be misled, and the answer was no. At the same time, it was debated whether automated decisions were valid in each case. In practice, the lack of regulation did not stop public agencies from digitalizing activities (see above), primarily within the areas of social insurance, social security, taxation, study administration, and environmental matters (see above). To a limited extent, certain cases were actually governed by special rules stating that decisions about, for instance, congestion tax or traffic offenses were to be made wholly or partly by automatic means.

A next major step was when the lawmaker decided to permit automated administrative decisions, as laid down in Section 28 of the Administrative Procedure Act. However, it is important to note that the rules in the Administrative Procedure Act are subsidiary in relation to the approximately 200 so-called national register laws

[21] Ethics Guidelines for Trustworthy AI (2019). High-Level Expert Group on Artificial Intelligence. European Commission, Brussels.

covering rules about personal data processing. Furthermore, Article 22 in the GDPR states the boundaries of automated individual decision-making including profiling (Article 4.4). The GDPR does not state a clear yes or no regarding the practice of legal automation. Over the years that the GDPR has been in force, it has given rise to quite intrinsic discussions on whether a data subject has a right not to be exposed at all to automated decisions, or whether he or she rather has a right to claim exceptions with reference to whether the protection is good enough in the supplementing rules that Swedish national law offer.

5 New Legal Infrastructures

To achieve good legal system management, the notion of infrastructure can be useful to reflect upon. The starting point is an understanding that society as a whole comprises both hard and soft infrastructures. In this context, law evidently refers to legal infrastructures, i.e., those parts of a legal system that form the bases and conditions for the rule of law in digital environments. Generally, this includes wholly or partly automated data processing, electronic documentation instead of paper-based hard copy, and mobile communication instead of landline-based communication.

To further elaborate upon the notion of infrastructures in the legal domain—or what can be referred to as legally relevant ICT features—the categories of these types of infrastructures should be briefly expanded upon. First, there is conventional software, that gives rise to issues concerning the transformation of legal information into code. Next, there are database technologies that serve as a basis for information retrieval, and the question of how to apply and evaluate recall and precision, given a certain coverage.[22] There are also information standards that require standpoints being taken concerning document structures and record linkages. Without going into further detail, mention should also be made of technologies and applications framed by AI, machine learning, cloud and edge computing, and social media. In short, this concerns the impact of machine intervention versus human intervention during decision-making. Such digital approaches and tools are not new. On the contrary, issues of this kind began to emerge several decades ago. Eventually, there will be yet other layers that arise hand in hand with, for instance, trust and power of information. From an infrastructural perspective or, if one would prefer, a power perspective, the attributes or practices that could be identified are marketing, ownership, and commercialization. And once again it is important to remember that the conditions for data collection and data management vary between the public and the private sector.

[22] Commonly the term *coverage* is used within the area of language technologies. In the legal domain, measurements concern for instance court cases and other factors, but it can also be used to reflect commercial activities.

Another important distinction concerns decision support systems versus decision-making systems. On legal consequences, deterministic (static) algorithms differ from dynamic algorithms. It is important to be aware of how matters of system design also differ between private and public sector solutions. Additionally, there are some differences between system development within the civil law system and the common law system.[23] From a holistic point of view, there are more legal constraints governing public system design, e.g., administrative procedure law. Furthermore, case law has a more fundamental standing in common law compared with civil law and the concentration of the latter on rules and regulations. When concluding what the law means in a certain situation, there is evidently a need for a legal method. This applies not only in traditional manual environments but also under digital conditions. The challenges can appear rapidly. For instance, who has the authority to state that a given court case is relevant when interpreting another one? A closely-related problem concerns linking. As every legal scholar knows, merely indicating a connection between two legal sources results in interpretation. This brings us to the classic issue of whether a legal source of some kind is relevant or not, or rather more or less relevant. There is no definite answer, so discussion will go on.

Here are a few final words on the future developments in the area of law and AI. First, the digitalization of society gives rise to new roles shaping the law.[24] More precisely, we can see the introduction of (a) legal developers, (b) privacy protectors, (c) data openers, (d) technology interpreters, and (e) security agents.[25] Tentatively a legal developer is someone who has taken or been given a role in the context of the transformation of software into law. From the tech side, we could imagine a person with an academic exam, a certificate, and other qualifications. From the legal side, we could accept similar qualifications. Of major importance is the acknowledgment of transformation itself and the need for skills to handle open texture in law so that the rule of law would not be hampered. Privacy protectors work with personal data and how such personalized data may be processed. Quite a few future tasks will be similar to what already exists today, but not entirely. For instance, would a privacy protector always reason in favor of the data subject, not at all taking other stakeholders' needs, such as researchers, into consideration? In contrast, data openers would always defend freedom of information and expression. That being the case, the Swedish principle of openness dating back to 1766 has a safe place in the law. The overall idea is that despite data being freely accessible, it might be easier said than done to extract the data due to regulatory complexity and other complications. Therefore, professional support for how to carry out record linkages are increasingly

[23] On ICT Law in the context of the common law system, see, for instance, Ashley (2017) and Murray (2019).

[24] Issues related to professional roles emanating from digitalization are well known also going back in time. Here is one example: Magnusson (1990).

[25] In Swedish, this list would read: *rättsutvecklare, integritetsskyddare, dataöppnare, tekniktolkar och säkerhetsagenter*. The idea and selection of this new group (categories) of potentially skilled workers in the Digitalised society was provided by Cecilia Magnusson Sjöberg. Kungliga Ingenjörsvetenskapsakademien (2022).

attractive. Technology interpreter is yet another role evolving in the future. The basis of their activities is traditional administrative procedure law. A non-Swedish speaking party would have the right to interpretation. Now, why should the right to interpretation not also be the case when it comes to technology and law? This would be particularly interesting within such legal frameworks such as the GDPR (see below). Lastly, the security perspective must also be considered. A security agent is someone who particularly maintains confidentiality, integrity, and accountability without being formally obliged to do so; an example of a security agent could be a regular office worker who has access to, or views, sensitive information.

It will be important to clarify the expectations of each role as regards proactive law (and possibly stronger preventive law), as opposed to the more traditional reactive law.[26] In the 1990s, politicians were quite active when it came to modern technologies. One rather spectacular approach initiated by *Toppledarforum* (Top Leaders)[27] at the time was to design and develop a completely new legal toolbox for Swedish constitutional acts, such as the Freedom of the Press Act, the Secrecy Act, the Instrument of Government, and the like, as if there was no legacy at all that stems from historical evolution.[28] These attempts were not successful. Simply put, the mindset of the Working Party was not adapted to successfully deal with the assignment. Actually, the overall ambition of the Working Party was almost spectacular beyond reason (no legacy). The important point that was made clear was how easy it is to complain about current legislation and how difficult it is to come up with new alternative rules. In other words, the lawmaker deserves respect also in our modern society despite not always getting a grip on regulatory management. Interestingly, in the 1990s, algorithmic decision-making was not explicitly addressed in combination with regulatory sandboxes;[29] such decision-making might, however, become the response to dissatisfaction with lawmaking of our time.

One critical success factor remains to be mentioned. This has to do with certain practically-oriented insights about legal system management. Based on theoretical studies and practical experiences, at least three major aspects can be extracted. First, it is important to understand that digitalization is seldom finalized—rather, it will usually continue interminably. This has to do with the fact that system design, development, implementation, and management are intrinsically ongoing activities. Therefore, to succeed, it is necessary to proactively prepare for long-term routines both of a technological and a manual character. Second, there is also a pedagogical aspect concerning when, how, and by whom this kind of information should be

[26] See further Stockholm Institute for Scandinavian Law (2006).

[27] *Toppledarforum* can during this time be described as a Working Party for development of the public sector. The so-called Lexit subgroup has been especially interesting from a legal point of view: Lexit 1995 Prestudy IT 2005 and Post Lexit including a legal panel, 1997. The equivalent of today is different activities on behalf of the Swedish Agency for Digital Government (DIGG) including a forum for top leaders, https://digigov.se/.

[28] In Swedish: *tryckfrihetsförordningen*, *sekretesslagen* and *regeringsformen*.

[29] The notion of regulatory sandboxes can roughly be explained as a protected digital environment where different tests are carried under the supervision of legal experts and ICT-professionals.

conveyed among those who participate in e-government from the suppliers' side. For instance, lawyers may—for better or worse—have quite different styles of problem solving. Some push, others pull. Similarly, when one wishes to keep the doctor away, one might opt for safe solutions (take the medicine), rather than taking a chance (sticking to coffee and tea). Evidently, this is similar to saying that engaging a lawyer (temporarily or permanently) does not solve legal issues per se. Third, there is a need for legal methods beyond the traditional legal sources (such as legislation and settled court cases), opening the door for the use of software and AI.[30] When digitalization is on the agenda, there is a need to weigh competing interests of different kinds. More precisely, advantages as well as disadvantages associated with ICT are commonly scrutinized. Such deliberations often take the shape of privacy vs. efficiency, the rule of law vs. trust, and software vs. printed material (see above). Collaboration and cooperation between lawyers and ICT developers has become more common, and at the same time, platforms and processes such as Future of Democracy—which organizes annual summits, among many other initiatives—are becoming more important.[31]

References

Ashley KD (2017) Artificial intelligence and legal analytics: new tools for law practice in the digital age. Cambridge University Press, Cambridge

Carlsson L, Magnusson Sjöberg C, Papadopoulou F (2017) The wired world of university teaching: legal challenges. ExTuto Publishing, Copenhagen

Crawford K (2021) Atlas of AI: power, politics, and the planetary costs of artificial intelligence. Yale University Press, New Haven and London

Department of Infrastructure (2021) Uppdrag att främja offentlig förvaltnings förmåga att använda artificiell intelligens [Assignment to promote the public sector's ability to use artificial intelligence], Dnr I2021/01825

Dexe J (2022) Transparent but incomprehensible. Investigating the relation between transparency, explanations, and usability in automated decision-making. Doctoral Thesis in Human-computer interaction, KTH Royal Institute of Technology, Stockholm

Digitaliseringsrättsutredningen (2018) Juridik som stöd för förvaltningens digitalisering. Betänkande av Digitaliseringsrättsutredningen [Law as support for administrative digitalisation. A report from the Digitalisation Law Inquiry], Swedish Government Official Report (SOU) 2018:25

Häggström O (2021) Tänkande maskiner: den artificiella intelligensens genombrott. Fri Tanke, Stockholm

[30] Much has been written—positive as well as negative—about artificial intelligence and modern technological societies. The approach varies considerably from one author to another. Here are some titles to illuminate this: Zuboff (2019), Crawford (2021), Häggström (2021), and Magnusson Sjöberg (2021a, b).

[31] Mention can be made that the first keynote in 2021 was by the author of this contribution. See: https://www.futureofdemocracy.se/summit-2021 (accessed on 29 August 2022).

Kungliga Ingenjörsvetenskapsakademien (2022) Digitalisering i välfärden: dagsläge och framtid. Rapport från IVA:s projekt Digitalisering – möjliggörare i framtidens välfärd, 2022. Tema: Människa – Teknik – Samhälle. Kungliga Ingenjörsvetenskapsakademien (IVA), Stockholm

Kurki VAJ (2019) A theory of legal personhood. Oxford University Press, Oxford

Magnusson C (1990) New roles in the shaping of the law. In: Seipel P (ed) From data protection to knowledge machines: the study of law and informatics. Computer/Law Series 5. Kluwer Law and Taxation Publishers, Deventer, pp 135–165

Magnusson Sjöberg C (2020) The digital person – a new legal entity? On the role of law in an AI-based society. In: Corrales Compagnucci M, Forgó N, Kono T, Teramoto S, Vermeulen EPM (eds) Legal tech and the new sharing economy. Springer, Kyushu, pp 49–59

Magnusson Sjöberg C (2021a) Legal AI from a privacy point of view: data protection and transparency in focus. In: Petersson S (ed) Digital human sciences. Stockholm University Press, Stockholm, pp 181–202. https://doi.org/10.16993/bbk.h

Magnusson Sjöberg C (ed) (2021b) Rättsinformatik: juridiken i det digitala informationssamhället, 4th edn. Studentlitteratur, Lund

Murray A (2019) Information technology law, 4th edn. Oxford University Press, Oxford

Stockholm Institute for Scandinavian Law (2006) Scandinavian studies in law, 49 a proactive approach. https://www.scandinavianlaw.se/49-a-proactive-approach-may-2006/. Accessed 30 June 2022

Suksi M (2022) Lagbundenhetskravet vid automatiserat beslutsfattande i myndighetsverksamhet enligt finsk rätt. In: de Vries K, Dahlberg M (eds) Law, AI and digitalisation. Iustus, Uppsala, pp 157–178

Utredningen om en väl fungerande ordning för val och beslutsfattande i kommuner och regioner (2021) En väl fungerande ordning för val och beslutsfattande i kommuner och regioner [A well-functioning order for elections and decision-making in municipalities and regions], Swedish Government Official Report (SOU) 2021:16

Westman D (2021) AI, big data och upphovsrätten. In: Magnusson Sjöberg C (ed) Rättsinformatik: juridiken i det digitala informationssamhället, 4th edn. Studentlitteratur, Lund, pp 639–668

Zuboff S (2019) The age of surveillance capitalism: the fight for a human future at the new frontier of power. Public Affairs, New York

Concluding Reflections on the Digitalization of Government Functions Through Automated Decision-Making, with Some Wider AI Issues

Markku Suksi

Abstract It appears that society is undergoing a paradigm shift due to digitalization and automation. The increasing use of automated procedures poses a significant challenge to the rule of law; accordingly, law-makers have become more active in regulating algorithmic systems in different ways. With new, dynamic ideas being formulated about how to regulate such systems, the professions needed in the future are also still in their inception. The growing importance of automated systems of decision-making, together with the increasing sophistication of different software, may start to dominate decision-making and different procedures in society in a manner that is not necessarily in consonance with the principles of the rule of law, at least in the relationship between public authorities and individuals. In the private sphere, the use of advanced AI technologies has been subject to less regulation than in public decision-making, but the impact of the use of algorithmic systems in the private sphere has the potential to overshadow even the traditional role of public authorities.

Keywords Automated decision-making · Rule of law · Paradigm shift · AI legislation · AI professions

"Paradigm shift" is a familiar concept in most fields of science. Usually, this term refers to a profound change in a field of science, i.e., that the foundations of scientific perception and activity are fundamentally altered. For at least the past 15 years, we have been in the midst of a paradigm shift that affects not only one field of science, but several fields of science simultaneously—and society as a whole. Some of the most significant technological developments today come in the form of increasing dependence on algorithmic systems used to control everything from mobile phones, to heating systems, to various stock market transactions around the globe. Furthermore, Spotify's algorithm has the ability to suggest what music I might like, Google seems to predict what searches I am conducting, and Amazon promotes the book I

M. Suksi (✉)
School of Law, Åbo Akademi University, Turku/Åbo, Finland
e-mail: markku.suksi@abo.fi

M. Suksi (ed.), *The Rule of Law and Automated Decision-Making*,
https://doi.org/10.1007/978-3-031-30142-1_10

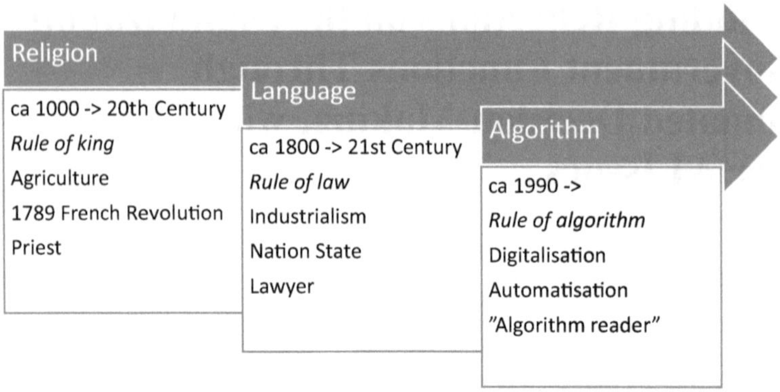

Fig. 1 Paradigm shifts (source: Suksi 2017, p. 291)

might want to read next. Online news outlets, many of which used to be available in paper and ink, also seem to mysteriously know what commercials might be relevant to me right now, and subsequent models of news and information companies may soon rely upon the production of content tailored to the individual reader, or "consumer" depending on one's view. The self-reinforcing bubbles in social media have likewise been gaining traction for over a decade, heightening the chances for manipulation of national elections and referendums. Various digital platforms thus now know an astonishing amount of information about the user. ChatGPT and similar generative algorithmic systems are about to change the way in which texts are produced and various tasks in the working life are carried out.

Theories of digitization and the use of algorithms originated from perhaps as early as the 1960s, but back then, computers were so undeveloped that they were unable to run all the data that would have been needed for the various things that scientists wanted to explore using computing power. Moreover, data in digital form did not exist to the extent that anything sensible could have been made of the limited accumulations of data. It is only in the past two decades that both computers and data sets have reached such levels of sophistication that an efficient use of algorithms can be achieved. But now that the floodgates have opened to an algorithmization of various activities, it appears the technological change is reaching its anticipated seismic proportions: such ongoing change affects the mode of production in society, the way in which society is governed, and all other aspects of society (see Fig. 1).

A first profound paradigm shift took place when agrarian society underwent industrialization, particularly from the nineteenth century to the last half of the twentieth century. Until about the nineteenth century, society had been arranged so that the legitimacy of the exercise of power was based on religion. God gave the temporal power to the king, who exercised power in relation to individuals. In this *Rule of King* (or Rule of God, if you want) agriculture was the dominant mode of production. A central profession in that epoch was that of the priest, who interpreted the will of God—a will that would at the same time be the king's will—and who told what religion required of individuals for them to reach a good life, especially after death. This traditional structure of the exercise of power began to crumble with the French Revolution in 1789, but it took decades before the following paradigm superseded the older one.

The paradigm that followed was, and is today, based upon language and has existed from about the nineteenth century to the present. The norms established in society have followed the principle of the *Rule of Law* and have served as the basis for the industrial mode of production in which the factors of production could be legally separated from the person who owned them, e.g., by founding a limited liability company. The Rule of Law has also been made possible by the nation-state, which generally assumes that society is language-based, and that legislation is usually enacted in a language that creates the legitimacy of the state and of the exercise of state power, preferably based on the election of representatives of the people to a legislative assembly. The central profession that characterizes this paradigm is that of the lawyer, who explains how laws enacted by the lawmakers should be interpreted.

However, as indicated earlier, this language-based legitimacy construct appears to be undergoing a paradigm shift and may be transitioning into a new kind of existence that is increasingly algorithm-based. This development has taken place from about the 1990s and is characterized by an increasing digitization and automation of various functions, both in terms of the mode of production in relation to goods and services, but also in terms of the actions and decisions of public authorities. The legitimacy of governing society in this way is based on the algorithm: computational systems make no mistakes when reading ones and zeros. We do not know yet what the hallmark profession of this new society will be, but for the sake of simplicity, I would venture to call this profession "algorithm reader": a person who can explain to other individuals why the machine did what it did.[1] At the stage when this new, developing paradigm comes to the fore and overtakes the current paradigm, we may be able to talk about a transition from the Rule of Law to *the Rule of Algorithm*. The individual's attachment to algorithms usually results from consent, such as agreement to terms and conditions of an application, to a software license or to the use of personal data for various purposes.

The concept of artificial intelligence (AI) is naturally linked to this new society that is emerging, and different techniques for the use of algorithms and, above all, of different techniques for algorithmic decision-making, are being developed and taken into use. An example of algorithmic decision-making would be when a bank or other credit institution grants loans based on the information entered by the customer on the bank's website in combination with credit and other information that the bank finds in various registers and online. Another example would be when a company recruits staff through the use of AI, when an employer controls the work of

[1] In her chapter in this volume, Cecilia Magnusson Sjöberg singles out five future roles (or new professions) that may fit under the general title of "algorithm reader": legal developers, privacy protectors, data openers, technology interpreters, and security agents.

employees by means of various AI applications or when a self-driving trolley for goods makes its way through the city streets to deliver the goods purchased online, which the online store's algorithm may have recommended to the customer. Facial recognition could also be mentioned, for example, for access control or at larger public events, as well as recognition of emotions by reading faces. China has been a prominent user of facial recognition and emotion recognition, linking these AI traits to a vast amount of other data about the individuals. AI can thus already be used by some authoritarian states to strengthen their own power in relation to individuals.

The use of algorithms can include a wide range of technologies, as demonstrated by the European Union's (EU) original proposal for AI legislation, which enumerates such technologies. The two main groups of algorithmic decision-making that we can identify are rule-based algorithmic systems and algorithmic systems based on machine learning. AI usually means algorithmic systems that use machine learning as the method to come to the conclusion about some matter. It is this machine learning AI that we experience when we use Spotify, Google, Amazon, and others that try to predict, for example, our preferred music, the questions we want to ask, or the books we would like to order. AI systems that use machine learning are often based on the so-called Bayesian statistics, which differ from traditional statistics (but also fuzzy methods and soft computing may be possible). The subtlety of Bayesian statistics comes from the fact that they can make accurate forecasts of future behavior based on a large amount of information about past behavior. Rule-based systems, on the other hand, may not constitute AI in the strict sense, as rule-based systems do not attempt to emulate human intelligence, nor predict anything, although they actually can emulate subsumption.

In the private sector, the use of algorithmic decision-making methods, or algorithmic support for decision-making, have been relatively unrestrained by overarching legal principles of a constitutional nature. The main limitation on the use of algorithmic systems in the private sector is the principle of non-discrimination, a principle which is rooted not only generally in humanity but also in international law and, above all, national constitutional law. The principle of non-discrimination is needed to counteract, inter alia, the so-called algorithmic bias, i.e., biases in algorithmic decision-making that favor certain persons or treat other persons in a disadvantageous way.

In the public sector, things are much different. Constitutions impose many specific requirements on ordinary human decision-making, and the starting point is that at least the same requirements that apply to human decision-makers should also apply to algorithmic decision-makers, perhaps even more so. But at the same time, there is something that can drive digitalization and automated decision-making in the public sector and encourage this development, namely the requirements of efficiency and even explicit requirements of speedy decision-making, as is the case in Section 21 of the Constitution of Finland. Combined with scarce tax revenue for the state and municipalities, the requirement of decision-making without delay means that the automation of various decision-making procedures of a mass nature is an obvious area where this new way to decide matters can be developed and expanded. It is also possible to reduce government expenditures, by using algorithmic decision-making to replace large numbers of human administrators who would otherwise need to be employed to handle large numbers of individual cases.

In fact, both the Social Insurance Institution of Finland (SII) and the Tax Administration of Finland have pioneered the use of automated decision-making procedures in Finland: the SII has certain automated decision-making procedures, including decisions on the renewal of student financial aid. The Finnish Tax Administration likewise utilizes similar automated tools. It is undeniably quicker to process documents using such tools, but these processes are by no means problem-free: the Deputy Parliamentary Ombudsman has examined some of the Tax Administration's automated decision-making systems and has come to the conclusion that these systems lack legal basis and are therefore unconstitutional. The Chancellor of Justice has also reviewed a number of automated decision-making systems within the SII and concluded that these systems do not meet the requirements of the Constitution either. What is common is that these supervisors of legality have found unlawfulness of various kinds in the use of automated decision-making. They call for legislation on automated decision-making. Such legislation has also been required by the Constitutional Law Committee of the Parliament of Finland, which in five opinions has taken a critical approach to various aspects of automated decision-making proposed by the Government for various governmental functions, such as the handling of personal data by the Migration Administration.

The Constitutional Law Committee's criticism of automated decision-making in the Government proposals particularly concerns circumstances such as shortcomings in the implementation of principles of good government laid down in Section 21 of the Constitution, uncertainties with the transparency of automated decision-making in light of Section 12 of the Constitution (freedom of expression and right of access to information), and the concretization of the responsibilities under Section 118 of the Constitution, about liability of public servants, that should apply to all decision-making activities, including algorithmic ones.

At the same time, it is clear that the Constitutional Law Committee would like a more holistic approach in relation to the regulation of this new technology for decision-making. It is not enough to include various provisions on automated decision-making in substance legislation, but the Committee expects that general administrative law legislation on automated decision-making will be created, such general legislation that ensures good government, legal responsibilities and accountability for public servants, and transparency in automated decision-making. Only after such legislation is in place, and when the parameters for the use of automated decision-making have been clarified, can provisions on the introduction of such decision-making procedures be introduced into substance legislation.

As a consequence of this approach of the Constitutional Law Committee, requiring prior guarantees of legality before automated decisions are made, general legislation on automated decision-making concerning, inter alia, the Administrative Procedure Act has been adopted. Since 1 May 2023, Finland has a general regulatory framework in force that defines the way in which legislation allows automated decision-making by public authorities, with a more or less pronounced ban on the use of machine-learning methods for automated decision-making in the exercise of public authority. Rule-based methods should thus be the only ones allowed for fully automated decision-making in government activities. However, it may happen that authorities could to some extent use machine-learning methods when AI is used in a decision support capacity where a human decision-maker makes the final decision and also takes responsibility for the decision. The regulatory situation is thus different in Finland than in, for instance, Sweden, where the legal requirements are more relaxed concerning the use of automated decision-making by public authorities.

The exclusion of machine-learning techniques from the field of fully-automated decision-making in government activities is a desirable and a necessary development for many different reasons. The most important reason is the maintenance of the rule of law as a fundamental principle of society. The rule of law, in its ideal form, presupposes that public power is exercised within a legal framework that makes the exercise of power foreseeable based on legal rules. The rule of law presupposes that the content of the exercise of public power will also be governed by legal norms, which means that citizens must be able to know everything essential about how power will be exercised, not just who or what will exercise that power. In this context, it is possible to define the rule of law as a principle of legality, i.e., that the exercise of public powers can always be linked to an Act of Parliament and ultimately to the Constitution. This requirement of legal basis, normally included in the constitutions of countries, applies to human decision-making and, therefore, it should, of course, also apply to algorithmic decision-making. It is not acceptable that algorithmic decision-making in government activities would be allowed to operate outside the rule of law framework, or that algorithmic decision-making in government activities could fall outside the requirements of the rule of law.

Administrative decision-making by a public authority is fundamentally about legal decision-making: a norm established by the legislature is set in relation to the facts relevant to an individual case, and the conclusion, the administrative decision, follows through a subsumption of these facts in relation to the norm. It is this subsumption that reconciles the administrative decision made based on the law enacted by the Parliament and completes the legality required by the rule of law. Only a rule-based automated procedure can achieve this direct link between the administrative decision and the statutory provision. If an automated decision-making system would be created so that it works based on machine learning, such a machine-learning decision-making system would have to use, as training materials, the previously-made administrative decisions in the same case category, after which the new decision would be a prediction based on the previous administrative decisions, i.e., a forecast using Bayesian statistics.

However, an administrative decision cannot be forecast, nor can it be a prediction based on previously-decided similar cases, because then the administrative decision is not primarily based on law, but on the previous decisions. In other words, at best, only an indirect link to the statutory provision would exist in a machine-learning environment. Machine learning could possibly be used in connection with semi-automated decision-making, in a supporting function, where an official makes the final decision after the computer program has proposed a certain decision based on an algorithmic analysis of the decision basis. However, in such a situation, the office holder would nevertheless be obliged to carry out the subsumption that the rule of law requires.

The Finnish Parliament is not the only legislator currently considering legislative measures concerning algorithmic decision-making. Several others, including EU legislators, i.e., the European Parliament and the Council of Ministers, are currently drafting and weighing proposals on this topic. In April 2021, the European Commission proposed the enactment of an EU Regulation on AI. This AI Act, if approved, would regulate all uses of algorithms, ranging from robotic arms performing simple, repetitive tasks, to the use of algorithms in complex machine-learning situations. In other words, an EU-level AI Act would apply to all robotics and any algorithmic system, both algorithms that are completely risk-free for humans, but also, of course, algorithms that pose low or—more importantly—high risks to humans.

Under the original proposal for this AI Act of the EU, the regulatory framework would apply both to the private and public sectors. Of course, if the public sector is using algorithms the AI Act will virtually always designate such uses of algorithms as "high-risk," as personal data in various sensitive areas is involved. The EU proposal for an AI Act cites Article 114 of the Treaty on the Functioning of the European Union, i.e., regulation of the internal market, as the legal basis for the Act. This means that the European Commission considers, in its proposal, that algorithms are perceived as goods that can be sold and bought in the internal market, and at the stage when the algorithm and software become ready for placing on the market, they would need to be reviewed and categorized at different levels of risk. It looks as if this EU proposal for AI legislation might lead to the EU gaining legislative competence in a new area, an area that in the future is sure to be extremely significant, considering the shift towards a digital mode of production that is taking place. It is possible that the AI Act of the EU is passed by the end of 2023.

The efforts of national legislators, and the EU legislator, in the field of automated decision-making and AI indicate that the "sovereign", the legislator, is fighting an impending paradigm shift that the algorithmization of society will perhaps usher in, at least over a longer period of time. The question is thus, is it possible to fight this major change? And in the long run, is it even possible to regulate AI? AI is perhaps a phenomenon similar to the climate: the legislature cannot regulate the climate, but it can hopefully regulate the activities that bring about harmful climate change and the consequences of climate change. Far in the future, it may appear that, like the climate, AI had its own unstoppable course that led to a change in the basic structures of society. We have not reached such a point yet, however, so now the efforts of legislators feel relevant, although at the same time, there are those who may think that one should not at all control the development of AI, but that one should allow the development of AI to remain free from the limitations of legislation. In any case, what happens is that it is often forgotten, when designing automated decision-making systems at and for public authorities, that these systems need to comply with the requirements of the current legislation. Such omissions should not be allowed to happen in a state operating under the rule of law.

In his book *The Concept of Law*, H. L. A. Hart theorizes on the determination of the locus of sovereignty in society by referring to the rule of recognition: sovereignty is where the rule of recognition points at.[2] In Hart's case, the rule of recognition is with the Parliament of England, the laws of which have been recognized as legitimate and binding by public authorities and courts in the UK (although those legislative powers today have been, in many areas, decentralized to Scotland, Wales, and Northern Ireland). The intention is not to engage in a lengthy argumentation of a theoretical kind here, but instead to raise the—perhaps rhetorical—question: could the developments within the area of social media lead to a situation where individuals increasingly recognize the algorithm-based software systems of large tech corporations, which guide individual conduct in various ways, as the sovereign or sovereigns whose norms individuals follow? Could a "metaverse" of some kind offer an alternative to real life and also to the real public authorities?

A legal relationship of a horizontal kind is normally formed by accepting the terms of use of a software, giving rise to a commitment under private law to the owner of the software. Most users give their consent without much reflection and are thus granted access to an algorithmically-operated environment for some service where the proprietary power is great and the rights of the user are often quite limited. A question of a philosophical nature: could an ever stronger horizontality of this kind at some point replace or make obsolete the vertical dimension in which a state and its public authorities exercise public powers in relation to individuals? Already now, social media companies are under pressure from politicians and some social media users who would like to see the companies exercise more editorial judgment, when moderating and even censoring certain types content,[3] such as nudity or hate speech, often with the help of AI,[4] which means that the platforms are exercising power over their users. Adding to this, EU legislation requires social media companies to censor content in some instances.[5] Artificial general intelligence could perhaps assume a position akin to public authorities, in the event that such an advanced form of AI is ever developed, but is it already possible to see signs of a shift of the rule of recognition in society in a manner that might lead, for the individual, to a clear dominance of the horizontal relationship over the vertical relationship? Perhaps so. However, judging from law-drafting projects that are ongoing in various states

[2] Hart (1961).

[3] Gillespie (2018).

[4] However, some human consideration is probably also used, as might be the case in China in relation to censorship of political content that deviates from the general policy of the country. See Gillespie (2018), p. 115.

[5] See Regulation (EU) 2021/784 of the European Parliament and of the Council of 29 April 2021 on addressing the dissemination of terrorist content online. Under Art. 3(1) of the regulation, the competent authority of each Member State shall have the power to issue a removal order requiring hosting service providers to remove terrorist content or to disable access to terrorist content in all Member States. The Regulation applies as of 7 June 2022. Under the Regulation, terrorist content must be taken down by the platform operator within one hour after it is identified online on on-line platforms offering services in the EU.

and in the EU, the ordinary forms of legal orders are preparing to fight back to prevent a shift of the rule of recognition from the lawmaker exercising sovereign powers to software that attracts almost all the attention of the individual.

It is also possible to raise a rhetorical question following from the utilitarian thinker Jeremy Bentham: can a system that operates based on the algorithms within social media produce a situation where the "pleasure and pain" that is most relevant for an individual is increasingly controlled and allocated by an algorithm, not anymore by the system of public authorities and courts based on the rule of law? It appears as if AI, in this respect, has already evolved into a serious competitor to public authorities. From this perspective, a "metaverse" of some kind may possibly become more significant to an individual than real life—by extension making the rules of the "metaverse" more significant than those enacted by real, human public authorities.

Therefore, although today we think about the grounding of algorithmic activities of public authorities in the rule of law, it is also possible to start to envision a shift in the manner in which the individual is bound to norms, a shift from the ordinary lawmaker to an algorithmic governance mechanism that is based on consent of some kind. The control, or at least influence, that social media, for instance, exert on individuals can be considerable. In case the consent given to the operator of software becomes the main form of commitment and obligation of an individual to services that she or he needs, it might be that the legal bindingness takes place almost entirely in the horizontal sphere by means of contractual constructions. The rule of algorithm may then grow stronger to the detriment of the rule of law. As a consequence, the rule of law might be pressed to the background while the rule of algorithm positions itself in the fore. At such a point, the ordinary legal basis for the actions of public authorities may become increasingly weaker, perhaps even irrelevant. However, at least for the time being, the existing legal orders are taking active measures to maintain their relevance as the main regulators both of public and private powers and activities.

References

Gillespie T (2018) Custodians of the internet: platforms, content moderation, and the hidden decisions that shape social media. Yale University Press, New Haven & London

Hart HLA (1961) The concept of law, 2nd edn. Oxford University Press, Oxford

Suksi M (2017) On the openness of the digital society. In: Lind A-S, Reichel J, Österdahl I (eds) Transparency in the future: Swedish openness 250 years. Ragulka Press, Tallinn, pp 285–317

Index

M. Suksi (ed.), *The Rule of Law and Automated Decision-Making*,
https://doi.org/10.1007/978-3-031-30142-1

MIX
Papier aus verantwortungsvollen Quellen
Paper from responsible sources
FSC® C105338

If you have any concerns about our products,
you can contact us on
ProductSafety@springernature.com

In case Publisher is established outside the EU,
the EU authorized representative is:
Springer Nature Customer Service Center GmbH
Europaplatz 3, 69115 Heidelberg, Germany

Printed by Libri Plureos GmbH
in Hamburg, Germany